Philip K. Dick

CRITICAL EXPLORATIONS IN SCIENCE FICTION AND FANTASY
(a series edited by Donald E. Palumbo and C.W. Sullivan III)
Earlier Works: www.mcfarlandpub.com
Recent Works: 46 *Nature and the Numinous in Mythopoeic Fantasy Literature* (Christopher Straw Brawley, 2014)
47 *J.R.R. Tolkien, Robert E. Howard and the Birth of Modern Fantasy* (Deke Parsons, 2014)
48 *The Monomyth in American Science Fiction Films* (Donald E. Palumbo, 2014)
49 *The Fantastic in Holocaust Literature and Film* (ed. Judith B. Kerman, John Edgar Browning, 2014)
50 *Star Wars in the Public Square* (Derek R. Sweet, 2016)
51 *An Asimov Companion* (Donald E. Palumbo, 2016)
52 *Michael Moorcock* (Mark Scroggins, 2016)
53 *The Last Midnight: Essays* (ed. Leisa A. Clark, Amanda Firestone, Mary F. Pharr, 2016)
54 *The Science Fiction Mythmakers: Religion, Science and Philosophy in Wells, Clarke, Dick and Herbert* (Jennifer Simkins, 2016)
55 *Gender and the Quest in British Science Fiction Television* (Tom Powers, 2016)
56 *Saving the World Through Science Fiction: James Gunn* (Michael R. Page, 2017)
57 *Wells Meets Deleuze* (Michael Starr, 2017)
58 *Science Fiction and Futurism: Their Terms and Ideas* (Ace G. Pilkington, 2017)
59 *Science Fiction in Classic Rock: Musical Explorations of Space, Technology and the Imagination, 1967–1982* (Robert McParland, 2017)
60 *Patricia A. McKillip and the Art of Fantasy World-Building* (Audrey Isabel Taylor, 2017)
61 *The Fabulous Journeys of Alice and Pinocchio: Exploring Their Parallel Worlds* (Laura Tosi with Peter Hunt, 2018)
62 *A Dune Companion: Characters, Places and Terms in Frank Herbert's Original Six Novels* (Donald E. Palumbo, 2018)
63 *Fantasy Literature and Christianity: A Study of the Mistborn, Coldfire, Fionavar Tapestry and Chronicles of Thomas Covenant Series* (Weronika Łaszkiewicz, 2018)
64 *The British Comic Invasion: Alan Moore, Warren Ellis, Grant Morrison and the Evolution of the American Style* (Jochen Ecke, 2019)
65 *The Archive Incarnate: The Embodiment and Transmission of Knowledge in Science Fiction* (Joseph Hurtgen, 2018)
66 *Women's Space: Essays on Female Characters in the 21st Century Science Fiction Western* (ed. Melanie A. Marotta, 2019)
67 *"Hailing frequencies open": Communication in Star Trek: The Next Generation* (Thomas D. Parham III, 2019)
68 *The Global Vampire: Essays on the Undead in Popular Culture Around the World* (ed. Cait Coker, 2019)
69 *Philip K. Dick: Essays of the Here and Now* (ed. David Sandner, 2019)

Philip K. Dick

Essays of the Here and Now

Edited by DAVID SANDNER

CRITICAL EXPLORATIONS IN
SCIENCE FICTION AND FANTASY, 69
Series Editors Donald E. Palumbo *and* C.W. Sullivan III

McFarland & Company, Inc., Publishers
Jefferson, North Carolina

This book has undergone peer review.

ISBN (print) 978-1-4766-7789-7
ISBN (ebook) 978-1-4766-3919-2

LIBRARY OF CONGRESS AND BRITISH LIBRARY
CATALOGUING DATA ARE AVAILABLE

Library of Congress Control Number 2020006106

© 2020 David Sandner. All rights reserved

No part of this book may be reproduced or transmitted in any form or by any means, electronic or mechanical, including photocopying or recording, or by any information storage and retrieval system, without permission in writing from the publisher.

Front cover illustration by Cliff Cramp

Printed in the United States of America

*McFarland & Company, Inc., Publishers
Box 611, Jefferson, North Carolina 28640
www.mcfarlandpub.com*

Table of Contents

Acknowledgments   vii

Introduction to Philip K. Dick Now That He Is Philip K. Dick
    DAVID SANDNER   1

FUTURE ECOLOGIES

Philip K. Dick's Futuristic Ecologies
    URSULA HEISE   14

From Soft Totalitarianism to TV Introjection: Philip Kindred Dick and the Tube
    UMBERTO ROSSI   32

Voices, Consciousness and the Bicameral Mind: *A Scanner Darkly* on the Road to Julian Jaynes' Psychology
    RICHARD FEIST   46

Ubik Does Not Yet Exist: Reading *Ubik* as a Case of Extro–Science Fiction
    SEAN MATHAROO   61

Rereading Dick's Mainstream Fiction within a Science Fiction Framework
    GABRIEL CUTRUFELLO   71

Evolving Dickian Criticism: *The Exegesis* and Pierre Teilhard de Chardin
    MICHAEL KVAMME-O'BRIEN   83

Philip Dick, the Earthshaker
    GREGG RICKMAN   99

Galactic Pot-Healer: A Singular Way Station
    GARY WESTFAHL   107

Archaeologies

The Philip K. Dick Society: A Preliminary Archaeology
    Jonathan Lethem   116

PKD at California State University, Fullerton: A Question-and-Answer Session with Nicole Vandever and Paige Patterson
    Tim Powers *and* James Blaylock   137

PKD Goes to the Movies: A Panel Discussion
    Daniel Gilbertson, Gary Westfahl *and* Paul Sammon   153

Dick's SoCal Dream
    Jonathan Lethem *in Conversation with* Samuel Sousa   171

Appendix: Images and Ephemera from the 2016 Philip K. Dick Conference   187

About the Contributors   213

Index   215

Acknowledgments

Associate editors Jaime Brody and Christine Granillo read submissions and edited for the collection. As English master's students at CSUF, Jaime, then–President of the Acacia Graduate Student Group, and Christine, then–President of the Creative Writing Club, helped plan, organize, and run the 2016 Philip K. Dick Conference. Their work has been invaluable throughout the process.

I am grateful for the hard work and dedication to student success by my conference collaborators, Cliff Cramp, art professor, and Patricia Prestinary, special collections librarian. I am lucky to have such great colleagues. The project began as a challenge to students, and many students in a number of my classes over the course of about three years went beyond the call and achieved remarkable things. In particular, Nicole Vandever, then–President of the Science Fiction and Fantasy Club, deserves credit for time and effort organizing and doing essential groundwork. I also want to acknowledge the institutional support at different stages of the overall work of the conference and collection by the Patrons of the Library, the Pollak Library, Associated Students, the College of Humanities and Social Sciences, and especially my home department, the English Department.

Finally, for Amy and Adele, who make things worth doing at all.

Introduction to Philip K. Dick Now That He Is Philip K. Dick

David Sandner

Returning to PKD

> I should yield to reality. I have *never* yielded to reality. That's what SF is all about…. The SF writer sees not just possibilities but *wild* possibilities. It's not just "What if—" it's "*My God*; what if—" in frenzy and hysteria. The Martians are always coming.
>
> —Philip K. Dick, "Introduction to *The Golden Man*" (1980)

Philip K. Dick wrote visionary science fiction set in futures that feel like our present. The "Martians" landed a long time ago, and land continually. "The Empire never ended," Dick wrote (repeatedly, in all capitals, throughout his novel *VALIS*), referencing his paranoid vision of a ubiquitous repression, stretching through time to the Roman Empire (and his "past life" remembrance of persecution there), and out to alien overlords whose powers reach even into our minds. "They" have already taken over and we are left but to seek the trace of their dominion—secret, hermetic, complete—over us in opaque and doubtful signs left in unlikely corners of the world. This intense paranoia is the uneasy, palpitating heart of the fiction PKD left to us. The surprise is that his paranoia, decades after his death, should remain something that feels frighteningly relevant, here and now.

American society has become only more anxious and uncanny since he wrote. His works speak to contemporary fears of being continually watched by technology. They speak to the paranoia of modern life in which we watch ourselves and lose our sense of identity. When corporations have "human rights" and AI personalities (Siri, Alexa, and on), the Turing Test is a relic because we are all robots: who will find who to be a fake? We are but commodities … consumers, cogs. Philip K. Dick's novels and short stories create alternate worlds, alternate histories, and alternate identities which challenge us to see reality, maybe for the first time. "If you find this world bad," he once warned in the very title of a speech, "you should see some of the others." In *Philip K. Dick: Essays of the Here and Now*, we seek PKD as if for the first time, looking for his traces in the places he lived, in the SF community he came from, and in his influence on contemporary American literature and culture, and beyond.

The collection's guiding insight is: the contexts in which we understand PKD have changed. Philip K. Dick is not the same Philip K. Dick he knew. Around the time of Dick's death (as Jonathan Lethem explains in the present volume) exactly one of his works was in print—*Blade Runner*, with its original title in small letters underneath. Now? Lethem presided over the hardcover Library of America volumes of Dick's collected novels and more, including the once-unpublishable *Exegesis*, and many more trade paperback collections and editions flood the market to meet a ravenous demand for everything by and about Dick.

The question is: if Philip K. Dick has changed from the Philip K. Dick he knew ... if the world, too, has shifted into something he dreamed up ... how are we to find him? Who is Philip K. Dick? Why is he?

Finding PKD

> My grand theme—who is human and who only appears (masquerading) as human? ... Without answering it adequately, we cannot even be certain of our own selves. I cannot even know myself, let alone you. So I keep working on this theme; to me nothing is as important a question. And the answer comes very hard.
> —Philip K. Dick, "Afterthoughts by the Author" (1977)

Does Philip K. Dick need introduction in the form of a biography? Even more to the point: if you've read this far, do you? But the collection, it seems to me, is constrained to create one, invoking a simulacrum of his life for consumption. I shall be brief...

Born in 1928 in Chicago, Philip Kindred Dick lived most of his life in California. He briefly attended the University of California, Berkeley, but dropped out after one year. In 1952, he began writing professionally and proceeded to write numerous novels and short stories. He won the Hugo Award for best novel in 1962 for *The Man in the High Castle* and the John W. Campbell Memorial Award for best novel of the year in 1974 for *Flow My Tears, the Policeman Said*. In 1978, his novel *A Scanner Darkly* won a British Science Fiction Association award and, in 1979, a Graouilly d'Or from the Festival de Metz in France. He was nominated for other Hugo and Nebula awards. Philip K. Dick died on March 2, 1982, in Santa Ana, California, of heart failure following a stroke.

Since his death, his influence has only grown until he has become simply one of America's most influential writers. In addition to 44 published novels, Dick wrote approximately 121 short stories, most of which appeared in science fiction magazines during his lifetime. Although Dick spent most of his career as a writer in near poverty, many of his stories have been adapted into popular films and TV shows since his death, including *Blade Runner, Total Recall, A Scanner Darkly, Minority Report, Paycheck, Screamers,* and *The Adjustment Bureau*. Series include recent productions of *The Man in the High Castle* and *Minority Report*. In 2005, *Time* magazine named *Ubik* one of the one hundred greatest English-language novels published since 1923. In 2007, Dick became the first science fiction writer to be included in The Library of America series.

Cut to size like this, into a biography the width of a writing life, we might fit PKD into a taxonomy, pinned to the page; perhaps we could tuck him back into his genre; or we might offer a genealogy in which we note that his themes and style have become part of the "furniture" of science fiction, part of its generic conventions. We can point to him as a precursor to cyberpunk in SF and postmodernism out of it, and all that follows from those movements. We might name, among the influenced, such celebrated writers as: Jonathan Lethem, Ursula K. Le Guin, James Tiptree, Jr., Haruki Murakami, William Gibson, and Thomas Pynchon. (He was influenced in turn by Le Guin, Tiptree, and Pynchon.) Such a list might be greatly extended. But does such a safe approach capture the "authentic" Philip K. Dick? To do that, or pretend to do so, shouldn't our story be weirder?

Perhaps a narrower focus will draw the stranger details into relief: let us look closer for him where he lived at the end: Orange County, California.

Collecting PKD

> The two basic topics which fascinate me are "What is reality?" and "What constitutes the authentic human being?"
> —Philip K. Dick, "How to Build a Universe That Doesn't Fall Apart in Two Days" (1978)

In Special Collections at the Pollak Library, California State University, Fullerton, there's a picture of Philip K. Dick in the collection itself, sitting at a table, sorting manuscripts and other materials before donating them. The Special Collections Librarian showed me the photo as if it was a talisman, which I suppose it is—the promise of a presence ... if seeing is believing, which in PKD's work, it's not. Still, by such proofs do we map reality. In 1972, Philip K. Dick moved to Fullerton. He lived the last ten years of his life in Orange County, closely associated with CSUF. The late English Professor Willis McNelly helped Dick relocate to Fullerton. Of the University's relationship with the writer, McNelly writes: "In one sense, CSUF became a virtual home base for him. In fact, he was awarded the status of 'honorary student' by the student government and attended many of the music and dramatic activities on campus." Dick settled into North Orange County, enjoying a relatively stable and productive period in which he wrote important works. Eventually, he left his papers to CSUF's Special Collections. As McNelly describes it: "Dick gave us an enormous collection of books, manuscripts, and personal copies of his writings in all forms, as well as much unpublished material including several novels" (24). They form a key part of the remarkable SF holdings in the Pollak Library's Special Collections.

McNelly had taught some of the first SF classes anywhere, wrote early critical works, including *The Dune Encyclopedia* (1987), and realized the need for preservation of SF writers' manuscripts. As a result of his efforts, rare and now valuable manuscripts remain in the possession of the Pollak Library. Original copies of works such as *The Man in the High Castle*, *Fahrenheit 451*, and *Dune* all have a home here.

About the early teaching of SF in academia, McNelly wrote:

> In the early 1960s, the first academic SF class was taught at Cornell. Many scholars throughout the country ... joined to form the workshop on SF at the Modern Language Association and later the Science Fiction Research Association. Inspired by their example, I created the SF course at CSUF in the mid–1960s, one that proved so popular that eventually three and four sections were being taught each semester by English Department colleagues....

Having founded the collection with a rich selection of pulp magazines, including near-complete runs of *Amazing Stories*, *Galaxy*, *Weird Tales*, *Thrilling Wonder Stories*, and donated paperback and hardback SF books, McNelly's most important innovation came when he turned to the archiving of the papers of living SF writers:

> I joined the Science Fiction Writers of America (SFWA) and even spoke at one of their meetings at Berkeley in 1967 about the relationship of SF and the academy. Among the suggestions made for closer cooperation between the writing and academic communities was that writers try to preserve the manuscripts of their work in some place other than closet floors or basement shelves, thus making them accessible for scholars.... I wrote to every member of the SFWA urging that they donate their manuscripts to the Patrons of the Library at CSUF.
> We had manuscripts flooding in within weeks [19].

McNelly had the visionary idea that SF was not only worth reading, but worth studying ... and worth archiving for future scholars. As it turns out, the oddest addition to McNelly's archives came to be Philip K. Dick himself. After Dick had a break down in Vancouver, he had written to virtually everyone in the SF community, looking for a place to stay. He had many friends who loved him, but unsurprisingly—perhaps because they knew him—they turned down his request to come for a long stay. McNelly, who hardly knew Dick at the time, agreed, finding a place in an apartment with CSUF students. He sent students to pick Dick up at the airport. The now award-winning writer Tim Powers was one of them. You can hear his version of that epic meeting in the Powers and Blaylock Q-and-A in our volume. In any case, Dick came to stay in the OC, and it worked surprisingly well.

McNelly tells the odd story of how he invited Dick to Fullerton this way:

> I first met Phil Dick in 1972 at an academic gathering at the College of San Rafael. He introduced himself to me as "the world's greatest science fiction writer," a description I would not have disputed.... His ransacked house had been sold; he was on his way to Vancouver to deliver a speech that later became "The Android and the Human," one of his most famous pieces of writing—we have the original—and during that initial interview I suggested to him that we safeguard what manuscripts had not been lost in various moves by sending them to Fullerton. He expressed interest, but because of his obligations to Vancouver, he had not time then to send anything back to Fullerton with me [24–5].

Dick was in a certain amount of distress at the time, which would culminate in a crisis. Dick wrote to McNelly: "Anyhow, if I could make by degrees my way down to Fullerton, do you think it's the sort of place I might like to live, at least for a while?" (Timberg, "Part 2"). Here's how McNelly describes the event: "Later, after he recovered from a breakdown in Vancouver and needed a place to stay—in his own strange way he was homeless—I was able to arrange housing for him in Fullerton" ("The Science Fiction Collection," 24).

But McNelly also warned Dick about the place he was coming to, writing back:

> You must realize of course, that Fullerton is in the heart of darkest Orange County.... Upper middle-class suburbia ... OC is also the place where Nixon's representative in Congress is a card-carrying member of the Birch Society [Timberg, "Part 2"].

In a 1975 letter, Dick wrote of his move to the OC: "I have gone from the gutter to the plastic container" (Timberg, "Part 3"). But Dick needed to move, and it helped him that he moved here. As he later explained: "It wasn't until I left Canada and flew down here to Orange County that I got my head together and back to writing" ("Introduction," xviii).

In 1972, when Dick arrived at LAX, trying to leave behind his breakdown ... and a break-in and explosion at his Northern California house the year before ... he entered a productive decade. He wrote important works, publishing *Flow My Tears, the Policeman Said*, *A Scanner Darkly*, and *VALIS*, among others. While in Orange County, Dick witnessed what he called the "2-3-74" experience, in which perhaps God, or something in the shape of God, had spoken to him and awoke in him a knowledge of eternity. He called this experience "anamnesis," meaning the loss of amnesia. He would be inspired by this event to work on the vast materials now gathered in his *Exegesis* for the rest of his life.

Eventually, Dick deposited his papers in the Special Collections of the Pollak library on a "permanent loan" basis (receiving a small stipend to organize them). More recently, in just the last few years, after numerous earlier attempts that McNelly thought he had long ago resolved, the estate of Philip K. Dick has removed certain manuscripts from the collection. But many PKD manuscripts and first editions remain. The estate's stated plan had been to redeposit that bequest at the Special Collections Bancroft Library at UC Berkeley, but the plan broke down. Instead, the papers are currently out of circulation, stored somewhere by the estate, and can no longer be accessed by scholars. A great loss.

As for Dick himself, by the end of his stay, his 1968 novel *Do Androids Dream of Electric Sheep?* became the popular film *Blade Runner*. He died shortly before the movie was released but he was able to view pieces of his work alive on the screen and looked forward to its release with excitement.

Dick enjoyed the odd, built environments in the OC, like Disneyland, that, instead of trying to insist on being real, revel in being simulacra. He didn't head for the beaches and the sun; he liked the odder elements of the OC, the punk music and the other outsiders of its "plastic" culture, the students and the SF writers. He wrote novels set among its chain stores and peopled by those living outside its walled enclaves.

This place inspired him.

In *A Scanner Darkly* (1977), one of his best OC novels, we first meet the main character, Robert Arctor, "an undercover narcotics agent from the Orange County Sheriff's Department," giving a speech to "the Anaheim Lion's Club" while wearing his scramble suit, which protects his identity by blurring him behind multiple faces and bodies. He goes off script from his "prepared speech … from the PR boys back at the Orange County Civic Center" (24) and gets in trouble with his superiors. Ordered to return for a reprimand, instead, "he wandered down one of the commercial streets in Anaheim, inspecting the McDonaldburger stands and car washes and gas stations and Pizza Huts and other marvels" (27). He thinks:

> In Southern California it didn't make any difference anyhow where you went; there was always the same McDonaldburger place over and over, like a circular strip that turned past you as you pretended to go somewhere. And when you finally got hungry and went into the McDonaldburger place and bought a McDonald's hamburger, it was the one they sold you last time and the time before that and so forth, back to before you were born. Life in Anaheim, California, was a commercial for itself, endlessly replayed. Nothing changed; it just spread out farther and farther in the form of neon ooze.
>
> They had by now, according to the sign, sold the same original burger fifty billion times. He wondered if it was to the same person [28–29].

Locating Philip K. Dick in Orange County in both his life and his writing reveals a surprising "grounded" quality to his seemingly "far out" works. His name-checking of endlessly repeated chain stores, for example, is not just a postmodern literary "move" (although it can be profitably read that way), but an accurate rendition of the changes undergoing late 20th-century Southern California, a place which, with its massive influx of new residents, acts as a kind of petri dish for late 20th-century capitalism in its invention of new mass ways of selling and buying and living in a Disney-fied simulacrum of life. Equally, the science fictional elements, like the scramble suit, emerge as not just a "gesture" toward popular culture tropes (though they are certainly SF) but as a reflection of Americans' shattered selves under the piercing gaze of our hypertrophied surveillance society.

Mapping PKD's Legacy

> What does a scanner see? he asked himself. I mean, really see? Into the head? Down into the heart? Does a passive infrared scanner like they used to use or a cube-type holo-scanner like they use these days, the latest thing, see into me—into us—clearly or darkly? I hope it does, he thought, see clearly, because I can't any longer these days see into myself. I see only murk. Murk outside; murk inside. I hope, for everyone's sake, the scanners do better. Because, he thought if the scanner sees only darkly, the way I myself do, then we are cursed, cursed again and like we have been continually, and we'll wind up dead this way, knowing very little and getting that little fragment wrong too.
> —Philip K. Dick, *A Scanner Darkly* (1977)

Some 35 years or so after Dick sat in Special Collections organizing his manuscripts, I proposed the first Digital Literary Studies class for the English Department at CSUF. As a final collaborative assignment, our class, using the fact of Dick's presence on our campus, created our website, *Philip K. Dick in Orange County*. With the site, we intended to document and share CSUF's literary history by creating digital archives both aggregating and ordering what was out there into relevant links and commenting upon it from our own perspectives, and creating our own content through interviews, new explorations, and research, especially into our University's Special Collections.

We used various digital approaches to comprehend Dick's final ten years and the work he produced after his sudden move to Southern California. I chose the dark epigraph above for this section because I wonder: what would Philip K. Dick think of this project? I think he would enjoy the fame that the site reflects, but I'm mindful that it represents a kind of scanning darkly, too. I want to articulate the value of our class experiment, but I don't want to forget that the whole thing might have made Philip K. Dick uneasy. For he was there before us, of course, hyperaware in his work and life of living in a time of being watched, of us watching ourselves—of a surveillance society of scanners hacking secrets we sign away for free to entertainment conglomerates in hopes that someone or something, if only the "smart" pop-up ads that hone themselves in so sharply on our desires, might see us better than we see ourselves. But, who knows, perhaps Philip K. Dick, whose work is experimental in form and function, might have welcomed our odd intrusions in the spirit of newness itself.

We deployed free tools, mapping through Google Earth (and Google Maps) to spatially locate pertinent places important to Dick's life in Orange County. We also mapped two novels set in Orange County, *A Scanner Darkly* and *Radio Free Albemuth*, in order to see the relationship of the places important in his real life to the fictional settings of his OC novels. Further, we used Google Earth to create a literary tour of *A Scanner Darkly* in order to think about the way characters move about in the work ... and to think about how physical space controls the characters. In doing so, we sought to understand not just Dick's presence here and what it means to us but, further, how Orange County itself shaped his thinking and writing.

As the assignment was an experiment, I could not predict the results of our attempts to use different digital tools. What emerged felt unsystematic, governed by chance, but even that seemed to fit our subject, as Dick would sometimes write by consulting the *I Ching*. The success of the website with PKD scholars and fans led to my being asked to host the Philip K. Dick Conference at CSUF. I agreed, focusing scholarship on an assessment of PKD's legacy, his immense literary and cultural impact. "Here and Now" became our conference theme. A number of events related to the conference celebrated PKD's special relationship with our university: a curated movie showing and other talks before the conference; an opening night creative writing workshop by writers Tim Powers and James Blaylock, friends of PKD's and special guests to the conference; and a months-long Art Show inspired by Dick's work, curated by Cliff Cramp, art professor at CUSF, and a Special Collections Display, curated by me and by Special Collections Librarian Patrisia Prestinary, in conjunction with my students. At the conference, Ursula Heise and Jonathan Lethem gave keynotes, and other talks and essays from the conference can be read in the present volume.

When I was hired at CSUF, I did not know all the stories related here. No one told me, although I think my interest in SF was of some interest to my hiring committee—as I could teach those now dormant genre classes McNelly put on the books along with my "canonical" Romanticism courses. Dr.

McNelly, who had retired, passed away just after I was hired. I never met him. I knew Philip K. Dick had lived in Southern California, but I'm from the Bay Area and knew that history better. I had not made the connection directly to my university until I went to Special Collections. I went curious, but expecting little. Philip K. Dick, Herbert, Bradbury, all those pulps ... I had no idea. When I recovered from my shock, I went looking to find out why it was all here ... and what I might do to bring attention to it all and help preserve it. You hold one result of that intention in your hands (or view it on your screen).

Now, I can't imagine CSUF without him. I sometimes expect to run into Dick's simulacrum just disappearing around a corner of a campus building, or sitting on a bench across a busy freeway you can't seem to get across—or perhaps sitting at the back of some talk I'm giving, just shaking his head in dismay at the things I'm saying. Anyway, I think he would fit right in.

Writing Back to PKD

> "Reality is that which, when you stop believing in it, doesn't go away."
> —Phillip K. Dick, "How to Build a Universe That Doesn't Fall Apart Two Days Later" (1978)

The collection is divided into two sections: "Future Ecologies" concentrates on new studies of Dick's output from recent critical perspectives; "Archaeologies" reassess his received legacy from the vantage point of his new status as a "major American author" to evaluate, in the aftermath, just what happened culturally and critically to precipitate his extraordinary rise in reputation. Essays are drawn from the groundbreaking 2016 Philip K. Dick Conference and a call for papers that followed to add more content to the strong core of essays, talks, panels, interviews, and other works from the conference itself. Hosted on my California State University, Fullerton, campus, the conference brought scholars from around the world to the place where Dick left his manuscripts and papers—to the place Lethem refers to in his keynote as "ground zero for Philip K. Dick scholarship." Collectively, we sought new approaches to an author who has become iconic and to look beyond his "canonical" texts to assess a greater scope of his works now that editions of all Dick's fiction, and much more, are widely available, including strong editions of previously unavailable texts like the *Exegesis*.

Ursula Heise's "Philip K. Dick's Futuristic Ecologies," developed from her conference keynote talk, "Dick's New Natures," revitalizes Dick scholarship by arguing for the significance of Dick's visionary "future ecologies" to ecocriticism and the idea of the "anthropocene" today. Recognizing his built environments as not simply dystopian, but hybrid spaces as worth considering as "nature" as his androids are of being "human," Heise strongly returns us in a new way to Dick's own concerns with "reality" as the "built environment" in which we have our being.

In "From Soft Totalitarianism to TV Introjection: Philip Kindred Dick and the Tube," Umberto Rossi performs linked close readings across Dick's fiction centered on the television as the ubiquitous technology of the mid-20th century, and a key literary metaphor for Dick's construction of reality itself. Rossi explores the trope as both positive, a connector, as well as negative, a way of overseeing, erasing, and replacing what we see—working across Dick's work from his first stories to his final *VALIS* trilogy.

Richard Feist's "Voices, Consciousness and the Bicameral Mind: *A Scanner Darkly* on the Road to Julian Jaynes' Psychology" underlines Dick's use of philosophy in his fiction and, more specifically, moves literary scholarship beyond his explicit use of Joseph Bogen's idea of "two minds" in *A Scanner Darkly* to an examination of Dick's philosophical thought in the novel in relation to other early brain researchers, especially Julian Jaynes' work on the "bicameral mind."

New methods of reading develop in Sean Matharoo's "Ubik Does Not Yet Exist: Reading *Ubik* as a Case of Extro-Science Fiction," which uses the emergent theories of French philosopher Quentin Meillasoux. Matharoo uses Meillasoux to build insights into Dick's use of non-representational fiction, especially in the transformational power of the spray product Ubik in the novel of the same name, to force an experience of the world itself as something that exists prior to human ideas of representation.

Gabriel Cutrufello's "Rereading Dick's Mainstream Fiction Within a Science Fiction Framework" turns to Dick's neglected and once-unpublishable mainstream works and seeks to perform a "double reading," reading his mainstream works in light of SF scholarship on Dick, then reading his SF in light of the themes that emerge from his mainstream work. Instead of using science fictional "estrangement" to approach "simulation" and "entropy" (two major Dickian themes), his mainstream novels, such as *The Man Whose Teeth Were All Exactly Alike* and *Now Wait for Last Year*, focus on familiar domestic and economic relationships, but in a way that shows their reality, too, to be already attenuated. New insights emerge when the mainstream works take their place back in his body of works, allowing rich comparisons across the imaginary divide of the realistic novel and SF.

In Michael Kvamme-O'Brien's "Evolving Dickian Criticism: *The Exegesis* and Pierre Teilhard de Chardin," Dick's *Exegesis* is unpacked for its relationship to his overall output. The visionary experiences that precipitated the *Exegesis* led Dick to regard his SF as part of a process of spiritual evolution that Dick himself described as "much as Teilhard de Chardin describes in *The*

Phenomenon of Man." Kvamme-O'Brien draws on de Chardin to understand the teleological critical lens Dick developed to revise his view of his own works late in his life. New readings of key Dick works illuminate the meaning of Dick's visions to his constantly evolving understanding of his own fiction.

Gregg Rickman's "Philip K. Dick, the Earthshaker" asserts new ways to value PKD's still-much-neglected mainstream novels and his late, important VALIS trilogy, along with his celebrated SF novels. Rickman turns to a drafted outline for an unwritten early novel, *Earthshaker*, to find a theme, the Dionysian figure of the title, that he argues runs throughout much of Dick's work, moving across the traditionally separated "successful" SF and "failed" mainstream work, opening up new works for examination in light of Dick's entire output.

Gary Westfahl's "*Galactic Pot-Healer*: A Singular Way Station" reads Dick's neglected novel as an anti–PKD novel "written by a Philip K. Dick who fervently longs to stop being Philip K. Dick, a Philip K. Dick who longs to stop writing Philip K. Dick novels. And the novel can be interpreted as Dick's step-by-step instructions on how he can achieve that goal." Westfahl confounds our own hardened expectations of what a PKD novel must be and, in a close reading of the text, demonstrates how Dick, ever the trickster, went about unreading himself long before anyone else thought to try.

Jonathan Lethem's "The Philip K. Dick Society: A Preliminary Archaeology" constructs how early Dick scholarship sharpened the arguments that promoted the "Philip K. Dick" we now know, complete with seemingly unshakable literary credibility; Lethem delves deep into his personal (and CSU, Fullerton's) archives to reconstruct the importance of The Philip K. Dick Society, run by Paul Williams (famed rock critic), which for ten years after Dick's death published a newsletter, and much other related material, shaping Dick's legacy. Lethem, as a young writer, had been an integral member of the group.

CSUF alums, award-winning writers, and friends of Dick, Tim Powers and James Blaylock situate Dick specifically in time and place in "PKD at California State University, Fullerton: A Question-and-Answer Session with Nicole Vandever and Paige Patterson," describing the events from his first arrival at the airport, to becoming his friends and figures in his fiction.

Philip K. Dick's film legacy propels literary scholarship and is crucial in developing "Philip K. Dick" as a literary icon. The films influenced by Philip K. Dick receive their due in a wide-ranging conversation, "PKD Goes to the Movies: A Panel Discussion," with noted film scholars Daniel Gilbertson, Gary Westfahl and Paul Sammon. Both Gilbertson and Sammon discuss their friendships with Dick and how that led to their insightful criticism of films he influenced, including Sammon's chronicling of the making of the iconic movie *Blade Runner*. Movies discussed also include: *A Scanner Darkly*, *Total Recall*, *Terminator* (as indebted to "Second Variety"), *Minority Report*, *The Ad-*

justment Bureau, *C.L.A.W.* (the screenplay by Gilbertson which was almost produced, and led to a Dan O'Bannon adaptation version, and, eventually *Screamers*), the long-unproduced *Ubik* screenplay, and *Blade Runner 2049*.

Jonathan Lethem, in conversation with Samuel Sousa, explores "Dick's SoCal Dream," the powerful fabricated reality of Disney, Hollywood, and other uniquely Southern California forms of the imaginary and commodification that fascinated Philip K. Dick when he moved to Orange County.

In the appendix, "Images and Ephemera from the 2016 Philip K. Dick Conference," we draw on materials from surrounding events. As a precursor to the conference, the Hibbleton Gallery in downtown Fullerton put on a PKD art show in 2015. During the conference, the Atrium Gallery of the Pollak Library at CSUF mounted an Art Show and Special Collections Display centered on Dick's works. The appendix consists of images from these events, and, in the spirit of Paul William's creation of zines that invented rock criticism and as Lethem describes in his keynote, launched PKD scholarship, we include brief introductions from two student-edited zines, *Philip K Dick in Orange County* and *The Aramchek Dispatch*, that came out in conjunction with the two art shows. Writings by the zine editors, Christine Granillo and Nicole Vandever, and by me (as Conference Chair to the PKD Conference), informally situate Dick in Orange County, in history … and here and now.

WORKS CITED

Dick, Philip K. "Afterthoughts by the Author." *The Best of Philip K. Dick*. Del Rey, 1977. 443–450.
_____. *The Exegesis of Philip K. Dick*. Eds. Pamela Jackson and Jonathan Lethem. Houghton, 2011.
_____. "How to Build a Universe That Doesn't Fall Apart in Two Days." 1978. *The Shifting Realities of Philip K. Dick*. Ed. Lawrence Sutin. Pantheon, 1995. 259–280.
_____. "If You Find This World Bad, You Should See Some of the Others." 1977. *The Shifting Realities of Philip K. Dick*. Ed. Lawrence Sutin. Pantheon, 1995. 233–258.
_____. "Introduction to the Golden Man." *The Golden Man*. Ed. Mark Hurst. Berkley Books, 1980.
_____. *A Scanner Darkly*. 1977. Mariner Books, 2011.
_____. *VALIS*. Bantam, 1981.
McNelly, Willis E. "The Science Fiction Collection." *Very Special Collections: Essays on Library Holdings at California State University, Fullerton*. Edited by Albert R. Vogeler and Arthur A. Hansen. The Patrons of the Library, 1992. 17–26.
Timberg, Scott. "Philip K. Dick, an Uneasy Spy Inside 1970s Suburbia. Part 3: Philip K. Dick, the Last Decade." *The Los Angeles Times*. Jan 27, 2010. philipdick.com/mirror/articles/The_Last_Decade_3.pdf. Accessed 15 Nov. 2018.
_____. "Philip K. Dick in the Land of the Birch Society. Part 2: Philip K. Dick, the Last Decade." *The Los Angeles Times*. Jan 26, 2010. philipdick.com/mirror/articles/The_Last_Decade_2.pdf. Accessed 15 Nov 2018.

Future Ecologies

Philip K. Dick's Futuristic Ecologies

Ursula Heise

Philip K. Dick is one of the most influential American science fiction writers of the twentieth century. His storyworlds, characters, and style have shaped not only futuristic fiction from cyberpunk to video games, but have also made their way into science fiction film. It is easy to see what recurring themes have made his work a productive source for much subsequent thought and writing about human futures: his interest in simulated environments, technologically created humans, artificial memory, nostalgia for historical spaces and figures, and technologies that are hard to control once they are released into the world has resonated in many later engagements with the transforming impacts of information and communications technology as well as biological engineering. So have his characters' unreliable perceptions and anxious realizations that they cannot always tell what reality is or how they should relate to it—an ontological uncertainty that permeated a great deal of postmodernist literature and art.

Other dimensions of Dick's voluminous *oeuvre* have remained more anchored in the context of the 1950s and 1960s: his recurring explorations of nuclear war and its aftermath, for example, his characters' frequent lapses into paranoia or schizophrenia, and their experimentation with mind-altering technologies that range from drugs to "mood organs" that allow the user to dial a state of mind seem centrally tied to the Cold War and the California counterculture that he formed part of. Yet other aspects of Dick's novels and short stories have remained more idiosyncratic, especially his obsession with esoteric religious beliefs and occultism, which is particularly visible in his late works.

Rereading Dick's wide range of works from an environmentalist perspective is not an easy task, since his major interests undoubtedly focused more on the fate of the human than the nonhuman world, and on the transformative impacts of technology more than on ecological change. Yet in the context of the Anthropocene—that is, the idea that humans now live on a planet that they have so fundamentally and pervasively transformed that the traces of their activities will be visible in the Earth's geological strata for millions of years to come—many of Dick's settings, themes, and turns of plot begin to resonate with environmentalist thought in new ways. Three dimensions of Dick's fiction in particular stand out in this context: his conception of post-apocalyptic environments and the futures they offer, his vision of humans as "natural aliens" who might be forced by ecological change to inhabit their own planet as a novel ecosystem, and his foregrounding of the repairmen who maintain fragile new communities of humans and nonhumans with their often flawed technologies.

1. Apocalypse and Anthropocene

Many of Philip K. Dick's novels and short stories are set in ecological wastelands that have been generated by perpetual war or global nuclear conflagration. His short stories from the 1950s feature, for example, military confrontations between Russians and Americans that have ravaged both Earth and the moon in "Second Variety" (1953), and humans' successive wars with alien species over materials they seek to extract from the aliens' home worlds in "Some Kinds of Life" (1953). Several of his major novels from the 1960s, such as *Dr. Bloodmoney* (1965) and *Do Androids Dream of Electric Sheep?* (1968), are set in postnuclear scenarios of devastated natural landscapes, disintegrated societies, and the perpetual risk of violence at both large and small scales. For this reason, he is often considered a dystopian writer. Yet Fredric Jameson has noted how, in Dick's works as well as many other science fiction texts, "global cataclysm so often serves as a mere pretext for the dreaming of a far more positive Utopian wish-fulfillment ... the coming into being of a small community beyond big city or nation" (2005: 378): this pattern repeats itself from John Wyndham's *The Day of the Triffids* (1951) to James Howard Kunstler's *World Made by Hand* (2008) and Margaret Atwood's *MaddAddam* (2013).

But Dick's deepest interest may not have been the exploration of utopian or dystopian futures so much as the question of what it means to be human in environments that have been altered, for better or for worse, by advanced technologies, as many critics have noted.[1] His work has generally been analyzed according to two major avenues of interpretation. In one reading, Dick's technologically altered environments mark him as the quintessentially postmodern novelist of inauthenticity, simulation, and hyper-reality: the writer whose work abounds in robot animals and artificial humans, as well as in varieties of perception and experience so mediated by drugs, technological devices, and psychological fractures that the authentic and the inauthentic, perception and simulation, reality and hallucination often can no longer be told apart. His fictions, in this perspective, articulate some of the ontological skepticism about the nature of reality, representation, and self that more generally characterize postmodernist American fiction (see McHale 2003).

A second, related way of reading Dick's work puts the main emphasis on his reconceptualization of identity in a thoroughly technologized and mediated world. Dick's writings are populated—one might say overpopulated—with androids, robots, "robands," mental patients, mutants, persons with supernatural abilities such as telepathy, telekinesis, and precognition, and of course a wide variety of aliens: from the interstellar pollen called the "drifters" in *The World Jones Made* (1956) and the extraterrestrial amoeba in *The Simulacra* (1964) all the way to the mysterious Proxers in *The Three Stigmata of Palmer Eldritch* (1965), the warring "Starmen" and insectoid reegs in *Now Wait for Last Year* (1966) and the gigantic, protoplasmic Frolixan Morgo Rahn Wilc in *Our Friends from Frolix 8* (1970). Interpretations of this universe of human, quasi-human, and alien identities have often taken their cue from Donna Haraway's "Manifesto for Cyborgs" (1984). Haraway's manifesto took up a term that had been coined in the early 1960s and was mostly associated with masculinity, military, police, and surveillance by the 1980s, and turned it instead into a trope of hope for sociocultural revolution, suggesting a turn away from pure origins to mixed genealogies, pure blood to hybridity, and more generally a constructivist understanding of class, race, and gender. Some critics, accordingly, read Dick's fiction as critical of essentialist notions of identity and as consonant with the cultural investment in diversity that only manifested itself fully after his death in 1982.[2]

In the early twenty-first century, Dick's emphasis on environments where conventional notions of "nature," "authenticity," or even "reality" have lost much of their traction resonates in new ways. Fears about the destructive impact of atomic war have given way in public debate to dire predictions about the consequences of climate change, ocean acidification, pollution, biodiversity loss, and other dimensions of what has come to be called the "Anthropocene." Where Dick foresaw a world reshaped by technology in such a way that little that can be called "natural" is left, the concept of the Anthropocene seeks to capture a world in which the unintended consequences of human activity are pervasively reshaping the globe directly and indirectly, to the point where some environmentalists have understood climate change as the end of nature—a point that the writer and activist Bill McKibben made forcefully in his eponymous book (*The End of Nature*, 1989).

The term "Anthropocene," originally coined in the 1980s, gained notoriety after the publication of a brief article by the ecologist Eugene Stoermer and the atmospheric chemist Paul Crutzen in 2000.[3] The current geological era, the Holocene, they suggested, should be renamed the Anthropocene because of humans' pervasive and lasting impacts on global ecosystems—impacts that, the two scientists argued, will leave permanent traces in the Earth's geological strata. Whereas humans have for a long time altered the planet's biology, they have now also transformed the composition of its atmosphere and oceans: as the historian Dipesh Chakrabarty has put it, humans have become geological agents as well as biological ones (2009: 206).

It remains to be seen whether geologists will accept the proposition to change the current era's name. But in the meantime, the Anthropocene has taken on a cultural life of its own, with multiple exhibitions and symposia by museums, foundations, and research institutions in Europe, Australia, and North America, as well as a profusion of publications. It has become a shorthand for referring to climate change—although Crutzen and Stoermer understood it to include a much wider spectrum of transformations from land use and nitrogen cycles to species loss—and more generally to global ecological change. Often, it implies a narrative of decline, a deterioration of the global ecosystem caused by humans that is not likely to end anytime soon. Some journalists and scientists have taken the Anthropocene, on the contrary, as an invitation to reimagine environmentalism in the context of a world that has been humanly altered, but that can also be conserved, restored, and made more habitable for both humans and nonhumans. At least one writer, Diane Ackerman, has even appropriated it for a techno-utopian vision of the future in her book *The Human Age*.

The Anthropocene, then, has unfolded into not just one story about humans' histories and futures in their natural environment, but several different ones.[4] To the extent that these stories project future environments, species, and human ways of interacting with them, they are distant cousins of science fiction. And indeed, the idea of the Anthropocene itself, reliant on the figure of a far-future geologist discovering the traces of contemporary humans' activities in the Earth's strata, can be understood as a science fiction trope, as I have argued in more detail elsewhere (Heise 2016: 215–220).[5] This family resemblance between Anthropocene narrative and science fiction enables an environmentally oriented rereading of Dick's visions of Earth's futures—not to suggest that Dick was an environmentalist (he was not), but to highlight what understanding of habitats and nonhuman species his techno-futurist scenarios explicitly or implicitly rely on, and what this understanding might contribute to the reimagination of environmentalism in the Anthropocene.

2. Natural Aliens

Environmentalists themselves are currently rethinking their commitment to nature with the help of narrative strategies, themes, and tropes that typify science fiction. This is particularly true of books about climate change such as James Hansen's *Storms of My Grandchildren* (2009), which includes a chapter in which aliens arriving on Earth in the future lament the mess humans have made of it, or Naomi Oreskes and Erik M. Conway's *The Collapse of Western Civilization: A View from the Future* (2014), a science fiction novella in which a Chinese historian in 2393 looks back on the climate policy irrationalities of the late twentieth and early twenty-first centuries.

But it is also obvious in environmental writing that references science fiction more indirectly. Even before the concept of the Anthropocene began to circulate widely, the environmental studies scholar Neil Evernden put in question the idea that humans were originally at home in nature and lived in harmony with it until the advent of modernity. Tool usage, he argued, very early on effectively transformed humans into a different species than they had been before, and this transformation turned them into exotic organisms even in their place of origin, Africa.

> A person with a tool is capable of a kind of behavior which was formerly difficult or impossible. A man who invents a spear instantly becomes a new and more dangerous kind of predator. Both his life and that of his prey are radically transformed. The consequences of technology are subtle but extensive, and one such consequence is that humans cannot evolve *with* an ecosystem anywhere. With every technological change we instantly mutate into a new—and for the ecosystem an exotic—kind of creature. Like other exotics, we are a paradox, a problem both for our environment and ourselves.... For it is not just the biotic community that is puzzled by the arrival of the exotic; so too is the creature itself. Figuratively speaking, just as the environment does not know how to cope with the new creature, neither does the exotic know what it ought to do [Evernden 1993: 109].

For this reason, Evernden argues, environmentalists should consider humans "natural aliens" even when they inhabit the ecosystems in which they originally evolved.

The idea that humans might be aliens in their own habitats, or conversely that the planet they live on might have become an alien one because of their own impact on it, has also been deployed in more recent environmentalist writing. The well-known writer and activist Bill McKibben, founder and director of an organization that fights against the continued use of fossil fuels, uses the sci-fi trope of humans settling on an alien world to begin one of his climate change books, *Eaarth: Making a Life on a Tough New Planet* (2010):

> The world hasn't ended, but the world as we know it has—even if we don't quite know it yet. We imagine we still live on that old planet, that the disturbances we see around us are the old random and freakish kind. But they're not. It's a different place. A different planet. It needs a new name. Eaarth.... It still looks familiar enough—we're still the third rock out from the sun, still three-quarters water. Gravity still pertains; we're still earth*like*. But it's odd enough to constantly remind us how profoundly we've altered the only place we've ever known [2–3].

By asking us to look at our own planet as an alien one with a name that is difficult to pronounce, McKibben invites us to rethink even the most basic and taken-for-granted dimensions of daily life in view of fundamental ecological change.

This idea that humans might no longer be naturally at home on the planet on which they evolved, due to both intended and unintended consequences of their own actions, is also a recurring motif in Dick's fiction. Dick, of course, did not envision these scenarios in terms of climate change, which only became a frequent topic of scientific and public debate after his death (although one of his novels, *The Three Stigmata of Palmer Eldritch*, already features a world grown so hot that city dwellers cannot venture outside their "conapts" without special protection). Rather, it is nuclear fall-out after a global war that typically transforms nature in his fiction. While nuclear radiation leads to widespread death and devastation, it also sometimes generates new forms of life in Dick's imagination of the future: cataclysm not only gives rise to new forms of community—as Jameson points out—but also to new organisms and ecosystems. The short story "Planet for Transients," for example, which was first published in 1953, is set on the North American continent three hundred and fifty years after a global nuclear war. Instead of nuclear winter and the devastation of organic life, radiation has given rise to an explosion of new biological forms: the planet actually teems with life.

> To his right the towering column of orange shrubbery rose, wrapped around the sagging concrete pillar. Spread out over the rolling countryside was a vast expanse of grass and trees. In the distance a mass of growth looked like a wall, a jungle of creepers and insects and flowers and underbrush.... Two immense butterflies danced past him. Great fragile shapes, multi-colored, racing erratically around him and then away. Life everywhere—bugs and plants and the rustling small animals in the shrubbery, a buzzing jungle of life in every direction [327].

This planetary environment, obviously, differs sharply from the barren post-nuclear environments of "Autofac" (1956) or *Do Androids Dream of Electric Sheep?* in its exuberant explosion of life forms. But humanity in its conventional guise is excluded from this vibrant new biosphere. Old-style humans have had to withdraw to underground habitats and can only venture to the surface in space suits with lead lining to protect them from radiation, with oxygen tanks that provide them with air they can breathe, and with food supplies that are not radioactive. The story follows such an old-style human, Trent, on his quest for other remaining human communities, since basic supplies and technological devices in his own have finally run out. On his walk through the new jungles and grasslands, he encounters several of the novel human species that have evolved from accelerated mutation rates due to pervasive radiation. He encounters eight-foot-tall humans nicknamed "toads" for their horn-like bluish skin, shorter ones called "bugs" for their chitinous shields, "worms" who are blind and live underground, and "runners" who resemble humanoid kangaroos. All of them are adapted to the new radioactive environment: they move about outdoors with no special protective gear and nourish themselves from the foods the new ecology yields.

Trent, meanwhile, toils on in his heavy suit with dwindling oxygen supplies. He finally discovers a settlement of conventional humans outside Montreal, but it has been recently abandoned. Just as he radios this disappointing find back to his dispatcher in Pennsylvania, a spaceship appears and lands. A team of former residents of the community has come back to pick up supplies from the old dwellings—as it turns out, for a new settlement that the group has established on Mars. They offer to take Trent and his community of thirty along to their new village. "It's pretty dry and barren, but it's not radioactive," the crew leader, Norris, explains. He sees no possibility of restoring Earth to livable conditions for old humans. When Trent insists, "We're the true humans" (338), Norris responds:

> "Not anymore. Earth is alive, teeming with life. Growing wildly—in all directions. We're one form, an old form. To live here we'd have to restore the old conditions, the old factors, the balance as it was three hundred and fifty years ago. A colossal job. And if we succeeded, if we managed to cool Earth, none of this would remain."
>
> Norris pointed at the great brown forests. And beyond it, towards the south, at the beginning of the steaming jungle that continued all the way to the Straits of Magellan.
>
> "In a way, it's what we deserve. *We* brought the war. *We* changed Earth. Not destroyed—*changed*. Made it so different we can't live here any longer" [338].

In Norris's view, it is now humans who are "visitors on a strange planet." He explains: "Look at us. Shielded suits and helmets, spacesuits—for exploring. We're a rocket-ship stopping at an alien world on which we can't survive. Stopping for a brief period to load up—and then take off again.... Closed helmets. Lead shields. Counters and special food and water." (338). Humans can no longer inhabit Earth in any traditional way, whereas the "natives," as Norris calls them, are the new posthuman species who can build villages on the Earth's surface, breathe its air, drink its water, and eat its food (339). Old humans, by contrast, have become aliens on their own planet.

A parallel scenario unfolds in Dick's novel *The World Jones Made* (1956), a world in which nuclear war has given rise to a variety of mutants. The novel opens with the description of an artificial biosphere with atmospheric gases, flora, and fauna that differ significantly from Earth's.

> The temperature of the Refuge varied from 99 degrees Fahrenheit to 101 degrees Fahrenheit. Steam lay perennially in the air, drifting and billowing sluggishly. Geysers of hot water spurted, and the ground was a shifting surface of warm slime, compounded from water, dissolved minerals and fungoid pulp. The remains of lichens and protozoa colored and thickened the scum of moisture that dripped everywhere, over the wet

rocks and sponge-like shrubbery, the various utilitarian installations. A careful backdrop had been painted, a long plateau rising from a heavy ocean [1].

One of the main characters perceives this environment as completely alien during a visit: "Only greens and blues were visible. The whole tank resembled a marine world, rather than the land world. A damp world, hot, steamy, compact, and utterly unfamiliar" (Kindle edn.).

Located in San Francisco, the Refuge is inhabited by eight dwarf-sized mutants who believe they are among the victims of radioactive fall-out. Their bodies are perfectly adapted to their artificial environment, but they cannot venture outside, since they cannot survive in Earth's atmosphere and gravity for long. Instead, they face the prospect of spending their entire lives in the confinement of their artificial habitat. But, as is gradually revealed, these mutants are not in fact victims of radioactive contamination, but instead part of an ambitious biotechnological and ecological experiment. During a period of political turmoil and riots stirred up by a movement intent upon exterminating all the "drifters," primitive alien life forms that crash on Earth and are legally protected, the scientists in charge of the experiment fear that the rioters' resentment might extend to the strange inhabitants of the alien-looking biosphere. They therefore precipitously launch the mutants on the interplanetary mission they had long planned. The mutants crash-land on Venus and suddenly discover themselves biologically, if not otherwise, at home.

> The scene was unbelievable. For a time neither of … [the first two that emerge from the crashed spaceship] could grasp it. "We're back home," the boy murmured, dazed and confused. "Something went wrong. We went around in a circle."
> But it wasn't the Refuge. And yet it *was*. Familiar hazy hills spread out, lost in billowing moisture. Green lichens grew everywhere; the soil was a tangled floor of lush growing plants. The air smelled of intricate organic life, a rich, complex odor, similar to the odor they remembered, but, at the same time, far more alive. They gaped foolishly: there was no delineating wall. There was no finite hull confining it. The world lay stretched out as far as the eye could see. And above. The world was everywhere.
> "My God," Frank said. "It's not a fake" [144].

Well adapted to their new planetary environment, the mutants—who would most likely be called posthumans in more recent science fiction—begin to adapt terrestrial technologies to their new environment. They explore Venusian fauna and flora, invent new domestication strategies, and create the nucleus of a new civilization. The first Venus-born child turns out to be biologically posthuman, not a reversion back to the old human gene pattern: a signal at the end of the novel that the new species has fully adapted to its new environment and can expect to sustain itself into the long-term future.

At the same time, a few human refugees from the political upheaval on Earth create a habitat with terrestrial flora and fauna on Venus that mirrors the enclosed biosphere portrayed at the beginning of the novel. The refugees have brought along pigs, cats, and dogs, even bugs and mice, because, the father of the family explains, "'I wanted things to be natural.... I even boxed up some grasshoppers and flies. I want my world to be complete.... I want [my son] to know what he's going to be up against.... So he'll be prepared, when the three of us go back'" (198). "Natural," of course, cannot help but be an ironic description of a habitat that had to be artificially constructed and differs fundamentally from that of the surrounding Venusian ecosystem, and the ending of the novel puts in question whether return to Earth is a realistic expectation: the Earth family may be as confined to its artificial habitat as the new Venusians were back on Earth. Like Trent and Norris' species of humans in "Planet for Transients," which has been superseded by posthuman species adapted to a radioactive environment, the Earth biosphere in the Venusian scenario of *The World Jones Made* becomes a somewhat nostalgic remnant of an ecology from which the most recent humans have moved on. Who is the native and who is the alien? Who belongs in a particular ecology, biologically and psychologically? Domestication, biotechnology, and terraforming make the answers to these questions difficult and ambiguous as biologically altered humans travel to other planets and Earth itself changes under the impact of human technologies.

Like Evernden and McKibben, then, Dick sometimes imagines humans as aliens on their own planet as a new ecology emerges, and at other times envisions humans technologically adapting their own bodies to new environments at the same time as they reshape the new natures they encounter. Already in some of his texts from the 1950s, but especially in Dick's work from the 1960s, the new organisms and environments that emerge after a global cataclysm are entirely artificial biological or mechanical creations that develop a life and consciousness of their own. In the arc of Dick's fiction, the self-replicating and evolving war weapons of the short story "Second Variety" gradually transform into the intelligent human replicas of *Do Androids Dream of Electric Sheep?*. As Patricia Warrick has pointed out,

> [a]t first [Dick] presents electronic constructs as merely automatons; then they become will-less robot-agents of enemy or alien forces, while masquerading as humans. Next robots become increasingly more like humans, with a sense of personal identity and a concomitant will to survive; and finally robots actually become superior to humans. [1983: 191].

These products of biotech and robotics labs, whether they are imitations of animals or humans, increasingly replace natural ecologies that have been devastated by war or other technological impacts in Dick's fiction (Warrick 1983: 192; Heise 2003: 71–74). But if biological nature gives way to its mechanical or electronic simulations in Dick's later fiction, this does not imply that the question of humans' relationships to their environments disappears. On the contrary, many of Dick's texts raise questions similar to those that have recently been debated in the context of the Anthropocene: How do humans survive in an environment in which many fundamental processes have been altered by human activities, intentionally or unintentionally? How should they manage ecologies that are at the same time pervasively domesticated and yet often outside human control? What responsibilities do humans have in repairing ecological damage? How do environments that have little original or "wild" nature left change individual and collective identities?

These questions unfold most obviously in Dick's best-known novel, *Do Androids Dream of Electric Sheep?*. The novel's human characters are confronted with two different sets of artificial beings. On one hand, they encounter human-like androids that have been manufactured for use in the off-world colonies where most humans live after planet Earth has been radioactively contaminated during World War Terminus, a global nuclear conflagration. Androids are theoretically not allowed to go to Earth, but some of them do so illegally to escape from the hardship of their enslaved lives in the Martian colonies. Arresting and killing them is made difficult by their close resemblance to "normal" humans, to the point where their difference can only be detected with the help of a psychological test that focuses on their inability to empathize with animals. On the other hand, humans keep robotic animals when they cannot afford costly real animals, which have become exceedingly scarce because of the war and radioactive fallout. While taking care of the remaining animals was a legal obligation in the aftermath of World War Terminus, it has become part of social etiquette by the time the plot starts. Robotic animals have mechanical parts and control panels, so their artificiality can be easily enough established by anyone who cares to look closely.

Even though humans and androids live in artificial environments, the critic Susan M. Bernardo has argued, both long for an authentic connection with the planet in what she calls "terraphilia." But this longing "can have no consummation because the world for which they long does not exist. Simulation and substitution are the ways they deal with this deficit and manage to create a sense of place from an initially broad idea of space and environments" (2014: 156). This terraphilia, in her reading, is the true marker of humanity in Dick's storyworld, as opposed to empathy, which is again and again held up as a standard of humanness but does not in the end unequivocally distinguish industrially manufactured from biologically born humans (Bernardo 2014: 168). Along somewhat different lines, Sherryl Vint has highlighted the importance of animals in the novel and the way in which the devotion and care for animals, whether they are mechanical or biological, defines humanness.

Both critics capture the continuing importance of nature in the depopulated and media-saturated world of postnuclear San Francisco in *Do Androids Dream of Electric Sheep?*. Crucial scenes for both of their readings as well as my own earlier engagement with the novel in the context of species extinction (Heise 2003) occur when two of the novel's protagonists, the animal repairman J.R. Isidore and the android hunter Rick Deckard, unexpectedly encounter what appear to be authentically wild animals. Isidore finds a spider in his apartment at a time when he is also offering sanctuary to three of the hunted androids, with whose predicament he has genuine compassion. Isidore takes his discovery of the spider as a sign from Wilbur Mercer, the central figure in a religious practice that in Dick's future society involves the use of "empathy boxes." These technological devices enable the citizens of this future to immerse themselves in a religious ritual in which they empathically connect with each other as well as the aged Wilbur Mercer, an old man who combines features of Sisyphus and Christ in his recurring ascent to a hill, fall into a netherworld, and resurrection.

But when the androids see the spider, they begin to perform a playful quasi-scientific experiment on it that consists of cutting off its legs consecutively to see how many it needs still to be able to walk—until Isidore snatches the animal from them and drowns it in the kitchen sink to end its suffering. The scene is clearly designed to generate revulsion and induce readers to question their own sympathy with the androids, who up to this point in the novel had been portrayed as victims of unwarranted discrimination and prosecution. In their total lack of empathy not just for the spider but for Isidore, their host, whose agitation and dismay at the mutilation they ignore, the androids seem to confirm what the reader had previously been invited to view as dubious stereotypes—their inhuman lack of compassion with other living beings. But as many critics have pointed out, the scene is not nearly as clear-cut as it appears at first sight, since mutilation and experimentation on invertebrates is of course part of normal human practice: children as well as scientists routinely injure, kill and dismember animals, either for play or for the acquisition of scientific knowledge. So Dick's portrayal of the androids may be aimed less at discrediting their humanity than at questioning the inhumanity that we routinely accept as part of "normal" humanness. Isidore's own reconnection with wild nature appears to be real enough, but he himself exists at the margins of this future society: mentally disabled because of radiation, he is denigrated by "normal" humans and legally outlawed from migrating to the colonies.

Isidore's discovery of the spider is echoed in a scene near the end of the novel, when Deckard leaves San Francisco for the first time. Exhausted after a risk-fraught hunt for six androids, he seeks spiritual restoration in a barren stretch of land north of San Francisco that resembles the desolate virtual landscape on display in empathy boxes. Deckard experiences a similar fusion with Mercer in the desert-like landscape even without the help of an empathy box. Right afterwards, as if to confirm his extraordinary vision, he spots an animal in this unlikely setting: "An animal, he said to himself. And his heart lugged under the excessive load, the shock of recognition. I know what it is, he realized; I've never seen one before but I know it from the old nature films they show on Government TV. They're extinct! he said to himself" (236). Like so much else in the novel, Deckard's reaction to what turns out to be an extinct species of toad is both deeply spiritual and unashamedly materialist. He takes the discovery to be a gift from Mercer, at the same time that he considers the compensation he might receive: "Something about a star of honor from the U.N. and a stipend. A reward running into the millions of dollars" (237).[6]

But when Deckard returns home and happily shows his wife the toad, she discovers almost immediately that the animal has a diminutive control panel on its belly, proving that it is yet another artificial replica. This makes Deckard's discovery of it no less miraculous: it is as mysterious how an electric toad would have continued functioning in the Northern California desert without any maintenance as it is that a biological toad would have sustained itself in a radioactive landscape. In a sense, then, the discovery of the toad might still be taken as some kind of religious epiphany, and Deckard is not as disappointed by its artificiality as one might have expected. He emphasizes that "'it doesn't matter. The electric things have their lives, too. Paltry as those lives are'" (241). This statement has often been taken as the novel's ontological summation, emancipating androids and artificial animals alike from their secondary and discredited status. Katherine Hayles, for example, has highlighted "the mixed condition of humans who are at their best when they show tolerance and affection for the creatures, biological or mechanical, with whom they share the planet" (1999: 191).

As I argued in an earlier reading of *Androids*, Deckard's reference to "electric things" (which the androids in the novel are not) and his characterization of their life as "paltry" make his statement a bit less of a full-throated embrace of cyborgism than it might seem (Heise 2003: 74). But however this may be, Deckard's statement certainly does attribute life to robotic animals, in a final twist on the considerations of nature in the novel that puts humans' empathic care for the natural world, and animals in particular, ahead of principled ontological definitions of what "nature" or "animals" might be in a global ecology pervasively transformed by humans. Whatever has a claim to life has a claim to human empathy and care—and that might include creatures that are wild and ones that are not, humanly altered or unchanged, organic or mechanic: this is as close as Dick's novel comes to a definitive pronouncement about humans' future relationship to nature. Deckard's wife, Iran, highlights this attitude by ordering a supply of electric flies for the toad because, she declares to the supplier, her husband is "devoted" to the animal (244). Not only does this perspective invert that of Dr. Frankenstein in Mary Shelley's foundational novel, in that Dick's characters are endorsed to the extent that they take responsibility for their creatures regardless of whether they are products of nature conventionally understood or not, it also speaks to contemporary environmentalists' concern with how to value ecosystems and organisms that, in the Anthropocene, have been definitively transformed by humans.

3. Repair, Maintenance and Care: Dick's Handymen

As a character type, J.R. Isidore in *Do Androids Dream of Electric Sheep?* highlights another dimension of Dick's futuristic ecologies: the maintenance and repair of systems perpetually prone to malfunction or failure. Isidore is dismissed as a "chickenhead" or "anthead" by other characters in the novel because his mental faculties have been damaged by radiation. His own limits and the discrimination to which he is subjected, though, have endowed him with extraordinary capacities for empathy. Not only does he have a unique talent for persuading grieving customers of a deceased pet animal to assuage their loss by acquiring an artificial animal, he is also so attached to the robot animals that he at one point mistakes a dying mechanical cat for a real one and speaks to it tenderly and encouragingly until it stops functioning.

The handyman or repairman with an uncanny knack for fixing troublesome appliances and broken artifacts, and sometimes also a genuine affection for both organic and mechanical fellow beings is a staple of Dick's fiction, as both Darko Suvin and Jameson have noted (Suvin 1983: 87; Jameson 2005: 378): for example, Thomas Cole in "The Variable Man" (1953); Leon Cartwright, the "electronics repairman and human being with a conscience" in *Solar Lottery* (1954: 17); the time-traveling swibble repairman in "Service Call" (1955); Jack Bohlen, the protagonist and repair technician in *Martian Time-Slip* (1962); Hoppy Harrington, the thalidomide victim in *Dr. Bloodmoney* (1965), who starts out learning television repair and becomes a handyman without hands; Bruce Himmel, the quality-control inspector who refashions defective starship guidance units into small autonomous robots in his free time in *Now Wait for Last Year* (1966); Joe Fernwright, the ceramics repairman in *Galactic Pot-Healer* (1969); and Nick Appleton, the tire regroover at the center of *Our Friends from Frolix 8* (1970).

The importance of characters who know how to repair broken-down devices and systems in Dick's fiction highlights how fragile the social, ecological, and technological networks are that his imagined communities rely on. The scenarios in which the futuristic repairmen carry out their work range across a wide spectrum, from the postapocalyptic community in Marin County in *Dr. Bloodmoney* that comes to depend on Hoppy Harrington and the precarious settlements on Mars where Jack Bohlen works in *Martian Time-Slip*, to the interstellar war efforts to which Thomas Cole is recruited even though he is just an uneducated and civilian handyman from an earlier time period. But all of these scenarios feature political, military, corporate or scientific authorities who are unable to control the technologies they have deployed and to manage the ecologies that have emerged from human use and abuse. In these situations, the repairmen intervene, sometimes in minor and sometimes in major ways, sometimes by legal and sometimes by illegal means, to help restore some degree of functionality and livability.

In at least one case, this intervention ends badly, not because the handyman proves incapable of solving practical problems, but because his success makes him too powerful: Hoppy Harrington turns into a tyrant and lethal danger for the postwar community that has made use of his talents and finally has to be killed to allow the community to continue in *Dr. Bloodmoney*. But in most other cases, Dick's repairmen contribute in at least a minor way to the success of a major enterprise, as Joe Fernwright does in helping the monstrously large alien Glimmung lift a sunken cathedral and thereby bring back an extinct civilization in *Galactic Pot-Healer*. And in some cases, the handymen's talent goes beyond mere repair: the most talented among them are able to take a broken device and develop it to a higher purpose. In this vein, Bruce Himmel indignantly defends broken spaceship units from being "groonked," consigned to the junk heap, and converts them into tiny robots that develop a social life of their own in *Now Wait for Last Year*. In "The Variable Man," similarly, Thomas Cole is recruited to complete a device that humans plan to deploy in their war against the ancient and powerful empire of Proxima Centauri. Originally, the inventors had intended to design a spaceship able to travel at the speed of light, but since the vehicle exploded on re-entry into normal space at the end of its journey, they work to convert it for use as an interstellar bomb of unprecedented power. Cole completes the construction that they were unable to finish on time for a decisive battle, and the bomb is sent to Proxima Centauri—but it does not explode. As the military leadership resigns itself to defeat, they discover that Cole has opened up interstellar travel beyond Proxima Centauri instead, by successfully converting the bomb into the functioning spaceship that it was originally designed to be.

In an indirect way, Dick here anticipates one of cyberpunk author William Gibson's basic tenets regarding matters of technology, namely that "the street finds its own uses for things" (1986: 186). Like Gibson, Dick foregrounds characters who are not formally trained or officially in charge of a particular technology, but amateurs and bricoleurs with talent and a passion for a particular art form or technological device. They end up being able to develop it in ways unforeseen by those who designed it and were supposed to control it. As the cases of J.R. Isidore and Bruce Himmel highlight, this reappropriation and reinvention of technology often takes them to the fuzzy borderlines between the inanimate and the animate, object and organism, technology and ecology.

Isidore's care for mechanical animals in need of repair leads him to empathize with the organic but equally artificial androids and thereby to function as a yardstick for what counts as human in *Do Androids Dream of Electric Sheep?*, in an anticipation of Rick Deckard's later insight that technological artifacts possess a life of their own that it is worth respecting. Himmel's tiny robot carts analogously develop a society of their own and even enter into fights for dominance and survival:

> The cart was pursued by another of its kind. They met, in a tangle of newspapers and bottles, and then the debris trembled and bits flew everywhere as the carts fought it out, ramming each other head-on, trying for the cephalic unit in each other's center … now one … seemed to be triumphing. It withdrew and, like a goat, maneuvered to locate itself for the coup de grace. While it was positioning itself the damaged one, in a last burst of native wit, popped into the sanctuary of a discarded galvanized zinc bucket and was out of the fray. Protected, it became inert, prepared to wait things out, forever if necessary…
>
> "I won't hurt you," Eric said to it, crouching down in order to get a better glimpse of it. The damaged thing, however, remained where it was. "Okay," he said and straightened up. "I get the idea." It knew what it wanted.… Even these things, he decided, are determined to live.… They deserve their opportunity, their minuscule place under the sun and sky [*Now Wait for Last Year*: 248–249].

Jameson calls this emergence of new mechanical life forms "a very modest salvationism … from a very imperfect landscape" (2005: 382). Modest it may be in this particular case, but the development of new species from dystopian landscapes through the tinkerer's dedication and knowledge also signals hope. Like Deckard's acknowledgment of new forms of life in the midst of a postnuclear wasteland, Eric Sweetscent, the protagonist of *Now Wait for Last Year*, ends up recognizing the right of new techno-organisms to form part of the ecologies of the future.

In some of Dick's fictional scenarios, recognizing the rights of new species that have emerged from transformed landscapes also includes granting them sovereignty over those territories. Let me return, to conclude, to the short story "Planet for Transients." Trent expresses the hope that even after he and his friends join Norris' settlement on Mars, they might come back to Earth to visit at some point.

> Norris smiled ruefully. "I hope so too. But we'll have to get permission from the inhabitants—permission to land.… We'll have to ask them if it's all right. And they may say *no*. They many not want us" [339].

Co-existence of a variety of species here turns into a scenario in which humans might not only have to ask permission to return to the habitat in which they evolved, but in which they might have to yield their dominance indefinitely to species that are better equipped to manage the ecosystem than they have been.

All three of the major tropes in Dick's fiction that I have highlighted here—postwar environments, the portrayal of humans as aliens on a planet that they have transformed beyond recognition, and the power of the handyman-tinkerer to catalyze new forms of life at the edge of technology and biology—emerged out of the landscapes of pessimism and devastation occasioned by the Cold War and the threat of global nuclear war. In the early twenty-first century, we reread these tropes from amid a different scenario of global threat, that of the Anthropocene and its scenarios of climate change, pollution, ocean acidification, biodiversity loss, and other ecological crises. The power of Dick's fiction in this context lies in its invitation to rethink some of the story templates on which environmentalist thought and writing have conventionally relied, and to move beyond narratives of a past natural home, harmony, or balance that we might return to. In the context of the Anthropocene, science fiction stories like the ones I have discussed here, which envision humans as aliens on a planet they themselves have irreversibly altered, take the risks of global ecological crisis for human and nonhuman life seriously, but also invite us to imagine new forms of agency and life emerging from the landscapes of change.

The anthropologist Anna Tsing, along similar lines, has used her exploration of matsutake mushrooms and the ecologies, economies, and communities that have developed around them to ask more broadly what might emerge from the damaged landscapes of the Anthropocene:

> Without stories of progress, the world has become a terrifying place. The ruin glares at us with the horror of its abandonment. It's not easy to know how to make a life, much less avert planetary destruction. Luckily there is still company, human and not human. We can still explore the overgrown verges of our blasted landscapes—the edges of capitalist discipline, scalability, and abandoned resource plantations. We can still catch the scent of the latent commons [2015: loc. 4147].

In rereading Dick in the Anthropocene, his postnuclear landscapes turn into our own environments threatened by climate change and species loss, and his natural aliens, human and nonhuman, into figures of thought for thinking about our own multispecies communities—including a few robots.

Notes

1. See, for example, Houschwitzka.
2. Both of these readings, legitimate and important as they are, also face difficulties. Dick's and his characters' investments in religious and other kinds of supernatural experience, the persistence of heroic and villainous figures in his plots, and Dick's own negative pronouncements about the figure of the android in his essays are not always easy to compatibilize

with the relativism concerning culture and identity that is sometimes ascribed to him. For a fuller discussion, see Heise (2003: 71–74).

3. See Stoermer and Crutzen (2000) and Crutzen (2002).

4. For a more detailed discussion of these narratives, see Heise (2016: 201–209).

5. As noted in *Imagining Extinction*, I am indebted to the identification of the far-future geologist as a science fiction trope to Gerry Canavan (2016: 218n6).

6. See Vint for a detailed analysis of how human-animal relations are caught up in commodification.

Works Cited

Ackerman, Diane. *The Human Age: The World Shaped by Us*. Norton, 2014.
Bernardo, Susan M. "A Case of Terraphilia: Longing for Place and Community in Philip K. Dick's *Do Androids Dream of Electric Sheep?*" *Environments in Science Fiction: Essays on Alternative Spaces*. Ed. Susan M. Bernardo. McFarland, 2014. 154–170.
Chakrabarty, Dipesh. "The Climate of History: Four Theses." *Critical Inquiry* 35, 2009, 197–222.
Crutzen, Paul J. "Geology of Mankind." *Nature* 415, 3 January 2002, 23.
———, and Eugene F. Stoermer. "The 'Anthropocene.'" *Global Change Newsletter* 41, 2000, 17–18.
Dick, Philip K. "Autofac." 1956. *Robots, Androids, and Mechanical Oddities: The Science Fiction of Philip K. Dick*. Ed. Patricia S. Warrick and Martin H. Greenberg. Southern Illinois University Press, 1984. 145–166.
———. *Do Androids Dream of Electric Sheep?* 1968. Del Rey, 1996.
———. *Dr. Bloodmoney*. 1965. Houghton Mifflin Harcourt, 2012.
———. *Galactic Pot-Healer*. 1969. Houghton Mifflin Harcourt, 2013.
———. *Now Wait for Last Year*. 1966. Houghton Mifflin Harcourt, 2011.
———. *Our Friends from Frolix 8*. 1970. Houghton Mifflin Harcourt, 2019.
———. "Planet for Transients." 1953. *The Collected Short Stories of Philip K. Dick*. Vol. 2. Citadel Twilight, 1990. 327–339.
———. "Second Variety." 1953. *Robots, Androids, and Mechanical Oddities: The Science Fiction of Philip K. Dick*. Ed. Patricia S. Warrick and Martin H. Greenberg. Southern Illinois University Press, 1984. 38–76.
———. "Service Call." 1955. *Robots, Androids, and Mechanical Oddities: The Science Fiction of Philip K. Dick*. Ed. Patricia S. Warrick and Martin H. Greenberg. Southern Illinois University Press, 1984. 129–144.
———. *The Simulacra*. 1964. Houghton Mifflin Harcourt, 2011.
———. *Solar Lottery*. 1955. Houghton Mifflin Harcourt, 2012.
———. "Some Kinds of Life." 1953. *The Collected Short Stories of Philip K. Dick*. Vol. 2. Citadel Twilight, 1990. 109–118.
———. *The Three Stigmata of Palmer Eldritch*. 1964. Houghton Mifflin Harcourt, 2011.
———. "The Variable Man." 1953. *The Collected Short Stories of Philip K. Dick*. Vol. 1. Citadel, 1987. 163–220.
———. *The World Jones Made*. 1956. Houghton Mifflin Harcourt. 2012.
Evernden, Neil. *The Natural Alien*. 1985. Second edition. University of Toronto Press, 1993.
Galvan, Jill. "Entering the Posthuman Collective in Philip K. Dick's *Do Androids Dream of Electric Sheep?*" *Science-Fiction Studies* 24, 1997, 414–429.
Gibson, William. "Burning Chrome." 1982. *Burning Chrome*. Ace, 1986. 168–191.
Haraway, Donna J. "A Cyborg Manifesto: Science, Technology, and Socialist-Feminism in the Late Twentieth Century." 1984. In *Simians, Cyborgs, and Women: The Reinvention of Nature*. Routledge, 1991. 149–81.
Hayles, N. Katherine. *How We Became Posthuman: Virtual Bodies in Cybernetics, Literature, and Informatics*. University of Chicago Press, 1999.
Heise, Ursula K. "From Extinction to Electronics: Dead Frogs, Live Dinosaurs, and Electric Sheep." *Zootologies: The Question of the Animal*. Ed. Cary Wolfe. University of Minnesota Press, 2003. 59–81.

_____. *Imagining Extinction: The Cultural Meanings of Endangered Species*. University of Chicago Press, 2016.
Houswitschka, Christoph. "Dystopian Androids: Philip K. Dick, *Do Androids Dream of Electric Sheep?* (1968) and Ridley Scott, *Blade Runner* (1982)." *Dystopia, Science Fiction, Post-Apocalypse: Classics—New Tendencies—Model Interpretations*. Ed. Eckart Voigts and Alessandra Boller. TWissenschaftlicher Verlag Trier, 2015. 121–138.
Jameson, Fredric. *Archaeologies of the Future: The Desire Called Utopia and Other Science Fictions*. Verso, 2005.
McKibben, Bill. *Eaarth: Making a Life on a Tough New Planet*. St. Martin's, 2011.
_____. *The End of Nature*. 1989. Random House, 2006.
Suvin, Darko. "Artifice as Refuge and World View: Philip K. Dick's Foci." *Philip K. Dick*. Ed. Martin Harry Greenberg and Joseph D. Olander. Taplinger, 1983. 73–95.
Tsing, Anna Lowenhaupt. *The Mushroom at the End of the World: On the Possibility of Life in Capitalist Ruins*. Princeton University Press, 2015.
Vint, Sherryl. "Speciesism and Species Being in *Do Androids Dream of Electric Sheep?*" *Mosaic* 40.1, 2007, 111–126.
Warrick, Patricia S. "The Labyrinthian Process of the Artificial: Philip K. Dick's Androids and Mechanical Constructs." *Philip K. Dick*. Ed. Martin Harry Greenberg and Joseph D. Olander. Taplinger, 1983. 189–214.

From Soft Totalitarianism to TV Introjection
Philip Kindred Dick and the Tube

UMBERTO ROSSI

> The debased form of power is to be on TV talk-shows.
> —Philip K. Dick

Media feature prominently in Dick's *oeuvre*: the electro-mechanic or electronic ones, from radio to vinyl records, but also the older ones, such as newspapers and books, not to mention the earliest forms of digital devices—e.g., the hypertext of the Bible described in *The Divine Invasion*. Among these, television seems to be the one whose life, up to a certain point, runs parallel to that of the writer, so that he witnessed the advent of TV and what Cecelia Tichi called "the Twentieth Century television mentality" (5). A few dates may support this statement. Dick was born in 1928 and died in 1982; John Logie Baird, the British television pioneer, transmitted the first television picture in 1925; Philo T. Farnsworth, his American counterpart, followed suit two years later. Dick published his first short story, "Roog," in February 1953; according to media historian Erik Barnouw the age of TV started for good in that year, when restrictions on war materials caused by the Korean War were lifted. Hence travelling again through Dick's *oeuvre* looking for the Tube (as Thomas Pynchon called it), the telescreen (as it is named in a novel that powerfully influenced Dick, Orwell's *Nineteen Eighty-Four*), or, if we prefer, television (as we usually don't call the device, preferring its short acronym) may help us to connect in a novel fashion some of his narratives, at the same time placing them in their historical background via the evolution of the electronic medium that may well be said to have had the strongest impact on our world. Moreover, such a reading will allow us to spot traces of Dick's changing attitude towards TV: from threatening, overpowering technology with authoritarian implications to fixture in a world of trash, or *kipple*, as Dick called it. Besides, it may also be an opportunity to talk about novels and short stories that have not been paramount in PKD scholarship so far, but might yield important insights on the twisted worlds of the Californian writer.

Dick witnessed the advent of TV, as we can see in one of his mainstream novels, *Puttering About in a Small Land,* completed by May 15, 1957, but posthumously published in 1985. The novel does not seem focused on TV and its impact, but on the adultery involving TV/radio technician Roger Lindahl and housewife Liz Bonner. In its painstakingly built background, however, we are shown the rise of the TV in the early 1950s. Roger foresees the oncoming future of a TV society: "There's going to be television inside one year," he tells a radio retailer. "I read all the trade journals and I know: it's the truth. This time next year you're going to have as big a television inventory as everything else put together" (92). He is the typical Dickian little man, ultimately defeated by his ambitious wife, who takes advantage of the adultery to force Roger to sell his shop to Liz Bonner's husband Chick, a local businessman, turning it into an elegant establishment with lavish appearance called "L & B Appliance Mart," full of brand new TV sets (255–6).

Those TV sets might seem no more than stage props, because there isn't a single scene in the novel in which they are turned on, or we are told what they show; however, they are sociologically meaningful, as they are blatant status symbols, embodying the consumerist Fifties and their dream of affluence. They are part of the age like suburbs, commuting, nuclear families, psychoanalysis and psychiatry, *Peyton Place* sexuality, and the daily struggle of the man in the gray flannel suit, which is not just the title of Sloan Wilson's 1955 bestseller, but also Dick's main concern in that decade. In fact, Dick later remarked, "During [Eisenhower's] reign we all were worrying about the man-in-the-gray-flannel-suit problem; we feared that the entire country was turning into one person and a whole lot of clones" (376). Cloning was not yet part of the collective imagination in the mid–50s, so cultural and political homogenization will be enforced through the TV sets sold in the L & B Appliance Mart.

Dick's fear that TV was a vector of conformism and homogenization finds a more straightforward expression in his science-fiction narratives, such as his 1955 short story "The Mold of Yancy." This evidently bears relation to Orwell's *Nineteen Eighty-Four* (published just six years before) with its implacable telescreens, inasmuch as its protagonists wonder how the apparently democratic society of Callisto, with a respectable two-party system, can be "moving toward a totalitarian make-up" (*Minority Report* 455), as a computerized analysis of statistical data has ascertained. This story about a future totalitarian society is pivoted upon a TV celebrity, as we shall see; this does not come as a surprise, because, according to media theorist Gabriele Frasca, totalitarianism and the electronic media go hand in hand (124). We find this connection explained by Dick himself in his story: "A totalitarian state reaches into every sphere of its citizens' lives, forms their opinions on every subject" (55). Interestingly, such a definition is close to what one can find in the *Merriam-Webster Dictionary*: "of or relating to a political regime based on subordination of the individual to the state and strict control of all aspects of the life and productive capacity of the nation." Orwell showed how telescreens might ensure such a total and strict control of society, reaching into its citizens' lives; yet Dick's take on TV and its totalitarian potential departs from the televisual nightmare of *Nineteen Eighty-Four*. There is no violent coercion on Callisto: "This is a model democracy" (57), despondently comments one of the characters. We do not even have the blackshirts, as in the original totalitarian regime, Italian Fascism, which originated the adjective (first used by one of the opponents of Mussolini's regime, Giovanni Amendola, in 1923).

Callisto may not have a Duce, but it has Yancy, who appears on a TV set in a bar where the three Niplan agents investigating the totalitarian menace have met to compare notes. Yancy is just "a kindly-looking geezer" (58), a "[t]otally ordinary man.... Used to be a soldier; in the Mars-Jupiter War he distinguished himself—battlefield commission. Rose to the rank of major.... A sort of talking almanac. Pithy sayings on every topic. Wise old saws: how to cure a chest cold. What the trouble is back on Terra.... Very popular figure. Loved by the masses. Man of the people—speaks for them" (58). His military past notwithstanding, Yancy is very different from the Duce or the Big Brother: and yet he is absolutely charismatic. People on Callisto prefer whatever his testimonials advertise: Yancy plays croquet? "So now everybody plays croquet" (59).

We might see Yancy as an opinion leader, but—unlike today's opinion leaders, who interpret the meaning of media messages or content for lower-end media users—he seems to belong to a pre-modern age. His opinions "on every conceivable topic" (61) are based on "specific maxims drawn from mankind's rich storehouse of folklore" (61); he appeals, according to one of the members of his staff, "to a certain type of rural mind" (59). He is no metropolitan pundit, but a homespun philosopher who has his say on any conceivable topic of modern and future life.

Yancy is not a threatening "Big Brother," but a powerful persuader. And yet he doesn't seem to have an opinion on certain important but controversial topics. He is against war, but thinks "a man must come forward and fight a *just* war" (61–2). All in all, "[w]ith one sentence Yancy gave; with the next he took away. The total effect was a neat cancellation, a skilful negation. But the viewer was left with the illusion of having consumed a rich and varied intellectual feast" (62). Such a self-effacing persuasion is very effective: even a nine-year-old boy like Mike Sipling—the son of Leon, one of the writers of Yancy's speeches—knows that war is bad but "[w]e have to fight just wars, of course" (65). And how can one know which war is just? "When the time comes won't somebody say?" (66) is the boy's answer.

Yancy is endowed with a "televisional" or (to use a Pynchonian adjective) "tubal" quality: he looks as believable as any real-life TV celebrity, in his apparent harmlessness and vapidity (62). And it is thanks to him that "the first really successful totalitarian state was being realized:... harmless and trivial it emerged" (62–3). A state where "torture chambers and extermination camps" are useless because they are "needed only when persuasion fail[s]" (62), and on Callisto, persuasion is working perfectly. Here Dick foreshadows what J.G. Ballard styled "fascism lite" (Ballard 417) in one of the interviews he gave after the publication of his last novel, *Kingdom Come*, where he said that "our equivalent of the ranting führer is the cable channel chat show host" (417).

Yancy is indeed the supreme TV talk show host, just because he does not really exist. In fact, "The Mold of Yancy" may be said to go deeper into televisual (ir)reality than the 1964 novel stemming from it, *The Penultimate Truth* (1964). Here the American people miserably survive in underground shelters called Ant-tanks while on the surface of the planet a terrifying nuclear war rages, fought by the robots built in the shelters. The only contact with the outside world is cable TV, which also transmits the speeches of the president, Talbot Yancy. But in this novel Yancy has solidity: he/it is a simulacrum, an android, not the totally virtual entity à la Max Headroom of the short story:

> There it sat. Solemnly, at its large oak desk, with the American flag behind it. In Moscow another and identical sim sat ... the flag of the USSR behind it; otherwise everything, the clothes, the grey hair, the competent, fatherly, mature but soldierly features, the strong chin—it was the same sim all over again, both having been built simultaneously in Germany, wired by the finest Yance-men technicians alive.... The sim began to move.... "My fellow Americans," the sim said in its firm, familiar, near hoarse but utterly controlled voice.
> To himself Joseph Adams said, *Yes, Mr Yancy. Yes sir* [57–8].

Joseph Adams is one of the Yance-men, the writers of Yancy's speeches; he is perfectly aware that the president is an android, yet Yancy is so charismatic as to command respect and awe nonetheless. Interestingly, this android president is much more warlike than the virtual celebrity on Callisto; maybe in the countercultural Sixties, Dick could be more straightforward and let readers surmise who was the model of Yancy. It is only in 1978, however, that he clearly said that Yancy was based on Dwight D. Eisenhower (Minority Report 376).

There is a strong historical connection between TV and the public figure of the 34th president of the United States. Not only were Eisenhower's moves towards a negotiated solution to end the Korean War instrumental in unleashing the TV boom of the 1950s, but his electoral campaign was characterized by a careful use of TV, with an elaborate pageantry for each speech. The campaign was managed by Batten, Barton, Durstine & Osborn, or BBDO— one of the most important advertising agencies then and today—and based on a barrage of TV spots written by Rosser Reeves from the Ted Bates advertising agency (Barnouw 1968 299), another giant in the field. The spots sound strikingly similar to Yancy's informal style in Dick's story. For example, a citizen asked, "What about the cost of living, general?" and Ike answered: "My wife, Mamie, worries about the same thing. I tell her it's our job to change that on November fourth!" (Barnouw 1968 299).

The Democratic candidate, Adlai Stevenson, relied on his oratorical abilities instead, but his speeches did not fit the timing of TV programs. Barnouw suggests that Stevenson was defeated because he didn't want to be merchandised "like a breakfast food" (Barnouw 1968 299); surely the help of expert admen like Peter George Peterson, who invented the celebrated "I like Ike" slogan, paved the way for Eisenhower's victory. Stevenson seemed to be unaware that the age of TV politics had already begun, at least since 1948, when both the Republican and Democratic parties had chosen Philadelphia for their conventions because that city was on the coaxial cable linking New York and Washington (Barnouw 1968 257). However, it was the 1952 electoral campaign that saw a massive use of the new medium, at least on the Republican side. Television was also used to solve an embarrassing crisis involving Richard Nixon, the Republican candidate to vice-presidency, accused of having improperly received funds from his backers. Nixon replied by giving a television speech on September 23, 1952, where he gave an account of his finances and said that the only gift received from his electors was "a little cocker spaniel dog in a crate … sent all the way from Texas" (Barnouw 1970 301), which his daughters had called Checkers. This became famous as the "Checkers Speech," and the phrase came to mean any emotional speech given by a politician—another example of TV politics, which was not lost on Philip K. Dick.

In these works of the 1950s TV is a sort of alien invader, only apparently benevolent and familiar; no wonder then that TV sets are omnipresent in the fake town of the Fifties in which Ragle Gumm is imprisoned in *Time Out of Joint* (1959). They are an important part of the commonplace reality where the novel takes place, the apparently ordinary suburb with "Men clipping lawns on Sunday afternoon, while listening to the ball game on TV" (79–80). Interestingly, in this nameless, nondescript town TV has totally replaced its older relative, radio—a way to tell readers that the Tube is *the* Medium. Unsurprisingly we find it in *The Man in the High Castle* (1962), where it is the evil Nazi Germany, after having won World War II, which is introducing television. Since the radio is still the most common medium in these alternative 1960s, TV is news:

> The new *Life* … had a big article called: TELEVISION IN EUROPE: GLIMPSE OF TOMORROW. Turning to it, interested, she saw a picture of a German family watching television in their living room. Already, the article said, there was four hours of image

broadcast during the day from Berlin. Some day there would be television stations in all the major European cities. And, by 1970, one would be built in New York [77].

Here television is associated to Nazi imperialism. Barnouw remarkably called the third volume of his history of broadcasting in the U.S. *The Image Empire*, and argued that "[i]f the United States was a felt presence throughout the world, the rise of broadcasting had something to do with it. Almost everywhere American voices could be heard" (85). He refers to the radio, but it is difficult not to think that the political and economical hegemony called "American Empire" is also connected to TV; and in a novel in which the Third Reich rules the world, TV must be developed by Telefunken, not RCA.

However, in the Sixties, TV becomes more and more important in Dick's fiction, as we can see in *The Simulacra*, also published in 1964, that continues the discourse that was started with "The Mold of Yancy": here the President of the United States of America and Europe, the sfnal aggregation of the USA and West Germany where the novel takes place, is nothing more than the Yancy android (or simulacrum) with a German name (Rudi Kalbfleisch) and nickname (*Der Alte*, the old one). Here, too, the leader is not an autonomous and intelligent android (like those in *We Can Build You*, or in *Do Androids Dream of Electric Sheep?*): it is no more than a programmed electronic puppet. And Kalbfleisch is not a charismatic figure like Yancy: he is old, grey and boring, disliked by USEA citizens, and his successor will not be much better. Nicole Thibodeaux, the First Lady, describes the new *Der Alte* that is going to replace Kalbfleisch thus: "Old and tired.... A worn-out stringbean, stiff and formal, full of moralizing speeches; a real leader type who can drum obedience into the *Be* masses. Who can keep the system creaking along a while longer" (143).

The *Be* are the *Befehlträger*, the lower classes who must carry out the orders of the *Ge* elite, or *Geheimnisträger*, those who carry the secrets on which the USEA are based: among them, the fact that *der Alte* is an android, a simulacrum that only lives—like Yancy in *The Penultimate Truth*—when it is on air. In *The Simulacra* the charismatic leader is not *Der Alte*, but the First Lady, Nicole Thibodeaux. Since she is a dark-haired girl, sophisticated, sexy, and aggressive, one may suspect that the sources of Nicole's ascendancy over Americans in the novel have more to do with Dick's complicated psychology than with a real understanding of TV politics and the workings of a tubal society. Like other dark-haired girls in Dick's fiction (especially those belonging to the variety which Andrew M. Butler labeled "Bitch wife"), Nicole embodies an archetypal figure, "the image ... of the Bad Mother. Overpowering and cosmic" (98). Dick's peculiar use of psychoanalytical and psychiatric categories posits the First Lady as "a Magna Mater figure.... The great primordial mother" (184).

And yet, although the Great Mother that has enthralled and subjugated the USEA may have powerful archetypal and psychoanalytical undertones, she holds her power thanks to TV: she can avail herself of the Unified Triadic Network, which has replaced the three competing private networks of the Sixties, ABC, NBC, and CBS. This is at the same time Dick's ironical answer to Orwell's *Nineteen Eighty-Four* (Pagetti 8), with the Big Brother replaced by the Great Mother, and a corrosive satire of Camelot and the Kennedy myth, as Nicole looks definitely like a satirical portrait of Jacqueline Bouvier Kennedy Onassis, who was the First Lady while Dick was writing the novel (completed by 28 August 1963, three months before the Dallas assassination). Nicole and Jacqueline Kennedy have much in common, e.g., beauty, elegance, sophistication, a French surname, an upper-class background, high education, and interest for the arts. However, it is her role as a premier TV star that deserves attention.

Carlo Pagetti suggests that Nicole is a TV figure worshiped by unaware citizens (Pagetti 8): a TV celebrity, hosting programs like this:

> Have you even wondered what it would be like to descend to the bottom of the Pacific Ocean? Nicole has, and to answer that question she has assembled here in the Tulip Room of the White House three of the world's foremost oceanographers. Tonight she will ask them for their stories, and you will hear them too, as they were taped live, just a short while ago through the facilities of the Unified Triadic Network's Public Affairs Bureau [20-1].

Nicole *lectures* Americans, and seems determined to improve their education by means of cultural programs, as we can see in her introductory speech for a bizarre concert:

> and at our musical tonight ... we will have a saxophone quartet which will play themes from Wagner's operas, in particular my favourite, *die Meistersinger*. I believe we will all find that a deeply rewarding and certainly an enriching experience to cherish.
> And, after that, I have arranged to bring you once again an old favourite of yours, the world-renowned cellist, Henri LeClerc, in a programme of Jerome Kern and Cole Porter [168].

There is no need to explain who Cole Porter was, while Kern is the U.S. composer who wrote the 1927 musical comedy *Show Boat* with Oscar Hammerstein II. It is a grotesque mix of highbrow and lowbrow culture that is typical of Nicole's artistic events and programs, well represented by Ian Duncan and Al Miller's jug duo, using a typically popular musical instrument to perform Beethoven's late sonatas and Bach's *Goldberg Variations* (22), and striving to be selected for the White House musicals hosted by Nicole; but we might also say "emceed," and I think this is the keyword.

Nicole is above all a TV emcee of infotainment and talent shows whose charisma relies more than anything else on her beauty and polished manners, which make male USEA citizens fall in love (consciously or unconsciously) with the First Lady. That is what happens to Kongrosian (97), but also to

Ian Duncan, since there are remarkable amorous undertones in Ian's inner monologue upon meeting Nicole at the White House (161). Americans are star struck.

However, this "overpowering and cosmic" TV presence is no less an artifact than *der Alte* (and this is the second secret of *Ges*): she is an actress, Kate Rupert, the fourth to have played the part of the long time dead First Lady. She has "no real authority, in the ultimate sense" (166) because she is just the White House TV host, a political emcee who presents a variety of "entertaining" materials. Although one of the characters complains that "the TV had become educational, not entertaining" (17), the descriptions of Nicole's programs call in doubt the meaning of the adjective *educational* in that sentence. Her shows adapt highbrow "products" (e.g., Wagner) to pop combos (the sax quartet); "serious" musicians must play Jerome Kern and Cole Porter; even oceanography is made into a spectacle. It is then fitting that Nicole, the Oprah Winfrey of the USEA, is ultimately revealed to be an actress impersonating the original Mrs. Thibodeaux, just like a Marilyn Monroe or Elvis impersonator. TV presents us a debased reality of jug players and dancing papoolas— *bogus* papoolas, as a matter of fact. So far we have read narratives in which Dick envisions TV as a threatening presence, enforcing what we have called "soft fascism": a regime of televisual manipulation.

But a change takes place in the mid–1960s in Dick's approach to the Tube, as we can see in his 1967 short story "Faith of Our Fathers," appropriately published in the year of the Summer of Love, where Tung Chien, a Communist official in Vietnam, is given phenothiazine, a substance that suppresses the hallucinogenic drugs put in drinkable water by the world-wide communist regime, and sees the Party Leader on TV for what he really is: "The screen remained blank.... He faced a dead mechanical construct, made of solid-state circuits, of swivelling pseudopodia, lenses and a squawk-box. And the box began, in a droning din, to harangue him" (*We Can Remember* 265). What is on the screen is hideous, but real. Yet those who were given phenothiazine described twelve different "realities": "a *variety* of authentic experiences" (271). Chien saw the so-called Clanker (268), but there are also the Gulper, the Bird, the Clinging Tube, the Crusher. And when he finally meets the leader, he discovers something still different: "it was not, Chien realized, a mechanical construct either; it was not what he had seen on TV. That evidently was simply a device for speechmaking, as Mussolini had once used an artificial arm to salute long and tedious processions" (281). The Clanker is just another fake, not the ultimate reality—and yet this story complicates the picture, inasmuch as it is through a TV image that Chien begins his quest for the ultimate reality. In another novel belonging to the surrealistic-psychedelic phase of Dick's career, *Ubik* (1968), Glen Runciter warns his dead employees that they are not alive through TV commercials (110–1; 114–6); like in "Faith of Our Fathers," truth, albeit scrambled, can reach you through the Tube. TV is not just a propaganda tool, then; it may sometimes play against the powers that be, just like the U.S. television of the 1960s, gradually assuming a more and more critical attitude to the American involvement in Vietnam as the war escalated (Barnouw 1970 271–303), leading to Lyndon B. Johnson's famous sentence: "If I've lost Cronkite, I've lost Middle America" (reportedly uttered on February 27, 1968).

TV also plays an important role in one of the central novels in Dick's canon, *Do Androids Dream of Electric Sheep?* Though critics have not been able to answer the question posed by the title so far, it is certain that the androids in the novel watch TV, and are fond of Buster Friendly's program—not because he is "Earth's most knee-slapping TV comic" (52), but because they know that Buster is an android, too (159). And he has a revelation coming: "This is Buster Friendly, who hopes and trusts you're eager as I am to share the discovery which I've made and by the way had verified by top trained research workers working extra hours over the past week. Ho ho, folks; *this is it!*" (155). Buster's announced scoop is about Mercerism, the official religion of the future society depicted in the novel, which is based on the empathic experience provided by electronic boxes allowing believers to become Mercer himself while he is slowly killed by lapidation. This religious experience strengthens the faith of humans in Mercer and his message of universal empathy and justifies the discrimination of androids as they lack empathy. But Buster Friendly reveals that "the grey background of sky and daytime moon against which Mercer moves ... is artificial" (156); that the hill or mountain on which Mercer wearily climbs is fake as well, as explained by "a former Hollywood special-effects man, a Mr Wade Cortot" (156), who has also identified Mercer with Al Jarry, a ham actor "who played a number of bit parts in pre-war films" (157); Jarry is then routed out and his mind "scanned by telepathic means" (157), so that the rocks thrown at Mercer are revealed as "soft plastic" and his blood as ketchup.

"*Mercerism is a swindle!*" (158) proclaims Buster Friendly at the end of his program. But what sort of revelation can this be, coming from TV? Mercer appears, almost at the end of the novel, and helps Rick Deckard to retire the surviving androids. Moreover, he offers a sort of moral justification, telling him that killing androids "has to be done" (166), even though his religion condemns the killing of any form of life. And yet Buster Friendly's revelation is not given the lie by Mercer: paradoxically, the experience provided by the empathy boxes is a hoax, but Mercer exists nonetheless and his message saves Deckard (physically and spiritually). TV seems to be a mixed blessing in these narratives of the late Sixties, no more the purely evil medium.

Moreover, the specific features of TV seem to be infiltrating Dick's own fiction. We can see this in *Do Androids Dream of Electric Sheep?*, when John

Isidore, the special one, the saintly idiot who acts as a foil for Dekard, has a strange feeling while fusing with Mercer:

> He remembered the top, the sudden levelling of the hill when the climb ceased and the other part of it began. How many times had he done this? The several times blurred; future and past blurred; what he had already experienced and what he would eventually experience blended so that nothing remained but the moment... [22].

Empathy boxes offer a *repeated* experience—and this is exactly what TV offers its viewers. TV news are more often than not the repetition of dismal experiences[1]—aggressions, assassinations, terrorist attacks, wars, disasters—and this is what one also finds in one of Dick bleakest short stories, "A Little Something for Us Tempunauts" (1974), where repetition is caused by an accident that occurred during an experiment in time travel, which establishes a time loop subsequently sealed by one of the tempunauts, Addison Doug, by loading the time capsule on which he and his mates will travel with some extra weight. Dick himself explained just two years later that the story expressed "a vast weariness over the space program, which had thrilled us so at the start—especially the first lunar landing—and then had been forgotten and virtually shut down, a relic of history" (*CS5* 489). But, this is only a part of the story.

Dick's tale also features the funeral of the tempunauts that they will be able to attend thanks to ETA, or Emergence Time Activity: the living tempunauts join the motorcade following the coffins with the dead tempunauts. This climactic scene is seen "through prismatic binoculars," by "TV's top news and public event commentator, Henry Cassidy" who comments on the motorcade, comparing it to "that earlier train among the wheatfields carrying the coffin of Abraham Lincoln back to burial and the nation's capital" (341). Here Dick stages a live broadcast in its making, with the frantic communications between the TV crews, the commentator, the control room—and shows us how artificial that broadcast actually is: "'I grasp it now, Everett,' Cassidy broke in excitedly, since his authorized script read CASSIDY BREAKS IN EXCITEDLY." Another example is when Cassidy tries to stop Everett, the interviewer, because "a note was handed him in a swift scribble, reading: *Do not interview 'nauts. Urgent. Dis. previous inst*" (342).

The time loop is an anamorphic image of what had happened in the last eleven years in the U.S., the repeated funerals of people who were as famous as Lincoln, maybe even more: John Fitzgerald Kennedy, Martin Luther King, Robert Kennedy (Barnouw 1970 234–5, 316, 318). Their deaths were historical events, President Kennedy's assassination being "the first murder ever witnessed by millions" (Barnouw 1970 228); their funerals were broadcast by TV. These spectacular deaths (also including the live broadcast of Lee Oswald's assassination on NBC) were shown on TV, again and again, not only in the USA, but all over the world, so that Zapruder's film is now part of our collective subconscious. Thus, the solemn ending of the story acquires a new meaning: "This was his gift to them, the people, his country. He had bestowed upon the world a wonderful burden. The dreadful and weary miracle of eternal life" (*CS5* 352).

Shakespeare has Cassius asking, "How many ages hence/ Shall this our lofty scene be acted over/ In states unborn and accents yet unknown" (*Julius Caesar* III.1), to which Brutus adds "How many times shall Caesar bleed in sport?" How many times, Dick's short story implicitly asks us, shall the motorcade pass along Dealey Plaza, in front of the Texas School Book Depository? How many times will a Dallas policeman shout "Jack, you son of a bitch" (Barnouw 1970 233) after Ruby has fired his .38? The syntax of TV, its uncanny power to repeat historical events as if they were caught in a loop, shaped "A Little Something for Us Tempunauts," which could not have been written without the TV deaths and funerals[2] of the Kennedy brothers and Dr. King. By the end of the Sixties television's language seems to have been introjected into Dick's fiction.

A good example of such an introjection is *Flow My Tears, the Policeman Said* (published in 1974, although completed in 1970), whose protagonist is a TV star, Jason Taverner, singer and emcee of a show watched by thirty million people. We do not have the space tyrants or artificial U.S. presidents of earlier fiction: the superman at the top of Earth's future society is a TV celebrity. Taverner is a Six, one of the genetically engineered super-humans created forty-five years before the beginning of the novel; his different DNA code somewhat underlines the difference between him and his audience. His dialogue with his lover and colleague Heather Hart is all about the gap separating those who are on the active or passive side of the TV screen: the celebrities vs. the "ordinaries" (13), as Taverner calls them.

Taverner's tragedy is that he wakes up, after one of his former lovers (an ordinary) has tried to kill him, and finds himself in "a lousy, bug-infested, cheap wino hotel" (22), with a roll of banknotes but without his ID, in a totalitarian state where being without ID is the best way to get quickly killed or arrested by the omnipotent world police. Moreover, everybody seems to have forgotten Taverner, and in a TV culture this seems to be equivalent to being dead—or damned. In *Flow My Tears* obscurity is hell; and it is remarkable that, at the end of the novel, Jason Taverner escapes hell—ending his dangerous trip through the underworld of the future society depicted by Dick—when he finds one of his songs in a jukebox in a coffee shop (154–61): he becomes himself again when he is famous again. In the Epilogue of the novel we are told that his "TV ratings, which had dropped to a low point during the trial, rose with the verdict, and Taverner found himself with an audience of thirty-five million, rather than thirty" (201). Neilsen ratings win in the end—

and TV does not just broadcast jug players and dancing papoolas, but also a passable pop singer.

Something has changed indeed. TV has changed Dick's fiction, and the world, too. In *Penultimate*, "The Mold of Yancy," and *Simulacra*, those in power are on TV and manipulate the minds of ordinary people. In *The Divine Invasion* (1981), Dick's penultimate novel, things are quite different. When Gregg Rickman interviewed Dick asking for comments on all his works, he complained that "the whole idea of the Catholic-Communist world [in *The Divine Invasion*] is completely lost after they move over to the new world" (Rickman 189), and Dick agreed that "those guys are no longer in power in the new world." He was talking about the leaders of the two competing institutions ruling a future Earth and its colonies at the beginning of the novel, that is, the Christian-Islamic Church, whose supreme leader is the Chief Prelate, Cardinal Fulton Statler Harms, and the Scientific Legate, headed by the Procurator Maximus, Nicholas Bulkowsky. When the novel moves from that universe to another, more sustainable one (Rossi 2011 249–50), Statler Harms and Bulkowsky are demoted to officials of much less powerful organizations: the former has turned into a cardinal of the Roman Catholic Church, the latter into an obscure USSR bureaucrat. Rickman then noticed that "they're appearing on TV talk shows," and Dick's withering comment was that "the debased form of power is to be on TV talk-shows." In fact the Cardinal is professionally mistreated by the moderator of "an afternoon TV talk show" (196)—not even prime time!—and when he desperately tries to answer the barrage of sensational accusations, he is immediately stopped by the TV death sentence:

"I'm sorry, Cardinal ... but that's all the time we have…"
"Man is born in sin," Harms said, totally unable to gather his train of thoughts together.
"Thank you Cardinal Fulton Statler Harms," the moderator said. "And now this."
More commercials [197].

No more charismatic figures like Yancy or Nicole, cardinals and politicians are now just guests to be ridiculed for the sake of the ratings. TV is no more a docile instruments of totalitarian regimes, be they hard or soft; it is an alternate reality with its own logic—however twisted—that seems to have engulfed our everyday reality. This is what we have in *A Scanner Darkly* (1977), whose protagonist, undercover FBI agent Bob Arctor, is completely surrounded by a televisual surveillance apparatus, and has to endlessly watch videotapes of his daily life to work the riddle of his existence out—unfortunately failing in his self-viewing effort. I believe it is not a coincidence that Dick made Arctor quote another famous TV speech given by Nixon—not the successful Checkers speech, but the 17 November 1973 question and answer session with the press, shown on TV while the

Watergate scandal was raging, when the president declared "People have got to know whether or not their President is a crook. Well, I'm not a crook. I've earned everything I've got." This time the show was not as successful, because Nixon had to resign less than a year later; however, when accused of having turned into a drug addict, undercover agent Bob Arctor says "You're treating me like a crook. I am not a crook" (208). Televisual reality resurfaces in the novel.

We are in a TV reality, a debased reality that nobody seems to be able to control and govern; and at the end of one of his most interesting narrative experiments, *VALIS* (1980), a postmodernist hybridization of religious science-fiction and autobiography, he chose to leave us this self-portrait of the artist as a TV viewer: "My search kept me at home; I sat before the TV set in my living room. I sat; I waited; I watched; I kept myself awake" (228). It is a strange, suspended ending which strikingly echoes an important passage in Mark's Gospel (13:35–37), in which Jesus tells his disciples to wait for "the Son of man coming in clouds with great power and glory" (13:26); to watch, just like Phil Dick (the author himself appearing as a character in his own novel) sitting before the telescreen. Such a final image is of course open to interpretation, and its enigmatic character is surely something Dick wanted to impart to his narrative: it may be a commentary on the passivity of our civilization of screen watchers—then TV, now tablets, smartphones, and laptops—but one may also read it as an allusion to eschatological expectations: something will happen, the Kingdom will come, and that will be announced on TV. Is that hope or despair? It is hard to say: one may think that a Second Coming, or some other momentous event, may redeem even TV and its world of trash; but one could also suspect that even the Apocalypse, presented as TV news or discussed in a TV talk show, would be turned into a debased reality—just another piece of (garbage) reality TV. *VALIS* is a tremendously ambivalent narrative (with its split protagonist and complex games of truths revealed and then immediately denied), and its ending is coherently ambiguous.

Dick surely feared TV at the beginning, depicting it as a sort of sneaky alien invader or the tool of a soft form of totalitarianism, but in the 1970s he was well aware that he was living in a tubal society, and the subject in that socio-historical context is, as Gabriele Frasca has argued, someone speaking "from in front of a TV set" (Frasca 70, 160), someone reduced, like Bob Arctor, to an eye (Frasca 256), to a gaze, maybe to a human TV camera. Hence his narratives do not simply portray the advent of TV (and other electronic media), but have been shaped by those media, to an extent that this essay has only begun to fathom; being well aware that what we have found and will find in Dick's fictions is highly relevant to our understanding of our mediatic civilization.

Notes

1. Of course we are talking of vicarious experiences, but then one has to ask him/herself just how much of his/her life is made of such vicarious experiences nowadays; Baudrillard's simulacra come to mind.

2. When it comes to the death of President Kennedy, what was repeatedly seen in the 1960s was the funeral more than the assassination, as the Zapruder film was first broadcast on the late-night television show *Underground News* with Chuck Collins, originating on WSNS-TV, Channel 44, Chicago in 1970.

Works Cited

Ballard, J.G. *Extreme Metaphors*. HarperCollins, 2012.
Barnouw, Erik. *The Golden Web: A History of Broadcasting in the United States 1933–1953*. Oxford University Press, 1968.
_____. *The Image Empire: A History of Broadcasting in the United States. Volume III—from 1953*. Oxford University Press, 1970.
Dick, Philip K., *The Divine Invasion*, 1981. Corgi, 1982.
_____. *Do Androids Dream of Electric Sheep?* 1968. Granada, 1984.
_____. *Flow My Tears, the Policeman Said*. 1974. Granada, 1984.
_____. *The Man in the High Castle*, 1962. Penguin, 1987.
_____. *The Minority Report: The Collected Stories of Philip K. Dick Volume 4*, 1987. Citadel, 1991.
_____. *The Penultimate Truth*, 1964. Granada, 1984.
_____. *Puttering About in a Small Land*. 1985. Paladin, 1987.
_____. *A Scanner Darkly*. 1977. Granada, 1985.
_____. *The Simulacra*. 1964. Methuen, 1983.
_____. *Time Out of Joint*. 1959. Penguin, 1984.
_____. *Ubik*. 1968. Granada, 1973.
_____. *VALIS*. 1980. Vintage, 1991.
_____. *We Can Remember It for You Wholesale: Volume 5 of the Collected Stories of Philip K. Dick*. 1987. HarperCollins, 1994.
Frasca, Gabriele. *La Scimmia Di Dio: L'emozione Della Guerra Mediale*. Costa & Nolan, 1996.
Pagetti, Carlo. "Simulacri E Marionette." Dick, Philip K. *I Simulacri*. Tr. Maurizio Nati. Roma, Fanucci, 2002, 7–14.
Rickman, Gregg. *Philip K. Dick: In His Own Words*. Fragments West/The Valentine Press, 1988.
Rossi, Umberto. "Radio Free PKD." *Foundation: The International Review of Science Fiction*. Vol. 37, No. 106, Summer 2009 [i.e. 2010], 10–28.
_____. *The Twisted Worlds of Philip K. Dick: A Reading of Twenty Ontologically Uncertain Novels*. McFarland, 2011.
Sellars, Simon, and Dan O'Hara (eds.). *Extreme Metaphors: Interviews with J.G. Ballard 1967–2008*. Fourth Estate, 2012.
Tichi, Cecelia. "The Twentieth Century Television Mentality," Bisutti de Riz, Francesca and Rosella Mamoli Zorzi (eds.). *Technology and the American Imagination: An Ongoing Challenge*. Supernova, 1994. 3–15.

Voices, Consciousness and the Bicameral Mind
A Scanner Darkly *on the Road to Julian Jaynes' Psychology*

RICHARD FEIST

Introduction

In private correspondence dated January 1975, Philip K. Dick (hereafter: PKD) wrote that about ten months prior, he had started reading the work of research psychologist Robert E. Ornstein (Dick, *Exegesis* 67). PKD also notes that around the time of reading Ornstein he had written the rough draft of *A Scanner Darkly* (hereafter: SD). Although Ornstein made a large impression on PKD, three other psychologists should be considered when discussing this complex time in PKD's life (roughly 1973–76) and the philosophical and scientific ideas that he was encountering: Michael S. Gazzinaga, Joseph E. Bogen and Julian Jaynes. I will examine how Ornstein's, Gazzinaga's, and Bogen's work played a role in PKD's thinking in a couple of his essays and in the text of SD, and then turn to consider how Jaynes' work helped after *SD* to fill in what PKD called "some vital missing parts" (*Exegesis* 67). But these four are a subset of the scientists that PKD studied at the time. (Another example would be physicist Nikolai Kozyrev, who radically speculated on the essence of time.) A full discussion of all the scientific influences on PKD is far beyond the scope of this paper. In correspondence PKD specifically states that Bogen's and Ornstein's work forms the scientific foundation of SD (Herron 275). The work of the four, however, nicely fits with many of PKD's philosophical speculations and what he saw on the streets: that observations of his friends' drug-damaged minds convinced him that their behaviour had "…something to do with 'split-brain' phenomena of some obscure kind…" (Dick, *Exegesis* 67).

PKD's Philosophical Journey in Brief

To set the stage, I begin by a brief discussion of PKD's complex relationship to philosophy. He had little formal training and only at an introductory level, from September to November 1949, as an undergraduate philosophy major (Sutin, *Divine Invasions* 62). He studied Plato, no doubt learning the standard Platonic hierarchy of reality. This hierarchy is often taught in survey courses to undergraduates, namely, that reality is bifurcated and graduated. True reality is the non-sensorial, metaphysical world of the forms. The sensorial, non-metaphysical, empirical—that is, the physical—world, is a lower level of reality. The mind grasps the higher reality via a special, non-sensorial rational insight and grasps the lower reality through the senses. PKD recognized the problem of this division. Dividing reality into a hidden, but true world and an apparent, but untrue world, engenders skepticism. The senses cannot provide an accurate representation of true reality since the empirical world presented is not ultimately real. "Hence in novel after novel I question the reality of the world that the characters' percept-systems report" (Sutin, *Shifting Realities* 46).

By rejecting the empirical world as not-real, PKD moved on to study several of the philosophical tradition's great metaphysical systems. PKD states that of all the metaphysical systems he studied, he has: "the greatest affinity for that of Spinoza, with his dictum '*Deus sive substantia sive natura*'; to me this sums up everything (viz. God i.e., reality i.e., nature)" (Sutin, *Shifting Realities* 46). Spinoza's system identifies God and the world and explains why the mind's experience is largely illusory even though the mind is able, via reason, to penetrate this veil of illusion in order to access the divine truths.

There is another aspect of Spinoza's metaphysics that deeply appealed to PKD: that God and the self are, in a sense, identified. Simply put, Spinoza argued that the self should be thought of, in terms of its contents, as a modification of the divine essence. Moreover, Spinoza grounds the self's unity in God since the self, ultimately, is an idea in the mind of God (Spinoza 69–70). Understanding ourselves in terms of Spinozan metaphysics helps to understand some of PKD's seemingly bizarre statements, such as the following: "We are gloves that God puts on in order to move things here and there as He wishes" (Sutin, *Shifting Realities* 228).

The upshot of this metaphysics for PKD is that the mind is not a clear, self-subsistent entity, as Descartes taught. Nor is it a bundle of impressions and ideas, as Hume taught. Descartes and Hume both radically separated the mind from the world. But in PKD's embrace of Spinoza, the mind is linked directly to God; it is not isolated. In other words, in the depths of your consciousness, you are not alone.

PKD's philosophical journey towards the non-isolated mind correlates with the well-known story of his "vision" in February 1974. While at home recovering from surgery for an impacted wisdom tooth and treatment with sodium pentothal, he received a delivery of painkillers. The delivery person was wearing a piece of jewelry, a golden fish: the symbol of early Christianity.

Upon seeing this, PKD began having "visions" and thoughts that he was not a single being, but a spiritual entity.

Sutin traces out PKD's reactions to and writings on these "visions" in some detail, which is not necessary for my purposes here (Sutin, *Divine Invasions* 210–211). Overall, Sutin writes that PKD has a very scattered and piecemeal reaction to the "visions." Nonetheless, Sutin makes two relevant remarks. First, he states that PKD never accepted a physical cause for these "visions" (211). It is difficult to evaluate this remark given that Sutin does not argue, but simply states the point. But nuance is needed here since PKD closely follows the scientific results from brain research in an effort to make some sense not of the "visions" *per se*, but of the non-isolated nature of consciousness. This leads into Sutin's second remark: that PKD "…never settled on a name for the new, dual consciousness within him" (211). The notion of dual consciousness is precisely the theme that links the brain research psychologists with PKD since their work led to the "bicameral" view of the mind, that it is dualistic or two-chambered. With this philosophical background in mind, I now turn to Ornstein, Gazzinaga and Bogen. After showing their role in *SD*, I will then turn to a discussion of Jaynes and in what sense he "fills in the gaps" as PKD noted.

Ornstein, Gazzaniga, Bogen and Brain Research

Ornstein was, as PKD says, "the brain revolution person," and worked out of Stanford University's psychology labs in the 1960s and 1970s. In 1973 Ornstein published *The Nature of Human Consciousness: A Book of Readings*, which PKD mentions in his 1976 article "Man, Android and Machine." Here PKD discusses a new world-view, one that is essentially the Spinozian fusion of God and the world, but now uses the language from the pre–Socratic philosopher, Heraclitus. Again appearances are rejected and truth is located only in that beyond the senses. The only way to reach truth is to undergo some kind of fusion with God (Sutin, *Shifting Realities* 222). But the rephrasing of this world view continues as PKD employs more modern terminology. He stresses "man" and "human being" should not be understood via ontology or origin, but functionally, as "…a way of being in the world" (Sutin, *Shifting Realities* 211). PKD's illustrative example is of a machine stopping its activity and then assisting you. You would then say, "thank you," ascribing it intentionality. But no dissembling of machine will reveal that intentionality. The same failure holds for trying to locate the human soul in any particular human organ. PKD goes further: for the soul (or mind) is not a discrete object. Rather, the mind should be considered as interacting energy fields, not discrete particles. These mind/energy fields are constantly interacting with each other and with a much larger energy field, namely, the "noosphere," which is the analogue of God (223). Here PKD specifically rejects the "thing ontology" of the 19th century, that is, that the mind is isolated and (nearly) closed off from the world, except for the small amounts of data flowing in via the senses. PKD generalizes this and stresses that this "thingness" is something to be discarded in any talk of life. This is a subtle point. All life, then, is composed of mind/energy fields of varying complexity, from the plants to the ants and on up to humans. To link this with brain science of the day, PKD (rather tersely) writes: "But what we don't realize is that the billions of discrete and entirely ego-oriented left-hemisphere brains have far less to say about the ultimate disposition of the world than does the collective noosphere. [sic] Mind that comprises all our right brains and in which each of us shares" (223).

Provisionally put, the new view says that the left hemisphere traps us in an outdated ontology, but we could break free of it and tap into the right hemisphere's link to the larger noosphere. PKD says that it is "evident that more than anyone else Dr. Ornstein has pioneered the way to discover the new worldview…" (228). The way referred to here is the set of experiments conducted on split-brain patients. Indeed, PKD's enthusiasm for the brain research of Ornstein turned him into a follower of the psychologist, even going to the point of nervously writing the psychologist a fan letter (Sutin, *Shifting Realities* 229–231).

I have not discovered the specific brain research results of Ornstein that PKD drew upon. Hence, I am unable to draw any conclusions at this time. Nonetheless, there are two articles in Orstein's *The Nature of Human Consciousness* that play a large role in SD, by Gazzaniga and Boden. These articles help elucidate some of the points PKD made in SD, especially with respect to the concept of a mind. Gazzaniga nicely summarizes the various kinds of experiments that were done on split-brain patients, thus providing the material for SD's laboratory scenes, whereas Bogen's article provides more philosophical reflection on the nature of brain bisection. I begin with Gazzaniga.

Gazzaniga notes that one of the most startling results was that the split brain operation did not produce easily noticeable change in the patients' behavior or intelligence. Only under specialized lab conditions, where information was sent to a single hemisphere, were peculiar behaviors observed (Gazzaniga 88). Information was sent in two ways: visually (text and images) and tactilely (grasping objects). Patients could (orally and in writing) correctly describe visual and tactile information sent only to the left hemisphere. But patients handled information sent only to the right hemisphere quite differently. For instance, a picture sent to the right hemisphere evoked a random guess or no verbal reaction. Similarly, a tactile sensation sent to the right hemisphere produced either a random guess or no verbal reaction. Nonetheless, the right hemisphere does process information. For instance, a patient who received a picture of a spoon only in the right hemisphere was able to search (without looking) solely with the left hand through a collection of random objects and grasp the spoon. However, the patient could not say what he was holding.

Perhaps one of the most interesting results was the discovery of "cross cuing." Because the corpus collosum is cut, the hemispheres cannot directly communicate, but they now start communicating indirectly through the body. For instance, a flash of green light was sent solely to the right hemisphere. The patient would then simply guess the color. If he guessed correctly, green, then the patient would stick with that answer. But if he guessed incorrectly, red, then the patient would suddenly frown, shake his head and then guess green. Because auditory information goes to both hemispheres, the right side heard the left say "red" and knew that that was wrong. The right side communicated this by forcing a bodily reaction, a frown, a shake, cuing the left side that an error was made. The left side would then verbally correct the guess. Gazzaniga notes that these cross-cuing mechanisms can become extremely sophisticated, which shows "how difficult it is to obtain a clear neurological description of a human being with brain damage" (96). This notion of the difficulty of acquiring clear descriptions of the "inside" of minds, especially damaged ones, is a key theme in SD. (This nicely links up with St. Paul's view of seeing ourselves in a mirror darkly.)

Now I turn to some of Bogen's philosophical musings. He discusses a mode of thought that he deems "appositional" (144–9). Bogen is not convinced that it is straightforward to localize a function in a specific hemisphere; to say something like "function × is located in the right hemisphere" is highly contestable. Functions exist in the world quite differently than objects do. Objects are localized. Functions are not. Bogen holds that the difficulty of functional localization pales in comparison to that of ascertaining the basic, unitary functions of the brain. Is the love of children a single function? Is it a combination? Is the recognition of inanimate objects a distinct function from the recognition of animate objects (107)? This is a subtle point in the philosophy of science, namely, that the categories used in scientific investigation are not directly given by scientific data. Instead, they begin the process of organizing the data.

Bogen states that we should simply say that the left hemisphere is superior for language and the right for "non-language." But he admits that the term "non-language" is not clear, even misleading. In general, those suffering from left brain damage often use language, but in different ways. In brief, both hemispheres retain words, but the left hemisphere employs them in propositional structures (indicative sentences), whereas the right works very differently. Bogen says that science does not know much about how the right works, so he suggests the need for a word that is homologous in structure with the word "propositional" but sufficiently ambiguous to permit provisional use (147). Bogen coins the term "appositional," which says little except that the right has a capacity for "apposing or comparing of perceptions, schemas, engrams, etc., but has in addition the virtue that it implies very little else." Further research, Bogen says, would fill in the details.

A Scanner Darkly: *Reflections on Mind and Identity*

With this brain bisection background, I now turn to SD. There are three key sections of SD that are heavily based, although not exclusively so, on PKD's research on brain bisections: the first (85–91) and second testing scenes (160–2), and the test results scene (167–172). This also provides the stepping-stone to Jaynes.

In the first testing scene the doctors begin to quiz Fred. PKD uses an interrupted narrative in order both to model the disunity of consciousness and to illustrate the themes from his brain research. The doctors know that Fred's work requires that he masquerade as a doper, frequently ingesting brain-splitting Substance D. One doctor lays a lined card on the table, questions Fred, and then begins instructing Fred as to what he is to do. The doctor says, in the context of the novel: "Within the apparently meaningless lines is a familiar object that we would all recognize. You are to tell me what the … object is and point to it in the total field" (86). But PKD inserts the following as information for the reader, and it is inserted into the above where the ellipsis is indicated:

> Item. In July 1969, Joseph E. Bogen published his revolutionary article "The Other Side of the Brain: An Appositional Mind." In this article he quoted an obscure Dr. A.L. Wigan, who in 1844 wrote:
>> The mind is essentially dual, like the organs by which it is exercised. This idea has presented itself to me, and I have dwelt on it for more than a quarter of a century, without being able to find a single valid or plausible objection. I believe myself then able to prove—(1) That each cerebrum is a distinct and perfect whole as an organ of thought. (2) That a separate and distinct process of thinking or ratiocination may be carried on in each cerebrum simultaneously.
>
> In his article, Bogen concluded: "I believe [with Wigan] that each of us has two minds in one person. There is a host of detail to be marshaled in this case. But we must eventually confront directly the principal resistance to the Wigan view: that is, the subjective feeling possessed by each of us that we are One. This inner conviction of Oneness is a most cherished opinion of Western man…." [86].

The disunity of consciousness is modeled in that this passage is not introduced or commented or integrated into the actual text. It is, again, simply dropped in, like a voice from another location but within the context of the narrative. It fits, but there is a jarring sense to it.

This idea of voices from one "mind" or one side of a mind to the other is explicit during Fred's first visit to Room 203 is when the technicians explicitly ask him if he is experiencing "cross chatter"—in which one hemisphere attempts to communicate with the other (87). This is PKD's extrapolation of the idea discussed earlier by Gazzaniga, namely "cross cuing." Fred responds that he has not, at least no such experience he can recall. However, it is the case that Fred already has had experiences of voices from another mind. The first was done as foreshadowing, back at the beginning of the novel during Fred's speech at the Lion's Club. Fred deviated from the speech and as he did, voices from the audience cheered him on while a voice from the police headquarters was piped into his scramble suit and warned him to stay on message (19). However, Fred is not clear if it is one voice in his scramble suit or many (23). But the clearest example of voices heard, or cross chatter, is during the car breakdown scene. Here, Fred (also Arctor at this time) opens the hood, and hears loud voices singing in his head (63). There are two developments going on here. The voices are appearing but Fred's "mind" is separating from Arctor's since Fred is having difficulties remembering what occurred when he "was" Arctor. Now, to return to the laboratory scene and cross chatter, the doctor comments to Fred on the experience of receiving: "Thoughts not your own. As if another person or mind were thinking. But different from the way you would think. Even foreign words that you don't know. That it's learned from peripheral perception sometime during your lifetime" (87). It is not clear what "peripheral perception" means, but it would seem that ordinary experiences can sometimes feed information to one hemisphere alone. In any case, there are two key aspects here, first that the "other mind" that intrudes will think in a different way and second, that this other mind could even use foreign words. Gazzaniga does not talk of this kind of learning, but something like this arises in Bogen's paper.

Bogen points out that one of the most relevant "non-language" abilities of the right hemisphere is that "certain kinds of verbal activity (poetry) may first appear subsequent to an aphasiogenic left hemisphere lesion" (146). The notion that brain damage could lead to the appearance of poetry also occurs in several scenes of SD. There are various passages from Goethe (139, 141, 144, 145, 147) and another poet, Heinrich Heine (207). There is much to analyze in the various German passages, but this is beyond the scope of this paper. I will simply point out one passage from *Faust*, the famous "two-souls passage" (*Faust*, Part I, lines 1112–1117). This passage interrupts Fred, who in this scene is riding in a taxi, thinking about Arctor's behavior, possibly some suspicious behavior that Fred saw on the holo-scanners in Arctor's house. Fred thinks that perhaps he should bring one of Arctor's friends, Barris, in for questioning. Suddenly, Fred comes to the following realization: "What the hell am I talking about? I must be nuts. I know Bob Arctor; he's a good person. He's up to nothing. At least nothing unsavory. In fact, he thought, he works for the Orange County Sheriff's Office, covertly. Which is probably…" Now, simply dropped in, in German, is the two-souls passage:

> Two souls, alas, live in my breast
> One wishes to separate from the other
> One, with a crude lust for life
> Just clings tenaciously to the world
> The other soars powerfully above the dust
> To the far ancestral heights [author's translation, 145].

Clearly the separation of Fred and Arctor is complete—at least in a certain sense, which raises an interesting philosophical question, again about personal identity. Does Fred really know Arctor? In one sense, yes, because they are ultimately the same person—or at least they originally were. But in another sense, Fred does not really know Arctor because Fred is no longer conscious of his identity or origin with Arctor. All memory ties between them are gone.

I had referred earlier to the problem of functional concepts in Bogen's and PKD's notion that "human" is ultimately a functional term, not an ontological one. This combination of ideas arises in SD as well. After his botched speech to the Anaheim Lions Club, Fred (in Arctor guise) walks a public street, admiring the "marvels" of "McDonaldburger" stands and of carwashes. As he told the Lions Club members, when dressed and acting like a doper, the "other" dopers would welcome him, give him the "peace, brother" look. The "straights" of course, did not welcome him. Based on this concrete incident, found in everyday experience, Fred muses: "You put on a bishop's robe and miter, he pondered, and walk around in that, and people bow and genuflect and like that, and try to kiss your ring, if not your ass, and pretty soon you're a bishop. So to speak. What is identity? he asked himself. Where does the act end? Nobody knows" (20). The scope of the term "nobody knows" encapsulates both the concept of identity and a particular interpretation of identity as played out in human experience of identity as action or performance—as theater—and how the performance is properly received by the audience (i.e., the community in question). The inclusion of "so to speak" suggests skepticism, that there just may be nothing deeper than talk. Of course this could be read differently, that there is something more to being a bishop than being talked about as one or acting as one. Nonetheless, Arctor seems to settle on the "act interpretation" of identity, which is ultimately functional, not ontological. The upshot is that you are who others say you are.

This notion of functional, dictated identity is reinforced elsewhere. For instance, Arctor finds that his identity is most deeply challenged and distorted upon confrontation with power: the police. At the beginning of the confrontation the police car would pull up and the officer would give him a "an intense, keen, metallic, blank stare" (21). The officer might or might not beckon Arctor over. The officer's whim determined what happened after the stare. One's safety, one's security, was neither secured nor violated within a determinate structure, that is, a causal matrix. If it were, it would be possible to ascertain how the structure worked and thereby gain some control. One's security is secured or violated on the whim of the officer, a subjective state. As the officer asks to see his identification, PKD describes Arctor as "Arctor-Fred-Whatever-Godknew" (21). Power as a kind of voice, then, has an enormous effect on identity. Overall, the notion that one's identity, one's subjectivity, could be completely controlled by another's subjectivity, is a common existential theme, classically examined in the works of Hegel and in a more modern context by Sartre. It is the presence of the other, that is, the confrontation with another subjectivity, which motivates the subject's deepest reflections upon subjectivity. This shows the radical nature of the functional aspect of the mind or self.

Perhaps one of the most powerful—and difficult—philosophical elements of SD is the possibility of the non-countability of minds. This was suggested earlier in thinking about the mind as a kind of modification of God's essence or an energy field. The non-countability issue goes beyond the non-isolation issue. A single mind, or several minds, could be non-isolated. However, it still makes sense to talk about there being one mind there or several; there is at least a numerical discreteness—i.e., countability—even if the minds in question are not radically separate. This notion of non-countability is explored in a variety of places in SD, as when Arctor puzzles over whether anyone can actually know his own motives (50), but perhaps the most striking example is within the context of Arctor's musing on the outdated nature of sin. One could find oneself blamed for others' sins by accident, but accidental blame raises the debatable nature of a unique self-identity. This confusion over the number of selves emerges in the context of the discussion regarding the assignment of sin to a soul after death. Arctor cracks a joke that sin may be sloppily assigned, as the soul's sins are collected in a pickle barrel and then simply thrown at the soul after death. Of course other souls' sins might have been tossed into the mix and so there you will be, after death, dripping not only with your sins, but perhaps some of others.' Arctor's friend, Luckman, chimes in, saying that the mix-up of sins could be because people have the same name. The novel's Bob Arctor could inherit the sins of another person who happened to be named "Bob Arctor." But Arctor reflects more deeply on this question of overlapping sins, beyond the simple level of name confusion. Instead of saying that a single name, "Bob Arctor" could apply to several discrete selves, the reflection is now whether or not he, the Bob Arctor of the novel, is himself but one self. "How many Bob Arctors are there?" he thinks, and then further reflects:

Two that I can think of, he thought. The one called Fred, who will be watching the other one, called Bob. The same person. Or is it? Is Fred actually the same as Bob? Does anybody know? I would know, if anyone did, because I'm the only person in the world that knows that Fred is Bob Arctor. *But,* he thought, *who am I? Which one of them is me?* [74–75].

In this reflection, it may not simply be the case that different minds could be called "Fred" or "Bob Arctor" and that we are unsure of which, but that the very notion that experience can be coherently theorized as "the contents of one (or many) minds" may itself be problematic. This problem of correctly theorizing the mental environment was seen previously in Gazzinaga's discussion of cross cuing. It is of interest to note that the non-countability thesis of mind is the conclusion reached by Thomas Nagel in perhaps one of the most influential philosophical articles on this topic (Nagel). I have not seen direct evidence that PKD read Nagel, but it is quite fascinating to think that he may have reached the same conclusion.

There is much more to be said regarding PKD and brain research. But I now turn to PKD post–SD in order to bring in Julian Jaynes.

Enter Julian Jaynes

In his extensive study of PKD, Rossi writes that Julian Jaynes' work, *The Origin of Consciousness in the Breakdown of the Bicameral Mind* (OC), with its theory of right-brain hallucinations, is "quite important" for SD, but does not say how (Rossi 297). An historical sense might be ruled out since SD was published prior to OC. But PKD held Jaynes' writings to be important work. In correspondence PKD refers to his worthwhile purchase of OC and that it contains a "stunning theory" (Herron 275). In a letter to Jaynes he stated that the latter's theories enabled him to discuss his own "visions" without simply being called a "schizophrenic." PKD was so excited about Jaynes' theory that he claimed that it answered his lifelong questions, formed back in high school physics class (*Exegesis* 248). But perhaps SD's publication prior to OC's is not such a difficulty. PKD notes that after reading other works, like that of William S. Burroughs and his "virus theory" of words, he would re-read his own works to see he was on a similar path. He applies this backwards attribution to Jaynes's work (*Exegesis* 306). PKD also stresses how Jaynes' work is a foundation for *VALIS*; however, that discussion is beyond the scope of this paper.

Jaynes' work on the origins of consciousness is controversial. Some critics say it is a quasi-religious theory masquerading as science. That is, it is not even a traditional religious theory, which requires a transcendent god, but "religious" in its grand scheme of propounding a cosmological framework for history, both human and natural (Jones 170). Some treat Jaynes' theory as scientific, but simply wrong (Schiedermayer 30). Nonetheless, Jaynes' work could be argued (which I will not do here) as less controversial today than when it appeared (Kuijsten, *Consciousness*). Suffice it to say that Jaynes-like views on the constructive power of language, such as narrative theories of the self, are more common today than in the 1970s. (For a wide variety of discussions on Jaynes, largely in favor of his work and responding to Jaynes' critics, see Kuijsten, *Reflections*). Perhaps one of the most balanced pieces on Jaynes is a short work by Daniel Dennett. Dennett is an extremely harsh critic of religion and regards science as the prime (if not the sole) source of knowledge. As I pointed out with Bogen, scientific concepts are not handed to us; they are what we bring to organize the data. There is much disagreement amongst scientists and philosophers of science regarding the nature of science. But Dennett offers a view of how science does and should work. Science is a top-down method. For example, to understand a chess program, you cannot go bottom-up, starting by analyzing the components of the computer's central processing unit (Dennett 152). You need to start at the top: the concepts involved, the moves and strategy. Jaynes, Dennett says, does that with respect to the mind: "We first have to start from the topo, from some conception of what consciousness is, from what our own introspection is" (152). Dennett admits that such an approach is dangerous, that it invites all kinds of speculation, runs all kinds of risk of serious error, but for important science, "we really can't do without it" (152).

OC divides into three parts: his linguistic theory of consciousness, the thesis of the bicameral mind, and the remnants of bicameralism today. Jaynes argues that the history of investigations into the nature of consciousness have resulted in a failure. Indeed, that is arguably true today, since many still refer to the notion of consciousness, that is, the subjective feeling of lived experience, as perhaps one of the most difficult and intractable problems in philosophy and neuroscience. (The subjective feeling of consciousness must be kept distinct from the subjective feeling of perception.) For Jaynes, consciousness is a linguistic creation, specifically, a creation of metaphor. OC's discussion as to how metaphor generates consciousness is not easy to understand since it is not that metaphor simply generates the terms used in thought, but the actual consciousness experienced when language is employed. Nonetheless, Dennett regards this as Jaynes' greatest idea: that there are concepts that can be, in themselves, preconscious. For example, Jaynes points out that the bee has a concept of the flower, but is not conscious of it (Dennett 153). It is possible to even have a conceptual scheme that is preconscious. Ultimately, then, it is possible for consciousness to emerge as a linguistic-driven enhancement of this preconscious conceptual scheme. The upshot is that consciousness is not completely tied to brain structures but can emerge and change—even quite radically—without there being a physical change in the brain. In Jaynes' context, this is analogous to how a change in software can drastically change how a computer runs without any change in the hardware. (Anyone whose machine has had a virus is well-aware of that.) For Jaynes, the point is that the same brain structures can do different jobs at different times. Function and structure, then, are not tightly linked. Ultimately, this implies that human consciousness, the very way that humans experience their world, can change—and do so rapidly. Jaynes clearly says that our manner of experience today may not be how the humans of tomorrow experience the world (Jaynes 45).

This notion of a radical, rapid change in consciousness (without a corresponding change in brain structure) leads into the second part of Jaynes' work, namely, the historical thesis of the bicameral mind and its breakdown.

Subjective consciousness is more closely tied to the evolution of language (and especially writing) than evolution of the physical brain; hence it emerges much later in human history than typically thought. According to Jaynes, subjective consciousness emerges around 1200 to 1000 BC. Civilization prior to that date was organized on the basis of bicameral brain functioning, not a single consciousness. The bicameral brain was a split brain in which the speech of the gods was organized and originated in the right hemisphere and then heard in the left, thus engendering experiences that are much like the auditory hallucinations of a modern day schizophrenic (45). These piped in voices were heard in times of stress and uncertainty and when behavior for the common good was needed.

Because Jaynes' main idea is that the change in brain function occurred without a corresponding change in brain structure, there will not be biological evidence. The evidence for the change will be encoded in literary works and sculpture—essentially artistic products. As Dennett quips, one will have to read the "print outs" when looking for the lost changes that have occurred in the printer itself (153). Jaynes exerts much effort to provide evidence for the change in consciousness, such as examinations of ancient religions and the customs of antiquity. Literary sources also play an important role. For instance, Jaynes discusses the *Iliad* in the attempt to show that it reflects a bicameral view of consciousness (257–72). Jaynes' view of the *Iliad* finds some support from an earlier and well-known classics scholar, Bruno Snell. Like Snell, Jaynes tries to show that there is, in general, no consciousness in the *Iliad* (45). What takes the place of consciousness are gods. Externally, characters look as though they are authors of their own actions, but their "internal experience" would be one of hearing the god's dictates. Jaynes writes:

> In distinction to our own subjective conscious minds, we can call the mentality of the Myceneans a *bicameral mind*. Volition, planning, initiative is organized with no consciousness whatever and then "told" to the individual in his familiar language, sometimes with the visual aura of a familiar friend or authority figure or "god," or

sometimes as a voice alone. The individual obeyed these hallucinated voices because he could not "see" what to do for himself [75].

The bicameral mind made possible the civilizations of Mesopotamia, early Greece, and Egypt. The bicameral mind was replaced by subjective and personal consciousness due to three major factors: increasing complexity and size of communities that strained the power of the simple directives of the gods; development of written language; and increasing contact among bicameral peoples. Those who became conscious had an advantage; they could escape dictates of the gods, become more rational and ultimately learn more. Achilles is the paradigm bicameral man while Odysseus is the newly conscious man. But the bicameral mind has some vestigial remnants. It is still around in ecstatic religious experience, hypnosis, and schizophrenia (45).

PKD, too, thought that there was a time when the human mind was bicameral, but lost such a structure and became monocameral. PKD held that this loss of structure indeed cut humanity off from the gods, but for PKD it is interpreted in a largely Christian context. The loss of the mind's bicameral nature led to the Fall. "Our sin is self-centered monocamerality" (*Exegesis* 247). PKD eventually used Jaynes' thought to interpret his own experiences that he claimed were of a mystical nature when he writes that in 2-3-74 he became temporarily bicameral (247). Via what was then recent work in neurology, PKD held that bicamerality was, in a sense, making a comeback. He thought that humanity might achieve a greater freedom through this reemergence of bicamerality; here he puts a twist on Jaynes' views. PKD says that monocameral brains still receive commands from the Gods, but the monocameral brain is unaware of the Gods' presence and that the Gods are issuing commands. This is, to say the least, a radical state of oppression; the oppressed does not even realize that oppression is occurring. Through the reemergence of bicamerality, the Gods' voices will come to be seen as these voices and hence recognized for what they are and not simply obeyed. There is a kind of paradox in all this as it is by becoming bicameral that the mind becomes once again free and "whole" (29).

SD is indeed one of PKD's bleakest novels. One could say that the bicamerality that emerges in it is nothing short of catastrophic for those characters who experience it. The novel presents the monocameral Fred who splits into the bicameral Fred/Arctor and then eventually becomes the new monocameral Bruce. However, it is difficult to be certain of this emergence and disappearance of bicamerality since Bruce is an opaque figure in the novel. Nonetheless, Bruce seems to recognize, at the end of the novel, an inner core of freedom and wholeness. In the final scene, Bruce is out in the cornfields, taking orders to get back to work. Bruce has a radical sense of time dislocation in which he steps outside time altogether. Nonetheless, Bruce returns to work and, when nobody is looking, picks a *Mors ontologica* plant. He then slips this into his shoe, out of sight: "A present for my friends, he thought, and looked forward inside his mind, where no one could see, to Thanksgiving" (217). There is a region, deep in Bruce's mind, which nobody sees, and so remains outside of any gaze: human, god, or scanner. But it is a region that reconnects with others as the novel ends on a theme of friendship. It could be said that passing through bicamerality leads eventually to a kind of inner freedom. Once again, PKD wrote this prior to investigating Jaynes' work, but it is not difficult to see how SD, coupled with PKD's investigations into metaphysics and brain research, put him on the path for being, at least for a time, an enthusiastic recipient of Jaynes' work. Hence, it comes as no surprise the PKD thought Jaynes' work could be the scientific foundation for *VALIS*.

Concluding Reflections

PKD's thought surrounding and within SD is a fantastic mix of then cutting-edge brain science as well as traditional metaphysical systems. Indeed, I have only started to scratch the surface of all the thinking that lies behind this amazing novel. (For instance, there would be much to say about how PKD blends St. Paul's reflections on inverted sight in mirrors with topological properties of transformations.) But the key point that I wish to make in this essay is that the more one understands the various scientific and metaphysical ideas behind the novel, the clearer many of its scenes become. It clearly is a novel by a writer who has previously built up massive amounts of knowledge through studies in various areas.

PKD was a voracious reader and writer. He was not, strictly speaking, a scholar. Rather, PKD's attachment was truly to the ideas, not necessarily to how they were expressed in philosophical language or scientific theories. Hence, he was comfortable shifting from Spinoza to Heraclitus and on to Ornstein, Bogen and Jaynes, as if they were saying similar things in different ways. He, too, expressed himself and his ideas in various ways, which is, I think, the essence of what he meant when he referred to himself not as a novelist, but as a "fictionalizing philosopher" and that his story telling was a means to articulate his views (*Exegesis* 693).

WORKS CITED

Bogen, Joseph E. "The Other Side of the Brain: An Appositional Mind." *The Nature of Human Consciousness: A Book of Readings*. Ed. Robert E. Ornstein. W.H. Freeman and Company, 1973. 101–125.

Dick, Philip K. *The Exegesis of Philip K. Dick*. Ed. Pamela Jackson and Jonathan Lethem. Houghton Mifflin Harcourt, 2011.

———. *A Scanner Darkly*. Double Day & Company, 1977. Print.
Gazzaniga, Micheal S. "The Split Brain in Man." *The Nature of Human Consciousness*. Ed. Robert E. Ornstein. W.H. Freeman and Company, 1973. 87–100. Print.
Herron, Don, ed. *The Selected Letters of Philip K. Dick*. Vol. 5. Underwood Books, 1993.
Jaynes, Julian. *The Origin of Consciousness in the Breakdown of the Bicameral Mind*. Houghton Mifflin Company, 1976.
Jones, W.T. "Julian Jaynes and the Bicameral Mind: A Case Study in the Sociology of Belief." *Philosophy of Social Sciences* (1982), 153–71.
Kuijsten, Marcel. "Consciousness, Hallucinations, and the Bicameral Mind." *Reflections on the Dawn of Consciousness: Julian Jaynes Bicameral Mind Theory Revisited*. Ed. Marcel Kuijsten. Henderson, 2006. 95–140.
———. *Reflections on the Dawn of Consciousness: Julian Jaynes' Bicameral Mind Theory Revisited*. Ed. Marcel Kuijsten. Julian Jaynes Society, 2006.
Nagel, Thomas. "Brain Bisection and the Unity of Consciousness." *Personal Identity*. Ed. John Perry. University of California Press, 1975. 227–245.
Rossi, Umberto. *The Twisted Worlds of Philip K. Dick: A Reading of Twenty Ontologically Uncertain Novels*. McFarland, 2011.
Schiedermayer, David L. "Bioethics and the Breakdown of the Bicameral Mind: Sacks and Luria Revisited." *The Journal of Medical Humanities* 10.1 (1989): 27–44.
Spinoza, Baruch. *The Ethics and Selected Letters*. Ed. Seymour Feldman. Trans. Samuel Shirley. Hackett Publishing Company, 1982.
Sutin, Lawrence. *Divine Invasions: A Life of Philip K. Dick*. Caroll & Graf Publishers, 2005.
———. *The Shifting Realities of Philip K. Dick: Selected Literary and Philosophical Writings*. Ed. Lawrence Sutin. Vintage Books, 1995.

Ubik Does Not Yet Exist
Reading Ubik as a Case of Extro-Science Fiction

Sean Matharoo

"Friends, this is clean-up time and we're discounting all our silent, electric Ubiks by this much money. Yes, we're throwing away the blue-book. And remember: every Ubik on our lot has been used only as directed"
—Philip K. Dick (*Ubik* 1)

In the history of science fiction (SF), the provocative phantasmagoria of Philip K. Dick—which casts into ironically sharp relief the paranoid cries of a postwar American culture at grips with an accelerating capitalism—is singular. This is due in large part to the author's founding of an idiosyncratic style that is at once laden with philosophical concepts and "badly written." For Peter Fitting, the disconnect between anarchic creativity and pulp hackery that marks the Californian author's oeuvre draws attention to the subversive power of Dick's engagement with a non-representational aesthetics that deconstructs the metaphysical, representational, and, thus, bourgeois SF novel. He explains that the bourgeois SF novel "reinforces a transcendental conception of reality which mystifies the actual reality of the capitalist mode of production and the resultant repression and alienation" (Fitting 50). In Fitting's argument, Dick's *Ubik* (1969) is a prime example of a work that deconstructs this type of novel. It follows that the author's postmodernist blending of the boundaries between the high and the low, when considered alongside his deconstruction of the representational novel from which some purified meaning may be metaphysically derived, has allowed his works to persist in a comic mode, with Dick himself becoming something like the psychedelic jester of SF. Erik Davis perhaps puts it best when he writes that Dick was a "narrative trickster, a master mindfucker" (233).

At first glance, Fitting's articulation of *Ubik* as being committed to a non-representational aesthetics pitted against the metaphysicians of the bourgeoisie may seem somewhat at odds with the shadow world of unchecked obsessions that haunt Dick's later works, which together compose a nightmare galaxy intersecting with the apocalyptic dark side of countercultural dreaming, writ large. Indeed, the *VALIS* trilogy (comprising *VALIS* [1981], *The Divine Invasion* [1981], and *The Transmigration of Timothy Archer* [1982]), the posthumously published *Radio Free Albemuth* (1985), and the unfinished *The Owl in Daylight* evince not only a hacker-like figure attuned to the proletarian deconstruction of a repressive and alienating bourgeoisie, but also a tragic hero equipped with a philosophical rigor and an incredible imagination amplified by amphetamines utterly lost to the chaotic oscillations between rational speculation and paranoid delusion that ultimately paved the way for religious ecstasy.

Taking seriously these oscillations, this paper argues that the earlier *Ubik* may be read as providing another Dick in addition to Dick the psychedelic jester and Dick the tragic hero: Dick the purveyor of what Quentin Meillassoux identifies as "extro-science fiction" (XSF). For Meillassoux, unlike in worlds of SF, in worlds of XSF, experimental science cannot "deploy its theories or constitute its objects within them" (*Science Fiction* 6). Modifying and elaborating on the French philosopher's own reading of *Ubik* from *Science Fiction and Extro–Science Fiction* (2013), I demonstrate that the novel's non-representational aesthetics builds an XSF world in which the necessity of natural laws cannot be explained. It may thus be confirmed that Dick's book arrays a non-representational aesthetics against metaphysics and, by extension, the bourgeois novel of representation, supporting Fitting's argument.

Departing from Fitting, however, I will argue that the novel at once affirms that the only necessity is contingency and provides the immanent conditions for a future world of egalitarianism and universal justice by affording its readers the phenomenal experience of an XSF world. This argument is given additional substantiation by the titular Ubik: a mass-produced spray can whose divine intervention is to offer hope in the future by reversing processes of decay and resurrecting the dead. It should be observed that Ubik also appears throughout the book in the form of commercial jingles that introduce each of its seventeen chapters, exhibiting a Phildickian guarantee: capitalism and religion are ubiquitous (*ubik-itous*?) and, moreover, deeply intertwined. Yet, like Meillassoux's radical notion of the God that does not yet exist, Ubik is in the last instance revealed to be non-existent, but possible and, ultimately, contingent. This paper correspondingly contends that, when read with the philosophy of Meillassoux, Dick's visionary novel realizes its anti-capitalist critique and looks to the communist horizon by adopting a philosophically speculative position whereby thought is granted the ability to reach the absolute in neither theistic nor atheistic terms.

The first part of *Ubik*, a cult favorite and one of *Time* magazine's 100 best English language novels, takes place in the near future of 1992 and describes in a mostly linear fashion the corporate rivalry between Hollis Talents and Runciter Associates. Ray Hollis sells a purchasable service to customers looking to deploy telepathic psi agents to spy on others, while Glen Runciter sells a purchasable counter-service to customers looking to elude telepathic surveillance by deploying so-called "inertials" that can block parapsychological effects. These effects include, for example, the precog's ability to pick from and activate a variety of futures. The year 1992 is a time in which automated machines direct the flow of interpersonal relations, which have been reduced to a capitalist marketplace where even opening one's conapt door for a guest requires a nickel and strategically chosen music may be heard in a variety of spaces, from hotel lobbies to helicopters. Our guide here is protagonist Joe Chip, an unlucky and impecunious technician working for Glen Runciter, the latter of whom spearheads the company's efforts alongside his dead wife Ella who is cryogenically suspended in half-life, a state from which the wealthy living communicate with the (half-)dead in corporatized "moratoriums." Following Runciter scout G.G. Ashwood's discovery of Pat Conley—whose enigmatic talents allow her to alter the past and subsequently change the present—a ragtag group of intertials, including Joe, Glen, and Pat, are sent on a mission to the moon to expose secret telepaths working for business tycoon Stanton Mick.

Their plan goes awry when an explosion on the moon seemingly kills Glen, inaugurating the second half of the book in which time and space crack at their seams—a cracking that effects an absence of the natural laws that support the structure of reality. The narrative then erratically devolves by spatiotemporal interruptions into a baroque past of 1939, with Joe at one point remarking, "reality has receded; it's lost its underlying support and it's ebbed back to previous forms" (162). Yet, another mysterious force is at work that makes itself known via material manifestations of the supposedly deceased Glen Runciter, whose face begins to appear on coins and whose voice is heard on a hotel room's vidphone as the narrative moves backward in time. What follows is a disjunctive narrative in which Joe attempts to unearth the cause that will explain the deracination of reality presented in the novel's second half. But, Dick's deconstructive use of the non-representational against the metaphysical ultimately denies some causal explanation that might explain the world he renders. As readers, we are nevertheless urged to join Joe on his search as he assumes what Meillassoux calls a "science fiction imaginary" (7) that is a "matter of imagining a fictional future of science that modifies, and often expands, its possibilities of knowledge and mastery of the real" (*Science Fiction* 4–5). To this end, Joe hypothesizes that Glen is in fact alive and trying to communicate—from the future of 1992—with the Runciter Associates group, now frozen in half-life following the lunar explosion. Joe's SF theory seems to hold up as Glen eventually makes more explicit contact with the group by entering the world of 1939 and saving him from entropic biological breakdown with the help of Ubik.

In 1939, one encounters a baroque setting where Dick's penchant for the non-representational is most apparent. Rococo ornamentations have been "constructed to blend, to merge with shadows, to be at all times opaque" (173) and, bizarrely, robotic appliances malfunction before they are used, phone books become outdated, money becomes antiquated, elevators and cars revert to earlier models, flowers instantly die while coffee instantly molds, cigarettes crumble in the hands of smokers, and even human bodies decay at an accelerated pace. Toward the end of the novel, Joe, after receiving a traffic citation from the supposedly deceased Glen masked as a police officer, is directed to a spatiotemporal anomaly in the form of an abandoned drugstore from which he is to obtain a small supply of Ubik in order to stave off the process of material decay that, otherwise, will result in his own death. While the rest of the inertial group waits at a nearby hotel, Joe arrives at the drugstore which is itself caught between an even more distant past and the future of 1992. This contradictory anomaly—which strikes Joe as though it were "alive" (172)—is occupied by a pharmacist separated from Joe by an "epoch of time" (174). On the precipice between life and death, Joe ultimately fails to obtain a can of Ubik from him because, in a bitter moment of Phildickian irony, he does not have enough money and, even if he did, it would probably be of a later mint. Upon returning to the hotel to rejoin the group, it dawns on him that perhaps Pat's ability to change the present (of the "future" 1992) by altering the past (of, one presumes, 1939, although this is left unclear) is responsible for warping the real and causing the eventual deaths of the group members. Giving in to speculation, he pushes further and conjectures that she may even be a secret agent working for Hollis Talents, Runciter Associates' business rival.

Joe's fear seems to be realized when he confronts Pat in the hotel lobby and is suddenly struck by a blast, which leads to a protracted scene in which his rapid deterioration is described with a baroque focus on the non-representational. First, darkness "hummed about him, clinging to him like coagulated, damp, warm wool," although it, too, appears to be subject to some unknown rule of decomposition, turning into "horizontal lines of gray" (179). His own voice takes on a nightmarishly incomprehensible form, as though "it dipped shrilly, with unnatural overtones … it's speeded up…. High-pitched" (180). Joe then begins to feel an "oceanic pull … [that] had invaded him as an instinct, non-rational, impossible to explain" (181). Convinced that he has "slowed down, compressed by gravity," Dick writes, "[h]is world had assumed the attribute of pure mass. He perceived himself in one mode only: that of an object subjected to the pressure of weight. One quality, one attribute. And one experience. Inertia" (182). A cosmic reverie following this moment of impossibility is worth quoting at length:

> Metabolism ... is a burning process, an active furnace. When it ceases to function, life is over. They must be wrong about hell, he said to himself. Hell is cold; everything there is cold. The body means weight and heat; now weight is a force which I am succumbing to, and heat, my heat, is slipping away. And, unless I become reborn, it will never return. This is the destiny of the universe. So at least I won't be alone [187].

Has Joe actually died this time? Ironically directed to his hotel room by Pat, however, he subsequently finds himself overcome by "shapes in the carpet, swirls and designs and floral entities in red and gold," playing with the possibility that he has "devolved back millions of years to something that flies and coasts, using its skin as a sail" (190). Glen meets Joe in his room and gives him a can of Ubik, which instantaneously reverses the process of decay and allows him to be reborn: "the air flickered and shimmered, as if bright particles of light had been released, as if the sun's energy sparkled here in this worn-out elderly hotel room" (191).

What follows this quasi-mystical encounter with death and a solar rebirth delivered through non-representational aesthetics is a circuitous series of plot twists, each one seemingly providing a conclusive explanation for the novel's catastrophic regressions. First, Glen confirms Joe's theory that he is actually alive in 1992 and attempting to communicate with Joe and the rest of the inertial group, who are cryogenically suspended in half-life, yet somehow in 1939, so that he might save them with the help of Ubik. Second, it is revealed that Jory—a fifteen-year-old boy also frozen in half-life and in possession of an acute cephalic activity that allows him to consume other half-lifers and even interrupt communications between the living and the (half-) dead—has been guiding the book's narrative. Third, again on the brink of death, Joe meets Ella Runciter, a messianic figure who can miraculously conjure cans of Ubik in order to temporarily emancipate herself and others from Jory's cerebral vampirism and attain a "morally proper" (217) rebirth. Ella eventually saves Joe from death in 1939 by sending a factory representative and a technical consultant possibly named Myra Laney with a can of Ubik. Following a long paragraph in which Myra explains Ubik in technobabble, Joe addresses the can, contemplating sardonically, "We are served by organic ghosts ... who, speaking and writing, pass through this our new environment" (225). At the beginning of the seventeenth and final chapter, however, the possibility of scientific resolution is thwarted yet again as an explanation for the decomposition of the world is outright disavowed: in 1992, Glen sees Joe's face on a fifty-cent piece. Is Joe alive and is Glen the one who is frozen in half-life? Are they both frozen in half-life? What year is it? What is real? And, what is Ubik, anyway? As Dick writes on the final page of the novel, "This was just the beginning" (227).

In Meillassoux's reading of *Ubik*, he suggests that it exemplifies the type of SF tale that occurs "within an uncertain reality ... in which the real would go to pieces, progressively ceasing to be familiar to us" (*Science Fiction* 48). He continues, "the tale would multiply the breaks ... according to a progressive line of oppressive disintegration" (Meillassoux, *Science Fiction* 48). More generally, Meillassoux argues that, although we might encounter irregularities in SF worlds, new hypotheses could theoretically explain their irregularities. But, in XSF worlds similarly constituted in irregularities, though science may present problems, science cannot in principle explain their irregularities. Meillassoux does suggest that Dick's book might constitute a "Type-2" XSF world in which irregularity obliterates science but not consciousness, but he ultimately differentiates it from what he singularizes as XSF. For him, we are given a causal explanation for the disintegration of the world in the form of the Jory narrative in which Joe and the rest of the inertials in half-life are being consumed while the living Glen tries to communicate with them. However, given that Glen sees Joe's face on a coin at the end of the novel and that we are, thus, left without any causal explanation for the world's spatiotemporal collapse, I want to expand Meillassoux's reading to suggest that what we discover in *Ubik* is an XSF world in which the natural laws that supposedly support the structure of reality are altogether absent, thereby preventing scientific knowledge from being able to revise its theories through experimentation and furnish the world with an explanation. To push further, I postulate that Dick's novel, being independent of the stability of natural laws, cannot causally explain the necessity of natural laws; instead, it intimates that the only necessity is contingency.

In defense of this postulation, Joe's own decoding of the processes of spatiotemporal decay that define the XSF world of the book as a double movement is useful: "One is a going-away, so to speak. A going-out of existence. That's process one. The second process is a coming-into existence. But of something that's never existed before" (112). I argue that this double movement, while certainly not a causal explanation for the necessity of natural laws, reveals that the only necessity in Dick's book is contingency. In this context, staging a continued dialogue between Dick and Meillassoux is illuminating, as Meillassoux writes in "The Immanence of the World Beyond" (2010):

> I hold that the radical contingency of all things, their irrationality, is not the sign of thought's incapacity for reaching the ultimate truth of something. On the contrary, radical contingency is the very truth of all things. When we stumble upon the irrationality of all things, we do not come up against a limit to our knowledge; rather we come up against the absoluteness of our knowledge: the eternal property of things themselves consists in the fact that they can without reason become other than they are [446].

In other words, the only necessity is contingency, which is itself an absolute that may be thought. It should be said that the abolishment of the necessity of natural laws is desirable for Meillassoux because, he argues, it coextensively abolishes religious belief: the assertion of the necessity of natural laws is itself essentially a religious belief in something outside the realm of rationally understanding the absoluteness that is the necessity of contingency, or the "irrationality of all things." Implementing his speculative position into this paper, I claim that the world of *Ubik*—when considered with a focus on its non-representational aesthetics that makes a metaphysical reading untenable and with Joe's description of its constitutive double movement—is an irrational XSF world whose only condition of possibility is "radical contingency."

It should also be noted here that the strange temporality of Dick's novel is compatible with Meillassoux's own theory of time, which he calls in *Time Without Becoming* (2008) "Hyper-Chaos," whose "contingency is so radical that even becoming, disorder, or randomness can be destroyed by it, and replaced by order, determinism, and fixity" (25). That is, like Hyper-Chaos, which is a kind of ontologization of radical contingency, the double movement outlined above by Joe guarantees that things themselves in Dick's book "can without reason become other than they are" (Meillassoux, "Immanence" 446). And, because we can know the necessity of contingency absolutely, I claim that, by reading *Ubik* as a philosophically speculative work, we are afforded the phenomenal experience that comes with thinking a thing-in-itself—the absolute that is the necessity of contingency, or maybe, even, a spray can called Ubik.

Remember that Ubik appears throughout the book as a divine entity capable of reversing processes of decay and resurrecting the dead ... and as commercial jingles introducing each chapter. Of course, it should be said that it is also the title of the book. Quite importantly for us now, though, Ubik's manifestation at the beginning of the book's final chapter recalls John 1:1:

> I am Ubik. Before the universe was, I am. I made the suns. I made the worlds. I created the lives and places they inhabit; I move them here, I put them there. They go as I say, they do as I tell them. I am the word and my name is never spoken, the name which no one knows. I am called Ubik, but that is not my name. I am. I shall always be [226].

From this passage, one may follow Fitting and argue that Ubik is God *qua* exchange value (48–51). But, to consider Ubik in the context of an XSF world of radical contingency, one may alternatively say that Ubik is a "virtuality." Virtualities, Meillassoux explains, are "advents *ex nihilo*, since they proceed neither from an actually existing world, nor from physical potentialities, nor from some totality of possible worlds" ("Immanence" 461). Proceeding from the time of Hyper-Chaos, virtualities like Ubik are contingent and possible.

I thus contend that Ubik aligns with Meillassoux's radical idea of the virtual God that does not yet exist—a non-existent God that might nonetheless exist in the future. In critiquing a postmodernist fideism according to which it is impossible to establish the non-existence of God, Meillassoux attempts to resolve what he terms the "spectral dilemma": is it possible to live and not die with "those who have died horrendous deaths?" ("Immanence" 452). He determines that neither an atheistic nor a theistic response can resolve the dilemma because both the atheist and the theist succumb to despair when confronting it. Instead, he builds on his philosophy of "speculative materialism," formulated in *After Finitude* (2006), which responds to the problem of induction and mounts a defense of the necessity of contingency by dismantling the metaphysical principle of sufficient reason, sustaining the law of non-contradiction, and demonstrating that mathematics offers a non-anthropocentric and materialist way of thinking being *qua* being. Using this framework as a foundation for his later argument, Meillassoux articulates a position of "irreligion" ("Immanence" 444) capable of thinking the absolute, overturning fideism, and, perhaps, resolving the spectral dilemma.

To this end, Meillassoux suggests that the possible arrival of a contingent God that does not yet exist would, like Dick's Ubik, reverse processes of decay and resurrect the dead—though not necessarily. Furthermore, the thought of a contingent and possible redemption of our world, he says, might galvanize not religious belief, but a militant hope in a future egalitarian world of universal justice in the form of a "vectorial subject," or "one magnetically attracted by the vector of the emancipation to come" (Meillassoux, "Immanence" 463). From the novel position of irreligion, Meillassoux reappraises Nietzsche's ostensibly metaphysical concept of the eternal return to argue that the vectorial subject would be generated in response to the horrifying experience of an immortality brought about by the arrival of the God that does not yet exist. Because God does not exist in this world but may in a future world concomitantly redeemed of atrocities by its arrival, he is able to distinguish this experience as an "immanence … not of this world" that "consists in an existence in which death is not at all a definite interruption of our existence but a stage of our becoming which is canceled out by our ulterior rebirth" (Meillassoux, "Immanence" 468). Adhering to the necessity of contingency and his temporal theory of Hyper-Chaos, the "unforgiving repetition" ("Immanence" 468) of immanence, Meillassoux writes, is "immortality conceived as the endless perpetuation of existing life … because the only genuine meaning of the immanent [*l'ici-bas*] consists in upholding its continuation to infinity" ("Immanence" 469). The sufficient material conditions for life having been met in the form of immortality—an immanence freed from the grasp of metaphysics—he follows Marx and writes, "there will be *a communist life*, that is to say, *life finally without politics*" (Meillassoux, "Immanence" 473). It follows that the vectorial subject's task becomes the catalyst of the advent of an egalitarian world of universal justice.

By way of conclusion, let us recall the anomalous drugstore that Joe visits in 1939. Dick describes it as a contradiction trapped within itself: an "oscillation, each phase lasting a few seconds and then blurring off into its opposite, a fairly regular variability as if an organic pulsation underlay the structure" (172). As Meillassoux explains, contradictory entities like this one are incapable of changing "*because there would be no alterity for it in which to become*" (*After Finitude* 69). That is, by granting existence and non-existence at the same time to an entity, adherence to contradiction makes necessary that entity, in turn contradicting the necessity of contingency according to which everything could change for no reason at all. It now makes sense, then, that Joe is unable to obtain a can of Ubik from its pharmacist. Yet, Ubik in all its various forms, if understood to share an indexical relationship with the God that does not yet exist, is non-existent, possible, and contingent. Proceeding instead from the radical alterity of Hyper-Chaos, it is capable of changing without reason, giving supplementary support to this paper's reading of Dick's novel as a work of XSF whose non-representational aesthetics displaces metaphysics and, in their place, finds the "organic pulsation" that is the necessity of contingency. *Contra* Dick the psychedelic jester and Dick the tragic hero, then, Dick the purveyor of XSF gives expression to a world where everything could change for no reason.

To read the XSF world of *Ubik* is to phenomenally experience it as an extraterrestrial immanence that is thought by thinking the absolute that is the necessity of contingency all the way to infinity—a non-existent, possible, and contingent immortality we find *vis-à-vis* Ubik's powers of non-necessarily regenerating material life and resurrecting the material dead. And, because scientific discourse is unable to obtain a causal explanation for the necessity of natural laws, it suddenly becomes possible to imagine another world beyond the book's own pages. It may finally be said that *Ubik*, when read as a philosophically speculative case of XSF, provides the immanent conditions for the production of a vectorial subject committed to both the demolition of despair in the face of capitalism and the realization of an emancipatory political project that would give rise to a future world of egalitarianism and universal justice. As Dick reveals in the retroactively collected *The Exegesis of Philip K. Dick* (2011), a crushing meditation on gnostic theology and mystical experience, "Ubik talks to us from the future, from the end state to which everything is moving; thus Ubik is not here—which is to say now—but will be" (10). Ubik, like a world of egalitarianism and universal justice, does not yet exist. But, Dick gives us hope in its arrival.

Works Cited

Davis, Erik. *Nomad Codes: Adventures in Modern Esoterica.* Verse Chorus Press, 2010.
Dick, Philip K. *The Exegesis of Philip K. Dick.* Edited by Pamela Jackson, Jonathan Lethem, and Erik Davis. Houghton Mifflin Harcourt, 2011.
―――. *Ubik.* Houghton Mifflin Harcourt, 2012.
Fitting, Peter. "'Ubik': The Deconstruction of Bourgeois SF." *Science Fiction Studies,* vol. 2, no. 1, 1975, 47–54.
Meillassoux, Quentin. *After Finitude: An Essay on the Necessity of Contingency.* Translated by Ray Brassier. Bloomsbury, 2014.
―――. "The Immanence of the World Beyond." *The Grandeur of Reason: Religion, Tradition and Universalism,* edited by Peter M. Candler Jr., and Conor Cunningham. Translated by Peter M. Candler Jr., Adrian Pabst, and Aaron Riches. SCM Press, 2010, 444–78.
―――. *Science Fiction and Extro-Science Fiction.* Translated by Alyosha Edlebi, Univocal, 2015.
―――. *Time Without Becoming.* Edited by Anna Longo, Mimesis International, 2014.

Rereading Dick's Mainstream Fiction within a Science Fiction Framework

GABRIEL CUTRUFELLO

Introduction

While there has been significant scholarship on Philip K. Dick's science fiction (SF) over the years, there has been little attention paid to his mainstream fiction, which was written between 1949 and 1960. Scholars have noted Dick's desire to publish his early mainstream fiction and his failure at doing so (with the exception of *Confessions of a Crap Artist* [1975]) during his career. Lawrence Sutin notes that the rejection of the mainstream novels anguished Dick, but that he used that anguish to fuel his SF writing career (85). Prior scholarship demonstrates that Dick's mainstream novels open up new avenues of investigation into his *oeuvre* as well as offering a new approach to understudied aspects in his SF. The mainstream novels place greater emphasis on marital relationships in a way that Dick's SF tends to background in favor of the commonly studied themes of simulation, the android, and altered reality. Instead of using SF's estrangement of reality to refigure problems and create fresh perspectives for the reader, Dick's mainstream works take the familiar and illustrate how it is already strange. Furthermore, there are significant recurring themes that Dick uses in his SF writing (Levack and Godersky 140), which occur in the mainstream novels, and point to a focus on personal relationships that are not often highlighted in discussions of his sf texts.[1]

This essay will read *The Man Whose Teeth Were All Exactly Alike* (completed 1960; published 1984), within the framework of established scholarship on Dick's SF themes of the artificial and entropy ("kipple") in order to highlight the ways in which these two themes are developed in relation to Dick's focus on marital strife. These themes will then be reread back into select historically adjacent novels (*The Three Stigmata of Palmer Eldritch* [1964], *Martian Time-Slip* [1964], *Now Wait for Last Year* [1966], and *Do Androids Dream of Electric Sheep?* [1968]) to demonstrate the productivity of rethinking the combination of the artificial, entropy, and marriage in his more commonly studied SF. As noted by Williams, *The Man Whose Teeth Were All Exactly Alike* signifies a major shift in Dick's writing both structurally and thematically. Furthermore, Dick felt that this novel was his most successful.[2] While the first half of the novel focuses on the marital strife of the Dombrosios and the Runcibles, the second half of the novel focuses almost completely on a fake Neanderthal skull hoax and its fallout. Dick had an interest in forgeries and fakes, and the hoax perpetrated by Walt Dombrosio resembles the Piltdown Forgery that had been discovered in 1953.[3,4] Earlier readings of Dick's mainstream work argue that these novels present readers with protagonists struggling with their personal and economic relationships; an extended reading of the mainstream novel will highlight that these struggles are entangled with the previously defined SF themes of the artificial and entropy.

Prior Scholarship on the Mainstream Novels

Scholarship on the mainstream novels is thin. Scholars like Emmanuel Jouanne make passing reference to Dick's mainstream fiction, but infrequently study the novels, even though Jouanne notes that the mainstream novels do have some similar themes to the science fiction (234). Prior to the early 2000s, Kim Stanley Robinson's dissertation-turned-book *The Novels of Philip K. Dick* (1984) and Douglas Mackey's *Philip K. Dick* (1988) were the only scholarship discussing these works. The most recent addition to the scholarship on the early mainstream works is Christopher Palmer's *Philip K. Dick: Exhilaration and Terror of the Postmodern* (2003) and Charles Thorpe's "Death of a Salesman: Petit-Bourgeois Dread in Philip K. Dick's Mainstream Fiction" (2011). The newer pieces offer insights into how Dick's mainstream novels critique marital relationships and economic concerns of the mid-to-late fifties. In his chapter entitled "Mired in the Sex War: Dick's Realist Novels of the Fifties," Palmer suggests Dick's novels are a response to the newly mythologized suburban existence in America through his analysis of the marital strife in *Confessions of a Crap Artist* and *The Man Whose Teeth Were All Exactly Alike*. Palmer argues that the novels of this period "centre on conflict between the sexes, and … bitter marital conflict" (67). To the extent that he discusses the theme of the artificial in the novel, Palmer argues that the fake Neanderthal skull and the surrounding racial tension are "linked attempts to escape from that obsessive attention to the battle of the sexes that is so marked in this as in other novels of the series" (79). He sees these novels as the beginnings of Dick's critique of capitalist modes of living as well as his critique of large dehumanizing organizations that frequently figure in his SF works.[5] Charles Thorpe, on the other hand, refocuses scholars' attention on the mainstream novels' use of common themes to construct the dread that motivates the middle-class characters. Thorpe argues that sources of the dread that characters experience are social (413). While Thorpe's analysis is focused on the entrepreneurial motives of the male characters, it also suggests a way of understanding how entropy and marriage fit as themes within the novels and notes "a void opening up beneath the superficial order of their [the characters'] lives" (418). The void that threatens to engulf the order of the world is, in part, driven by the relationship between capitalist modes of circulation and the interpersonal relationships; in turn, this tension "reveals the vulnerability of personal bonds" (424). Thorpe's analysis of the mainstream novel returns to a short reading of select SF novels and focuses on the ways that the science fiction novels foreground petite bourgeois dread. Palmer's reading of the marital relationships in two of Dick's novels is instructive, and Thorpe's method of reading the themes that constitute what he calls "dread" in select mainstream novels and then back into the SF provides a useful methodology.

The Artificial and Entropy in Dick's SF

One of the primary characters in Dick's SF novels is the creator or "artificer" character (Suvin 11). A few of the more prominent examples of this character type would be Frank Frink, maker of fake historical objects and of jewelry in *The Man in the High Castle*; Pris Rock, the designer of the simulacra Edward M. Stanton and Abraham Lincoln in *We Can Build You*; and Emily Hnatt, the maker of pottery sold to be "mined" in *The Three Stigmata of Palmer Eldritch*. These character types are one aspect of a larger move on Dick's part to complicate and discuss the influence of commodification and its attending attitudes that help create and sustain the fetish of commodification. Scott Bukatman suggests that "Dick's novels and stories are 'about' the processes of reproduction ... that often transcend the concern of any particular work" (49). The characters who produce objects, often times fakes or replicas, are the ones who become the manipulators of the shared reality of other characters in the novel. Frequently, the novels focus on the protagonists' "dissatification with ... reality" and their focus on artificial or simulated objects (Fitting 101). Although Fitting specifically discusses *The Three Stigmata of Palmer Eldritch*, his argument holds true for many of Dick's novels and characters—as in the necessity of creating fake antiques in *The Man in the High Castle* for a livelihood or the addiction to "mood organs" in *We Can Build You* and *Do Androids Dream of Electric Sheep?*. The artificial often destabilizes binary relationships and leads to an entropic movement in the novels, often referred to as kipple. Fredric Jameson notes "kipple ... is Dick's personal vision of entropy, in which objects lose their form and ... [tend] to disintegrate under [their] own momentum" (17). In Dick's works, entropy disrupts the nature of the world and throws matter into disarray as well as disrupts the flow of time (Lem 54). Entropy in Dick's SF appears in spectacularly literal ways: the half-life world of *Ubik*; the hallucinations of Jack Isidore in *Do Androids Dream of Electric Sheep?*; and in "Null-O," a short story originally written in August of 1953 but published in 1958 (Levack and Godersky 142–43). Simulated people, objects, environments and entropic forces collide in Dick's novels to destabilize easy understandings of the world, and, in doing so, highlight the already existing problems found in more quotidian experiences.

Simulation and Entropy in The Man Whose Teeth Were All Exactly Alike

The Man Whose Teeth Were All Exactly Alike was the last mainstream novel that Philip K. Dick wrote during the early part of his career, in between writing *Confessions of a Crap Artist* and *The Man in the High Castle* (Williams i). The Dombrosios and the Runcibles have each been married for some time, and the discord in their relationships originates (as Palmer argues) from their attempts at maintaining acceptable gender norms along with separate domestic and business spheres. The couples live in the fairly rural area of Carquinez, located north of San Francisco. Walt Dombrosio works in the city for an advertising agency making models and mock-ups for product packaging. In the beginning of the novel, Sherry Dombrosio stays at home during the day, working on arts and crafts projects; as the novel progresses, she takes a job at Walt's company, displacing him as the breadwinner in the family. Leo Runcible is a well-known, but not well-liked, realtor in the area. He dreams that Carquinez will become a lively suburb of San Francisco and sees himself as a prime driver of the change. Janet Runcible, like Sherry, is a stay-at-home wife; but she seems to have no interests or drives other than alcohol and gossip. The Dombrosio and Runcible homes are scenes of unstable domesticity, each with its own unique reason for the instability. Sherry transgresses her prescribed "housewife" role because she comes from a wealthy family and eventually develops a career, while Janet is unable or unwilling to fulfill her prescribed duties as a wife.

These transgressions fuel the narrative action of the second half of the novel, which focuses on a hoax fabricated by Walt in his anger and boredom. Walt fabricates a fake Neanderthal skull using the remains of a "chupper," an earlier inhabitant of the area who suffered skull and jaw deformities due to polluted water, to trick Leo Runcible, who wants to use the skull to bring attention to the area and his real estate development plans. The hoax threatens to destabilize the characters' sense of history and reality as well as their marital relationships. More than any of the other mainstream novels Dick wrote during the 1950s, this one focuses extensively on the concept of fakes and the artificial. Through its focus on Walt Dombrosio's job as a packaging designer and the Neanderthal hoax plot that comprises the second half the novel, Dick seems to drop the theme of marital strife and turns the reader's attention to the role of the artificial (and its maker) and the destabilizing effects that simulation has on one's understanding of the world. Palmer notes towards the end of his analysis that the discovery of the fake skull ultimately links to instabilities of marital relations in the novels because it is the product of Walt's skill in creating models. Palmer argues that the narrative finally does connect the story line of the fake skull and the story line centering on the marital conflicts because the marital relationships have not advanced beyond primitive brutality and that this metaphorical "move back into the archaic" is a common element of Dick's SF (83).

Walt Dombrosio is the only character in the novel that could pull off the hoax, and his ability (as the artificer) invites a destabilized sense of reality. He has the professional knowledge and tools necessary to carry out the hoax, and he also has a history of creating elaborate hoaxes that, in the words of Mr. Wharton, the fourth-grade teacher, "test[s]… the ability to judge reality" (*Teeth* 57). Dombrosio's "skill" is alluded to early on in the novel during a description of his workplace, Lausch Company, which is responsible for designing packaging for consumer goods. The physical business is an artificial construct, which Walt has created:

> Here, on the main floor with its ceilings lost in the rafters, fluorescents on stems did the trick; no sunlight up here, as in the workshop. Cool and dim in the corners … the cellotex kept sounds from echoing and gave the premises that modern quality, that taste…. He himself had installed the cellotex and done the painting. Oddly, the cellotex had so diffused the sound of the receptionist's electric typewriter that no one could guess how large the place was. The sound appeared to recede. But actually Lausch Company was small. Doors that might have opened into labs actually opened onto storage closets. Now … he entered the secret area where the new containers were designed [*Teeth* 10–11].

In this early description, we see that the results of Walt's ability to construct artificial environments do not seem to be totally under his control; he installed the sound dampening cellotex to create a pleasing atmosphere, but his work ultimately confuses the senses of visitors who cannot determine the true size of the building's interior. The surprising result of his handiwork foreshadows the destabilizing effects of his hoax later in the novel when the skull's existence seems to erode the experience of reality instead of merely embarrassing Leo, which was Walt's original objective.

As Leo begins consulting experts in an attempt to verify the authenticity of the skull he has found, fact and feeling begin to blend and blur the boundaries between authentic and inauthentic. Doctor Freitas, a prominent anthropologist brought in to examine the skull and the area where Leo found it, explains to Leo that the authenticity and importance of the Neanderthal skull may be in doubt. Freitas tells Runcible, "It could still be authentic. And you could genuinely believe it authentic and yet it might be not. And so on. What you believe or what you want are of no matter" (*Teeth* 148). Yet this doesn't stop Leo, and he spends much of Freitas' visit trying to get a scientist to verify the authenticity of the skull before the doctor has completed his analysis. Leo's investment in the skull's authenticity is partly related to the loss of his reputation, but is also bound in his desire to reliably differentiate between the real and the fake. His faith is based on his intuition, in a similar way to how he feels about clients, and he does not want to hear the doctor's scientific opinion. As Freitas continues to collect samples and to explain the improbability of the skull's authenticity, Leo continues to question him about his feelings about the skull. Finally, Freitas admits, "If I had found it I would have had the instantaneous emotional reaction that it was genuine" (*Teeth* 151). Like the plastic model kits, the connection between thing and authenticity is ruptured leaving only the desire and subjective belief in a thing's authenticity. It is this subjective belief that in turn is destabilized, even after the skull is found to be a hoax.

Once the skull is discovered to be a fake, a professor from the University of California, Doctor Dudley Sharp, realizes that the hoax skull was modified from an actual deformed skull and a series of destabilizing realizations begin. The doctor, Wharton, Runcible, and Sheriff Christen set out to find where it had come from. They are finally led to the graveyard in the old location of Carquinez. Upon discovering the disturbed graves and another deformed skull, Wharton and the other searchers briefly discuss the authenticity of the (real) deformed skull:

> All at once he [Wharton] said, "Listen. This could be a fake."
> They glanced at him.
> "Of course," the vet said. "That would really be clever. They'd know we'd be coming here looking." He stood up, away from the open casket.
> "No end to it," Wharton said in a jerky, hectic voice [*Teeth* 180].

Wharton's observation that there is "no end" to the levels of simulation suggests a malleability of authenticity—once acknowledged it leads to a state that questions every experience with that particular object, so there is the possibility for a series of fakes always leading to another fake. In this case, Wharton is wrong; they have found the origin of the deformed skulls, and they quickly learn how they came about. However, the distrust of his own perception can never be reversed once he has learned he cannot always distinguish the fake from the real. The second discovery of the nature and cause of the deformity will bring on a form of entropic destabilization that affects both Dombrosio and Runcible and how they fear a future in which the children of the area physically de-evolve.

The novel's kipplization is figured through the breakdown between fact and fiction, and past, present, and future. These destabilizations are the direct result of the interactions with the Neanderthal skull; first as a hoax and then as it fits into the history of the town. The deformed skull comes from a local cemetery used by the older section of the town where the poor live. The deformity, known as the Chupper Jaw, comes from a lifetime of drinking water that has been contaminated by the lime pits that the poor worked at during the turn of the century. Unnamed chemicals, thought to be associated with the pits and the mining, apparently seeped into the ground water resulting in a birth defect, the jaw too large to speak with and apish in appearance.

There are two ways in which we see the kipplization of reality and history. First, the hoax tests the ability of the people to judge reality, creating a kind of reality breakdown. Second, the true origin of the skull and the history of the deformity greatly affect both Leo and Walt. Leo becomes obsessed with the idea that somehow the chemicals will leach into the current water system of the town, and he sinks all of his money into purchasing the water company, becoming financially insolvent in the end. Walt, having impregnated Sherry, becomes worried about his unborn child and wonders if the baby will have the birth defect. Both of these characters' concerns center around the idea the there is a threat of regression or de-evolution that is inherent with the deformity. Indeed, the deformity itself is linked specifically to the Neanderthal hoax. The hoax worked well enough to fool people visually precisely because the deformity created a skull that closely resembled that of Neanderthal man.

Ultimately, the fear of kipplization, presented through the imagery of degeneration, disturbs the two characters' sense of reality and ability to judge it correctly. Upon learning that the water may be contaminated in old Carquinez, Leo begins to concern himself with raising the money to fix the ailing water system of the town; however, Leo's concerns about the possible contamination of the water system are not valid. The current town of Carquinez is several miles away from the old one, and thus the lime pits that are the possible source of contamination, and the deformity has never been seen in newborns of the town. Leo's knowledge of the deformity—an image of degeneration—unleashes irrational fears. His business sense, never previously in question throughout the novel, suddenly breaks down, and his fears of kipple ruin him as a businessperson when he sells all of his real estate holdings. Walt suffers a similar breakdown concerning the threat of the Chupper Jaw. Walt's reality breakdown is figured as an uncontrollable dream: "In his mind he had a vivid image, almost a hallucination, of the future. All the details were there: they entered his mind in a throng. God, get away! he thought" (*Teeth* 211). The intrusion of these images, which last for five pages of the novel, signals a massive reality breakdown predicated on the discovery of an image of degeneration. The power of this break from reality is such that it is full of detail and devoid of any of the markers of a dream sequence. He sees a future in which his son is deformed with the Chupper Jaw. He has to take him to a special school with other children with the same physical deformity. In this sequence, Walt imagines his son as physically and mentally handicapped: "The little boy was looking up at her. The slow little face, the slow reaction. So dulled, he thought. So stupid. Attempting to understand" (*Teeth* 214). For Walt, the fear is of the total kipplization of his son; the boy will degenerate both physically and mentally.

The novel ends with the characters returning to their previous gender roles. Walt is once again "the man" of the house, and Sherry is once again confined to the home, pregnant with their child. Leo is entertaining local businessmen and their wives at his home with Janet performing the role of good hostess. The domestic and ontological instabilities present in the rest of the novel seem to have been surmounted in some way. However, beneath this calm return to normal lurks the very instabilities that both couples try so desperately to deny. Sherry and Walt relax at home; Sherry discusses how disgusted with her body she has become, and Walt has the dream about their deformed future son. Sherry's boredom with her role in the marriage has turned into hatred for Walt and her body; Walt's playful imagination seen in the beginning of the novel is no longer playful. Janet and Leo host an extravagant holiday party that they can't afford; Janet plays the good hostess, all the while sneaking drinks, and Leo launches into long discussions concerning the faltering water company. The Dombrosios act relaxed but are miserable; the Runcibles act wealthy but teeter on the edge of financial ruin. Although the marital relationships seem to be similar to those presented at the beginning of the novel, they are worse than before and could continue to degenerate. The only kind of change envisioned by either Walt or Leo is degenerative kipplization in the future generations of Carquinez. This is a paradoxical image of the shape of the future moving towards the forms of the past. The characters' realizations that they are unable always to perceive reality destabilizes the already shaky domestic scenes in the novel. Walt is no longer sure of the future of his unborn child, and Leo is no longer sure of the future of Carquinez. The concerns of both characters can be traced back to their interaction with the Neanderthal hoax that led to the discovery of the contaminated water.

Reading the Realist Novels Into the SF Texts

The failed marriages in *The Man Whose Teeth Were All Exactly Alike* drive the action of the novel and lead to reality breakdowns and kipple-like disorder; as such, the relationships are highlighted as a framing device, which

Dick employs in his SF novels as well. At the end of the novel, having resolved the tensions of reality-threatening events, the couples resume their marriages by returning to domestic scenes that have unresolved underlying tensions, and a new normal of unreality is put into place. This pattern is most apparent in this (and other) realist novels of Dick, and we can reread them back into the SF texts, recentering marital discord as the driver of intrusions of the artificial and kipple into the characters' lives, often leaving the characters in even more precarious states of marital disharmony than where they were when the novels started. For instance, much of the early action of *The Three Stigmata of Palmer Eldritch* is intertwined with Barney Mayerson's and Emily's failed marriage, which influences his decision to reject her pottery designs for the Perky Pat Layouts. *The Martian Time-Slip* begins with the Bohlens' failing marriage—Jack Bohlen suffers from schizophrenia, and Silvia Bohlen relies on pills to address her depression. They become involved with Arnie Kott and his ex-wife Anne Esterhazy's business machinations and Arnie's interest in Manfred Steiner's psychic powers. *Now Wait for Last Year* features the unhappy marriage of Eric and Kathy Sweetscent; the latter is driven to take JJ-180, which affects the user's perceptions, but also has the ability, depending on the particular user, to move him or her forwards or backwards in time and also sideways to parallel dimensions.[6] The Lilistar agents use the drug to force Kathy into becoming their spy, and she addicts Eric in a bid to resume their marriage. *Do Androids Dream of Electric Sheep?* starts with the Deckards' bitter bickering instigated by a disagreement over the mood organ settings; Iran insults Rick as a hired killer and accuses him of having "crude cop hands" (*Androids* 3-4). These brief descriptions highlight the regularity by which marital strife is used to frame the novels and that the discord is frequently intertwined with the reality altering drugs and devices common to Dick's SF. As in the mainstream novels, the marriages undergo changes due to other pressures during the course of the narrative, and, in the end, the SF novels return to these domestic scenes, but they have been altered in significant ways.

The damaged marital and domestic scenes at the end of the SF novels originate in the initial fragilities of the relationships involved and their interaction with the reality breakdowns that have occurred throughout the novel, leaving, finally, an altered and ominous domesticity similar to the end of *The Man Whose Teeth Were All Exactly Alike*. Barney and Anne, at the end of *The Three Stigmata of Palmer Eldritch*, share a realization that the stigmata brought on by the use of Chew-Z will be an ongoing "curse," "out in the open, ranging in every direction" (*Eldritch* 219). *Martian Time-Slip* ends with Silvia making dinner for Jack, where they come to an uneasy truce when Silvia mentions Jack's affair. This scene is interrupted when a far-future version of Manfred appears next door. In attempting to calm Silvia afterwards, Jack explains, "'It probably won't happen again…. But even if it does—'" (*Time-Slip*

262). The qualified statement with its trailing ending leaves no doubt that any domestic peace that the Bohlens have begun to develop could be disrupted in the future as a direct result of Jack's work with Manfred. In *Now Wait for Last Year*, Eric engages a taxicab in a discussion about whether or not to stay with Kathy, who has been damaged by her addiction to JJ-180. In the end, he decides to stay married to her, agreeing with the cab's analysis that "life is composed of reality configurations so constituted. To abandon her would be to say, I can't endure reality as such. I have to have uniquely special easier conditions" (*Last Year* 229). At the end of *Do Androids Dream of Electric Sheep?*, Deckard returns from his travel up north with the ersatz toad. Iran welcomes him home, but the final scene wherein she adopts a stereotypical marital love belies the marital dysfunction that is on display earlier in the novel. In this instance, she puts Deckard to bed by setting the mood organ for Rick and goes about ordering a habitat and fake flies for the android toad. In each of these examples, the relationships are frequently resumed in a diminished but continuing form. The diminishment often originates from the artificial and/or the reality breakdowns and its entropic effects, and the return to the marital relationships highlights the fractured state of the domestic scene at the end of novels. However, these marriages were never whole to begin with, and the new normal of these relationships should not be understood as a simple commentary that reality disturbances hurt traditional marital relationships; instead, these troubled relationships are the defining realities of the characters and frame the narratives. The alien incursions, time travel, alternate realities, and androids are the spectacular events that the characters experience as their mundane relationships fracture and disintegrate only to be reassembled in an even more unstable form.

Conclusion

Philip K. Dick once told an interviewer that science fiction could not adequately represent male/female relationships, and this was its primary failing ("Questionnaire" 67). The early mainstream novels explore the turbulent world of male/female relationships in a way that Dick felt SF novels could not. In *The Man Whose Teeth Were All Exactly Alike* and some of Dick's historically adjacent SF novels, strained marital relations are central to the plots and drive the action. Once the theme of the artificial is introduced, entropic forces are unleashed which erode shared understandings of reality, which, in turn, further degrade the already unstable marriages. The marital relationships central in the mainstream fiction are placed at the outer edges of the SF novels but are no less important for that. Studying Dick's mainstream novels deepens our historical understanding of Dick's work, since their period of production is the direct precursor to the most successful era of his career. The readings offered above demonstrate that the pivotal moments in these novels often center around the intersection of the artificial, kipple, and their association to marital relationships. Instead of using cognitive estrangement to present problems in a way that creates fresh perspectives for the reader, Dick takes the familiar and illustrates how it is already science fictional. The SF novels, full of androids and reality breakdowns, are often grounded in the already strange and terrifying martial relationships highlighted in the mainstream novels. The ongoing critical project of studying Dick's *oeuvre* requires that scholars take notice of these novels. They are not a footnote to Dick's work; rather, they are a chapter unto themselves.

NOTES

1. For a SF writer, Dick seemed to hold a rather pragmatic view of the limitations of the genre. In response to a question concerning the failings of SF, Dick replied, "SF fails to explore the depths of interpersonal human relationships, and this is its lack.... But SF (excepting Bradbury) is for younger, more optimistic people, who haven't yet suffered at the hands of life; quality fiction tends—and rightly so—to deal with the defeated, those who have lost the first bloom" ("Questionnaire" 64).

2. See *Philip K. Dick: In His Own Words* (1984). Dick states that the novel is a "hell of a good book.... And I'm hoping very much that it will sell. I read it over and I liked it a lot. I was reading the others and I didn't care for the others at all. But *The Man Whose Teeth* is really a very well written book" (Rickman 145).

3. Dick notes that after he published *Eye in the Sky* (1957) he received fan mail from Murray Teigh Bloom author of *Money of Their Own: The Great Counterfeiters*. Dick states, "As a matter of fact it was that book that gave me the idea of forgeries. He [Bloom] said a really good counterfeit coin can never be nicked. So there may be classes of counterfeiting that no one ever (catches) (sic)" (Rickman 78).

4. See J.S. Weiner's 1955 investigative book *The Piltdown Forgery*, which delineates the detailed history of the original "discovery" of the Piltdown man by Charles Dawson in 1912 to its eventual discovery and public disclosure of its true nature as a forgery on November 21, 1953.

5. In his chapter "The Short Stories: Philip K. Dick and the Nuclear Family," Palmer does read several short stories of Dick's that do focus on the nuclear family, but he does not seem to make an explicit connection between the readings of the mainstream novels and the appearance of family strife in the science fiction.

6. Kim Stanley Robinson argues, "Every aspect of the novel partakes of the harsh and strained nature of the time. All of the personal relationships in the novel are marred by suspicion, distrust and exploitation. The marriage ... is the most bitter in all of Dick's work, which is saying a lot: at one point, it is called 'legalized hate'" (79).

WORKS CITED

Bukatman, Scott. *Terminal Identity: The Virtual Subject in Post-Modern Science Fiction*. Duke UP, 1993.
Dick, Philip K. *Do Androids Dream of Electric Sheep?* 1968. Del Rey, 1996.
_____. "The *Double*: Bill Symposium: Replies to a Questionnaire for Professional SF Writers and Editors." 1969. *The Shifting Realities of Philip K. Dick: Selected Literary and Philosophical Writings*. Ed. Lawrence Sutin. Vintage Books, 1995. 63–67.

———. *The Man in the High Castle*. 1962. Vintage Books, 1992.
———. *The Man Whose Teeth Were All Exactly Alike*. Mark V. Ziesing, 1984.
———. *Martian Time-Slip*. 1964. Vintage Books, 1995.
———. *Now Wait for Last Year*. 1966. Vintage Books, 1993.
———. "Null-O." 1958. *The Collected Short Stories of Philip K. Dick*. Vol. 3. Citadel Press, 1987. 135–44.
———. *The Three Stigmata of Palmer Eldritch*. 1964. Vintage Books, 1991.
———. *Ubik*. 1969. Vintage Books, 1991.
Fitting, Peter. "Reality as Ideological Construct: A Reading of Five Novels by Philip K. Dick." 1983. *On Philip K. Dick: Articles from* Science-Fiction Studies. Ed. R. D. Mullen, Istvan Csicsery-Ronay, Jr., Arthur B. Evans, and Veronica Hollinger. SF-TH Inc., 1992. 92–110.
Jameson, Frederic. "Futuristic Visions That Tell Us About Right Now." *In These Times*, May 1982, 17.
Jouanne, Emmanuel. "How 'Dickian' Is the New French Science Fiction?" 1988. *On Philip K. Dick: Articles from* Science-Fiction Studies. Ed. R. D. Mullen, Istvan Csicsery-Ronay, Jr., Arthur B. Evans, and Veronica Hollinger. SF-TH Inc., 1992. 232–35.
Lem, Stanislaw. "Philip K. Dick: A Visionary Among the Charlatans." 1975. *On Philip K. Dick: Articles from* Science-Fiction Studies. Ed. R. D. Mullen, Istvan Csicsery-Ronay, Jr., Arthur B. Evans, and Veronica Hollinger. SF-TH Inc., 1992. 49–62.
Levack, Daniel J. H., and Steven Owen Godersky, comps. *PKD: A Philip K. Dick Bibliography*. Meckler Corporation, 1988.
Mackey, Douglas A. *Philip K. Dick*. Twayne Publishers, 1988.
Palmer, Christopher. *Philip K. Dick: Exhilaration and Terror of the Postmodern*. Liverpool University Press, 2003.
Rickman, Gregg. *Philip K. Dick: In His Own Words*. Fragments West/The Valentine Press, 1984.
Robinson, Kim Stanley. *The Novels of Philip K. Dick*. UMI Research Press, 1984.
Sutin, Lawrence. *Divine Invasions: A Life of Philip K. Dick*. Carroll & Graf Publishers, 2005.
Suvin, Darko. "The Opus: Artifice as Refuge and Worldview." 1975. *On Philip K. Dick: Articles from* Science-Fiction Studies. Ed. R. D. Mullen, Istvan Csicsery-Ronay, Jr., Arthur B. Evans, and Veronica Hollinger. SF-TH Inc., 1992. 2–15.
Thorpe, Charles. "Death of a Salesman: Petit-Bourgeois Dread in Philip K. Dick's Mainstream Fiction." *Science Fiction Studies* 38.3, 2011, 412–434.
Weiner, J. S. *The Piltdown Forgery*. Oxford UP, 1955.
Williams, Paul. Foreword. *The Man Whose Teeth Were All Exactly Alike*. By Philip K. Dick. Mark V. Ziesing, 1984. i.

Evolving Dickian Criticism
The Exegesis *and Pierre Teilhard de Chardin*

MICHAEL KVAMME-O'BRIEN

> Christ is seen in evolutionary terms paralleling or expressing the very evolution that (I believe) my work represents (and which I see in the macrocosm and in Valis). At a certain crucial stage of evolution toward complexification of structure (i.e., negentropy) the mundane passes over—in a quantum leap—into the divine; the man becomes Ditheon, Christ; macrocosm likewise (à la Teilhard and his Point Omega).
> —*The Exegesis of Philip K. Dick* (771)

Introduction

The publication of *The Exegesis of Philip K. Dick* (2011) has changed Dickian literary criticism. At just under one thousand pages, the published version of the *Exegesis* represents a mere fraction of Dick's eight-thousand-page manuscript, scribbled late at night with pen and paper between 1974 and his death in 1982. While reduced in size, the published *Exegesis* remains a mine of inestimable critical value. Dick wrote the *Exegesis* as a reflexive philosophical exploration of himself and his work following his visionary experience of the February 3, 1974 (which he named 2-3-74). He reported a visionary experience involving a pink beam of light emanating from God, which provided him with accurate information on his son's illness before it was discovered. This vision set off a cascade of psychological incidents within Dick's mind. Ultimately these psychic events lead Dick to the "outline of a new theology" (*Exegesis* 837). Reflecting on his SF *oeuvre* throughout the *Exegesis*, Dick concludes that his SF work had been subject to the process of spiritual evolution "much as Teilhard de Chardin describes in *The Phenomenon of Man*" (785). The purpose of this essay is to show how the theories of Pierre Teilhard de Chardin, especially his view that spiritual energy is the dynamic standard of the universe, can be used as a critical lens through which to view Dick's *oeuvre*. In Chardin's paradigm all things that exist, including the human intellect, evolve towards a state of ultimate being known as the Omega Point. By linking together analyses of *The Penultimate Truth* (1964), *Do Androids Dream of Electric Sheep?* (1968), *A Scanner Darkly* (1977), *VALIS* (1981), and the *Exegesis*, it can be shown how Dick's fiction progresses from a primary focus on political domination, through an emancipatory stage of material world-awareness, to a transcendental level of advanced philosophical and theological consciousness.

Dick suggests in the *Exegesis* that humanity is moving "toward a cosmic awakening something like the Omega Point suggested by paleontologist Teilhard de Chardin" (314). Dick views his own *oeuvre* as evolving towards "spiritual perfection" by culminating in the hyperpersonalised Omega Point embodied by Horselover Fat's "metapsychoanalytic" connection to the VALIS entity in *VALIS* (Stilling 91). The critical literature to-date on Dick's *oeuvre* does not expose the genealogical formation of Dick's spiritual self. Marxists such as Darko Suvin (1975) and Fredric Jameson (2005) do much to define the material aspects of Dick's political SF but avoid the point of his theological work. Kim Stanley Robinson's *The Novels of Philip K. Dick* (1981) (originally a Ph.D. supervised by Jameson) highlights the realism and capitalist critique of Dick's work. However, like Suvin and Jameson, Robinson does not properly address Dickian theology. Theologians and theologically-interested critics, such as Patricia Warrick (1987), Gabriel McKee (2004), and Marcus Boon (2015) do a good job of highlighting the themes of Dickian spirituality, but only mention Chardin briefly. Here's McKee touching on the importance of Chardin:

> Teilhard de Chardin describes God's action in the world as "God gathering to himself not merely a diffuse multiplicity of souls, but the solid, organic, reality of a universe, taken from top to bottom in the complete extent and unity of its energies." Teilhard de Chardin further describes this as a substantial transformation of the universe into God: "In order to create…. God has to inevitably immerse himself in the multiple, so that he may incorporate it into himself." Dick is in complete agreement with Teilhard de Chardin here, and in the *Exegesis* he frequently acknowledged the similarities between their theories. In Dick's terms, this incorporation is a form of transubstantiation: God, as a mimicking, undetectable being superior to human beings, is altering the substance of the universe and infusing it with and thus incorporating it into his infinite Being [McKee 61–62].

McKee quickly moves on. However, the present essay asserts that Dick's *oeuvre* can be more thoroughly read as Dick himself suggests we read it: as the literal embodiment of the spiritual energy that is Chardin's dynamic standard of the universe.

Pierre Teilhard de Chardin

Chardin was born in France in 1881 to parents of Catholic faith. His father, Emmanuel Teilhard, was a scientist who oversaw his children's education before they entered school. He encouraged Pierre's interest in the natural world by collecting plants and insects to bring home for him to study. Pierre's mother, Berthe de Dompiere, encouraged his spiritual interests.[1] She hung a picture of the Sacred Heart of Jesus in their living room. Chardin wrote about this picture in *The Heart of the Matter* (1979) stating, "It is in the Sacred Heart that the conjunction of the Divine and the cosmic has taken place.... There lies the power that, from the beginning, has attracted me and conquered me.... All the later development of my interior life has been nothing other than the evolution of that seed" (43). The combination of Pierre's parents' material and spiritual teachings later flowered into his theories on spiritual evolution.

Chardin studied mathematics, philosophy, theology and literature. He worked as a science teacher, priest and paleontologist. Whilst carrying out scientific research in China, he began documenting his hybrid philosophies in writing. In China he wrote "The Cosmic Life" (1919), "The Spiritual Power of Matter" (1919), and *The Divine Milieu* (1960). The Church banned publication of all his book-length works, including *The Phenomenon of Man* (1955), which later proved to be his *magnum opus*. In *Phenomenon*, Chardin presents his cosmological vision of the spiritual unity of the universe, defining material evolution as the physical manifestation of the universal dynamic standard of spiritual energy.

In *Phenomenon*, Chardin describes the universe as "a system by its plurality, a totum by its unity, a quantum by its energy" (48). The system of the universe is the interrelationship of its parts, the totum is the universe's total "order and design," and the quantum is the spiritual energy or "dynamic standard" that drives material evolution (49). For Chardin, because human consciousness is a component of material reality, it is subject to the same process of material evolution as the rest of the physical universe. Chardin's stages of evolution are "geogenesis" to "biogenesis" and then "psychogenesis" to "noogenesis" (201). While geogenesis and biogenesis are the evolution of mineral, vegetable, and animal life, psychogenesis and noogenesis are the evolution of human, psychic and spiritual life. Psychogenesis is the process whereby consciousness starts to appear in an organism. This happens when the "within" of the organism starts to reflect upon itself (68). Noogenesis is the perfecting of human consciousness, where individual minds evolve in a collective direction to form the "noosphere" (200). The noosphere is the "thinking layer" of the planet (202). The noosphere is also "the collective effect of human consciousness on the biosphere and the medium for the planet's evolution toward Point Omega" (*Exegesis* 934). Conceptualizing the evolutionary direction of human consciousness necessitates visualizing a spectrum of growth from something prior to something transcendent. The prior stages commence with geogenesis and the transcendent stages with psychogenesis. The transcendent final point of evolved human consciousness is "the Omega Point" (Chardin 294).

The Omega Point is achieved through "Christogenesis" (325). Christogenesis is the process governing all evolution through all its stages, according to Chardin. Geogenesis, biogenesis, psychogenesis, and noogenesis are all components of Christogenesis. Christogenesis draws all matter and spiritual energy towards a center. For Chardin, as a Christian (having grown up with a picture of the Sacred Heart of Jesus in his living room), the center of the universe is Christ. The spiritual energy of the universe is therefore a "Christic" energy (325). Christogenesis causes the collective human mind to evolve through the noosphere towards Christ to the Omega Point. In the Omega Point the collective human mind and Christ become one. Culminating at Point Omega the evolved consciousness of individual people is just as personalized as it is collectively unified. As Chardin states "Far from being mutually exclusive, the Universal and Personal (that is to say, the 'centered') grow in the same direction and culminate simultaneously in each other" (Chardin 285). Dick believed Chardin's process of spiritual evolution should be framed as a process of remembering Christ.

PKD and Chardin

In the *Exegesis*, Dick critiqued his own *oeuvre* as a composite whole, a plural system, self-referentially subject to the dynamic standard of spiritual evolution. Much of the *Exegesis* is given up to Dick retrospectively analyzing the significance of his own work. He writes: "I, consciously, don't write my novels ... my unconscious does" (29), arguing that his SF evolves from being largely unconscious of spiritual paradigms to becoming fully aware of them. In an *Exegesis* entry dated November 1974, Dick reflects that his visionary experience of the 3 of February that year may have been a remembering of "Immanent Mind within us and around us" (62). According to Dick, this visionary experience involving a pink beam of light emanating from God (which reportedly provided accurate information on his son's illness before it was discovered) signaled the presence of "the third point in human evolution" (62–63). Dick's third point of evolution is the psychogenesis of Chardin. Dick summarizes this stage as "the leap from inanimate to animate," which is the same leap as from biogenesis (material) to psychogenesis (spiritual) (62). Indicating this third stage leads to noogenesis (the generation of the thinking layer of the planet), Dick suggests his vision 2-3-74 represented "the perfecting and completing" of psychogenesis (62). He states 2-3-74 indicated a noogenesis that was "pushing beyond the threshold" of psychogenesis (62). For Dick:

> Consciousness occurs when unconsciousness has been energised to a purely quantitative point, and passes beyond.

It possesses immortality (through rebirth). It knows everything (through being gestalted from an almost infinite number of bits throughout space and time). Knowing it can't err, knowing it can't die, having a direct relationship with the Logos, or objective reality, or the Plan, it can make decisions partaking of Haggia Sophia: the wisdom of God [63].

This is where Dick explains psychogenesis (and thereafter noogenesis) better than Chardin. Chardin states in *Phenomenon* that "it is not easy" to be clear on how "the cellular revolution should express itself psychically" (97). But for Dick, it is simply because the entire universe "is made out of information" (VALIS 23).

Dick's SF *oeuvre* offers a perfect literary example of Chardin's view that spiritual energy is the dynamic standard of the universe. The three general categories of Dick's SF canon are (1) early-to-middle (2) middle-to-late (3) late-to-death (or 1. Dystopian, 2. Ontological 3. Theological).[2] Dick's dystopian period was dominated by material and political concerns, his ontological period by existential and exploratory matters, and his theological period by spiritual and transcendent themes. The dystopian period covers texts from *Solar Lottery* (1955) through *The Penultimate Truth* (1964) up to and including *Now Wait for Last Year* (1966). These texts are mostly realist critiques of dystopian America. According to Chardin's terminology, this period's themes are largely "geogenic" (i.e., relating to the formation of the earthly environment). Dick's period of ontological exploration runs from *The Crack in Space* (1966) through *Do Androids Dream of Electric Sheep?* (1968), from *Ubik* (1969) to *A Scanner Darkly* (1977). This is where he defines what it means to be human while exploring reality. In other words, the ontological period is dominated by "psychogenic" themes (i.e., themes relating to how mind inhabits matter). Finally, the late period, inspired by 2-3-74, comprises the visionary VALIS-trilogy in which Dick attempts to define the reality of his transcendental experience. The trilogy contains the theological SF texts *VALIS* (1981) and *The Divine Invasion* (1981), rounded off by the mainstream realist text, *The Transmigration of Timothy Archer* (1982), published posthumously. The texts in this period, *VALIS* especially, have strong noogenic themes (i.e., themes relating to the perfecting of human consciousness and the development of the noosphere).

2-3-74 and The Penultimate Truth

In an *Exegesis* entry dated March 3, 1980, while considering the mechanism whereby 2-3-74 could have given him specific information on his son's illness, Dick recalls the year he wrote *Penultimate* (1964). He states, "I can see that a decade before 3-74 I was subliminally aware of the problem that lay ahead and was already beginning to analyze it" (587). He states (in language reminiscent of Chardin's explanation that consciousness arises when energy reflects upon itself) that in 2-3-74, "my psyche reversed itself so that what was latent became actual" (588). In other words, his unconscious mind had been a repository for information his conscious mind had no previous access to. In this entry, Dick indicates his SF *oeuvre* unfolded through the same mechanism, suggesting *Penultimate* was an unconscious foretelling of what his later work would evolve into. Dick uses a metaphor in his March 3 entry to describe *Penultimate*. He suggests that the text, coming from the early-to-middle, dystopian period of his SF *oeuvre*, primarily offers a rudimentary geogenic (and biogenic) image of a dystopian earthly environment operating based on "a constant flow of traffic everywhere as if in a giant brain" (588). Dick's "giant brain" analogy highlights the psychogenic potential of the text.

Penultimate is geogenic because it describes the environmental impact of future warfare. Dick's examination of how the war impacts the human populace is biogenic. For Chardin biogenesis always holds the potential for psychogenesis. In *Penultimate*'s 2009 there is a war on Mars between the Earth's Eastern and Western blocks. Due to atmospheric damage both sides displace their populations to underground communities known as "tanks" (48). The tanks operate underground factories to produce robots, called "leadies" to fight in the overground war (18). The leadies fight large-scale battles across the planet's surface for two years. Although most of humanity is underground, protected from the destruction above, a small number of military personnel remain overground to co-ordinate the robotic war. Amongst these personnel are media technicians, known as "Yance-men," responsible for producing propaganda to control the tankers below, thus keeping them motivated in the war effort (97). The "Protector," a simulacrum of Eisenhower named Yancy, communicates the propaganda (14). However, it soon becomes clear to the overground leaders the war is not winnable. Supported by their robots, they end the war, dividing the remaining land and resources amongst themselves, not telling the civilians below, who keep producing robots for the elite to use as servants.

Dick states in his March 3 *Exegesis* entry that *Penultimate* illustrates the universe as it is on a material (geogenic-biogenic) level: "bloody with information" (588). While *Penultimate* was mostly about two protagonists with irreconcilable differences who meet each other, one from above ground and one from below, Dick's later metaphorical interpretation of the text as "a constant flow of traffic everywhere as if in a giant brain" (588) is correct. *Penultimate*, with its overground elite controlling resources, overground Yance-men controlling underground tankers, and underground tankers building leadies for overground use, is like a giant (geogenic-biogenic) brain.

This future society is an organizational system sustaining itself based on the careful co-ordination of information. However, Dick's March 3 entry further interprets *Penultimate* as a representation of the integration of individual and universal mind, with both conscious and subconscious psychogenic aspects. Referring to his own real-life and *Penultimate*, Dick states:

> Reality is a giant brain whose information content the faculty plunders for its own use, and, having acquired the information, in the right time period, it acts on it, against the universe if necessary. This is a survival tool. The workshop in which it was built is the workshop of dying organisms that did not develop such a talent, that could not see or acquire the information or if they did when the moment came they could not act on it—they knew what was going to happen and then they knew what was happening but they could not get it together and fight the antagonist off [588].

Regarding Dick's own life, the cognitive faculty he describes becomes for him the mechanism whereby 2-3-74 provided information on his son's undiagnosed illness. In the March 3 entry, Dick says this faculty caused his mind to overrun "external time, caused it to run backward in relation to myself, and extracted the information from the drastically altered world that I needed" (587). Such statements cause Warrick to describe Dick "as a contemporary thinker in the Gnostic tradition" (Warrick 179). Warrick suggests Dick is Gnostic because he believes "salvation through self-knowledge is the only means possible to man to heal his wounded psyche" (Warrick 179). For Chardin self-knowledge is available through psychogenic reflexivity. Dick's Gnosticism is remembering Christ through psychogenic reflexivity.

Dick suggests *Penultimate*'s plot is a metaphor for under-evolved spiritual cognition. For example, the underground tanker St. James tunnels up to the surface to obtain an artificial heart for his dying friend Souza. St. James acts like Dick's visionary faculty, plundering reality for his own use, acting against the (dis)order of the universe to cure his friend's disease. Tunneling up into the consciousness of the overground elite from below, St. James is like an unconscious archetype appearing in the egotistical realm of the bourgeois leaders. However, while St. James finds a heart and develops a relationship with the overground Yance-man Adams, who in-turn visits the underground tanks, neither St. James nor Adams develop the spiritual consciousness required to partner up to reform the dystopian system on Earth. The potential of the spiritual faculty remains unrealized on the individual and collective levels. Neither character undergoes psychogenic Gnostic revelation. The novel ends with "both of them without friendliness, and without warmth. Divided from each other absolutely" (190). Therefore, *Penultimate* can be placed within the geogenic phase of Dick's *oeuvre*, mostly related to the material formation of dystopian America. Psychogenesis is not fully realized within the materiality of *Penultimate*'s setting. If it had been, then the within of the material system represented by St. James and Adams spiritually-lacking relationship would have reflected upon itself more effectively and a more collective consciousness would have arisen.

Dick states regarding the success of the spiritual visionary faculty in his March 3 entry of the *Exegesis*:

> The final stage, that of seizing motor and speech centers, simply indicates the success of the faculty; its dynamism is found at the heart of the faculty in its unconscious or latent stage where it foreknew and analyzed. My ego, consciousness, went like an obsolete species whose time was over; I made way for the next generator of life which could do battle because it had long ago figured out who was after its neck and why and how and, most of all, what the proper response was. So it is in the nature of the faculty, this faculty, to know when it is needed and to advance control without negotiation and without explanation. But it let me see the world as it sees it, and what it sees is not what we see. The faculty has power over the outer world such as we cannot imagine, and, I realized even at the time, in 3-74, it has complete power over me—if there is a me anymore, now that the faculty has once come into conscious organization [588].

So, while St. James and Adams did not awaken the collective spiritual consciousness required to seize control of a diseased governmental superstructure together, Dick suggests 2-3-74 indicates this psychogenic faculty later awoke within him personally and *Penultimate* was an unconscious metaphor for the latent mechanism. The geogenic (and biogenic) foundation had been laid in *Penultimate* and Dick's *oeuvre* was entering its psychogenic stage. Reflecting back from 3 March 1980 to 2-3-74 and 1964 respectively, Dick envisaged how his own spiritual faculty had come into "conscious organization" as part of his individual psychogenic evolution. This is the faculty making way for "the next generator of life" in his *oeuvre*, by shifting the focus from the organization of the material world to how universal mind inhabits it.

The Penultimate Truth *vs.* Do Androids Dream of Electric Sheep? = *Psychogenesis*

In *Penultimate*, although underdeveloped in comparison to his later SF, Dick examines tensions between inner realities and outer realities (i.e., psychological/psychogenic vs. environmental/geogenic), using the character Adams. Adams is the surface-dwelling protagonist psychologically alienated from his humanity by the mechanistic speech-writing he performs. As a Yance-man "alibi" for the bourgeois control of Earth's material resources, he deceives the underground workforce by spinning propaganda about a fake war (Robinson 65). *Androids* presents similar tensions using characters such as Deckard and Isodore, but this time they are more evolved. Deckard is the "alibi" bounty-hunter stalking a group of rebelling androids; he is alienated from his humanity by the shallow materialism of the system, symbolized by his possessing an electric sheep for a pet rather than a real one. Isodore is a truck driver psychologically damaged by the radiation fallout of the apocalyptic war named "World War Terminus" (12). He is an empathetic individual who tries to make friends with a group of androids. Chardin had already thought about tensions between inner and outer realities before *Penultimate* was written.

Summing up the philosophical battle fought between materialists and divine philosophers for centuries, Chardin posits the following tension between inner and outer:

> On the one hand the materialists insist on talking about objects as though they only consist of external actions in transient relationships. On the other hand the upholders of a spiritual interpretation are obstinately determined not to go outside a kind of solitary introspection in which things are only looked upon as being shut in upon themselves in their "immanent" workings. Both fight on different planes and do not meet; each only sees half the problem.
>
> I am convinced that the two points of view require to be brought into union, and that they soon will unite in a kind of phenomenology or generalized physic in which the internal aspect of things as well as the external aspect of the world will be taken into account. Otherwise, so it seems to me, it is impossible to cover the totality of the cosmic phenomenon by one coherent explanation such as science must try to construct [58].

In *Penultimate* the outer material world and inner spiritual reality remain in conflict. However, this begins changing by *Androids*.

Dick's developing representation of tensions between inner and outer across *Penultimate* and *Androids* highlights a spiritual evolution shifting from the geogenic level to the psychogenic. In *Penultimate*, while Adams' inner alienation and "loneliness" is caused by the oppressive materialism of the outer world, he lacks the spiritual consciousness required to transcend it (1). Although Adams perceives the material cause of his inner condition, he is too self-centered to move beyond it. For example, while looking out his window at home, he can link the outer material reality of "dead trees" and a "darkness hanging and approaching," to his inner psychic life (1). He sees how this "fog can drift in from outside and get you" (1). However, unlike Isodore at home in *Androids*, who can experience the deafening silence that "flashed from the woodwork and the walls ... to supplant all things tangible," he is not aware this inner spiritual void reflects a lack of "God" in his world (16–17). While in *Androids*, Isodore can see beyond materialism to "sense the presence of life" within the android populace; in *Penultimate*, Adams never bridges the gap between himself and those further down the politically imposed ontological hierarchy (53).

Another example of the Chardinian psychogenic evolution of spiritual consciousness from *Penultimate* to *Androids* is the example of Adams' attempt to use a "rhetorizer" (1) to write a speech vs. Deckard's use of an "empathy box" to fuse with the spiritual entity Mercer (151). Fulfilling the cog-in-the-machine role of pumping out speeches to aid bourgeois control of the underground workforce, Adams is reliant on his rhetorizer to stimulate his own creativity. While his wife encourages him to just imagine "what finding a thriving, living squirrel would have meant," rather than have his machine do it for him, this proves beyond him (3). Adams is ignorant. He cannot remember what a pen is called and requires an entire robotic staff to source some paper. On the other hand, Deckard's use of the empathy box facilitates "mental and spiritual identification" (18) with the "archetypal superior entity" Mercer (182). Deckard's spiritual identification allows him to unify external and internal reality, to enter a psychogenic stage of reflexive conscious awareness where transcendence beyond shallow materialism becomes possible. Such reflexivity allows Deckard to ask questions Adams cannot, like "do androids have souls?" (117). Marking the evolution of Dick's *oeuvre* from Chardin's geogenic to psychogenic stages, Deckard exemplifies how the "within" of an organism starts to reflect upon itself. When Deckard states "I'm Wilbur Mercer" he shows that both he and his literary creator have become conscious of their own spiritual reality through Gnostic revelation.

Psychogenic Revolution: A Scanner Darkly

By the time *Scanner* was published, nine years after *Androids*, Dick's focus had become fully psychogenic. Matter is subject to mind in *Scanner*; the opposite is true in *Penultimate*. In *Scanner*, Dick assumes a universal metaphysical mind, which he splits into two characters who are the same person. This allows for a complete deconstruction of how mind inhabits matter and of how mind inhabits itself. Deconstructing how mind inhabits itself while inhabiting the material universe allows Dick the transcendence required to generate Chardin's "generalised physic in which the internal aspect of things as well as the external aspect of the world" are fully explained (Chardin 58). Throughout the text, all divisions between inner and outer are erased. In *Scanner* this generalized physic is a Gnostic function of Christogenesis (*Exegesis* 403). While Dick used a "big protagonist" vs. a "little protagonist" in *Penultimate* and *Androids* (Adams vs. St. Brose, and Deckard vs. Isodore), where the primary was an "alibi" for the system and the secondary a utopian "wish" for what the system could become, in *Scanner* there is no real distinction between either—one character represents both (Robinson 17–65).

Scanner is set on Earth in the future focusing on the everyday life of the drug-dealing protagonist Bob Arctor who lives in Orange County (in Southern California where Dick lived in the 1970s) in a house with other drug addicts. Arctor is an alienated individual living on the fringes of society. He rejected a superficially perfect suburban life searching for a more authentic existence. The novel's first half focuses on the idle musings of the directionless dopers as they play out various imaginary situations together while taking Substance D. Substance D is a highly addictive drug that splits the human mind in half, creating two distinct personalities. The action speeds up in the second half as Arctor starts forgetting he is also Agent Fred, an undercover narcotics officer whose identity is hidden from everyone, including the police, by his scramble suit, which affects others' ability to remember him. Eventually, due to an administrative error, Fred is tasked with observing Arctor. Dick then presents Arctor/Fred as carrying out surveillance upon himself through a holographic scanning device. This is where the title "A Scanner Darkly" comes from. Dick's allusion to Apostle Paul's biblical statement "for now we see through a glass darkly" brings a transcendent theological interpretation to Arctor/Fred's perspective on the surreal distortion between the boundaries of subject and object in *Scanner* (*The Bible* 553). Just as Paul's view of spiritual reality was limited (through a glass darkly) due to material restrictions, so are purely geogenic interpretations of reality restricted by a relative lack of psychogenic awareness.

Blending both little and big protagonists aids Dick's construction of Chardin's generalized physic in two ways. Firstly, the blend dissolves the subject-object divide, which allows Dick to show how mind inhabits matter (Palmer 177). Secondly, this blending allows Dick to show how mind reflects upon and inhabits itself. The first function (the dissolution of the subject-object divide) erases the inner vs. outer divide. This first function shows how the inner subjective state of a particular being is equitable with the outer objective reality of general being-in-itself.[3] For example, Agent Fred is introduced to the reader in Chapter 2 by the host at a gathering as an "undercover narcotics agent" wearing a "scramble suit" (*Scanner* 21). The scramble suit projects "every conceivable eye color, hair color, shape and type of nose, (and) formation of teeth" to make the user appear as "everyman" (23). Fred's identity is fluid; although he is an individual, he also embodies the general collective. Though the equivalence between Fred's inner state and general being-in-itself is visible from the outset, the overlap becomes more significant as his addiction to Substance D develops. Fred's spiritual ill-health as a fragmented drug-user becomes the spiritual ill-health of a fractured postmodern America in general actualizing Chardin's generalized physic. In *Scanner* capitalism and postmodernity are shown to be "death rising from the earth" because universal spiritual lack has caused a mindless human interaction with the natural environment (275). By the end of the novel for example, Arctor/Fred has become "a reflex machine, like an ant" growing Substance D plants for the government's New Path institute to sell (265).

The second function of assuming a universal metaphysical mind, highlighted by blending Arctor and Fred, shows how mind reflects upon and inhabits itself. Dick says regarding this function "it's almost as if in Scanner the Ur-personality which is and was not occluded was able to monitor the conscious occluded one, from a detached standpoint," reminiscent of Chardin's Christ spiraling all matter and spiritual energy upwards towards himself at the center (*Exegesis* 403). Initially it appears that Fred may be the Ur-personality observing Arctor. However, while Arctor/Fred's desire to take Substance D represents a desire to find a "saving Gnosis" (677) to provide transcendence over the material world (which does assist him to see himself and the "entire universe backward" in a partial Gnostic revelation), it also occludes him because it causes amnesia (212). Warrick likens Dick's Gnosticism to the Valentinian Gnostic belief: "each individual is a spirit, or pneuma, a fallen particle of the true God. He is trapped in the prison of material existence. He is asleep and ignorant of his condition. God sends messengers to call the sleeping spirit to awaken and remember its true destiny." (Warrick 180). By Chapter 10 Fred no longer remembers he is Arctor or that he is carrying out surveillance on himself. Presenting psychogenic evolution as a spiritual revolution (rather than a material one defined by Substance D), Dick starts firing German poetry into the mind of Arctor, revealing the Ur-personality to be a Christic messenger. The invasions are from Goethe's *Faust*. The following Faustian passage reveals the invasions as Gnostic:

> Two souls, alas, are dwelling in my breast,
> And one is striving to forsake its brother,
> Unto the world in grossly loving zest,
> With clinging tendrils, one adheres;
> The other rises forcibly in quest
> Of rarefied ancestral spheres [183].

The Goethe quote dispenses the psychogenic Gnosis that humanity is simultaneously material and spiritual. It likewise shows the evolution of true consciousness relies upon an organism's internal ability to reflect upon and transcend its material component. This is found in the contrast between "clinging tendrils" and "ancestral spheres," where a reflexive spiritual consciousness arises in an upward cycle from the tension between them. Arctor/Fred's ultimate Gnostic revelation is new-found faith in "Teilhard de Chardin" and "Christ (as) the final determination and Plasmatic Principle of the Universe" (Dick 127).

VALIS and the Noosphere

The late period of Dick's *oeuvre* comprises the VALIS-trilogy and was directly inspired by 2-3-74 and the *Exegesis*. *VALIS* itself contains a fictional version of the *Exegesis* written by Horselover Fat. Dick writes:

> Scanner is my true Paradise Lost (the story of the Fall) and VALIS Paradise Regained, the story of the restoration through Christ. Hence VALIS can only be truly understood if Scanner is taken into account. Bob Arctor on the last page of Scanner is Horselover Fat on the first page of VALIS—the two novels form a seamless whole [*Exegesis* 677].

Because *VALIS* represents "Man's restoration through Christ who brings him the saving Gnosis that in effect he has lost," which causes Fred/Arctor (and Fat) to be healed, Fat reaches the Omega Point that Dick claims his *oeuvre* has been evolving towards (677). In Chardin's Omega Point the collective human mind and Christ become one. In *VALIS* this Omega Point is achieved through Fat's noogenic hyperpersonalized "metapsychoanalytic" connection to the VALIS satellite (Stilling 91). The VALIS entity is symbolic of both the cause and ultimate goal of Christogenesis. That is, VALIS shapes the thinking layer of the planet and draws this layer unto itself. VALIS achieves this by firing information into Fat's brain and encoding the film Valis with clues as to the mechanism. Fat writes in his Exegesis that people "appear to be memory coils ... in a computer-like thinking system" in which there is "a failure of memory retrieval" (*VALIS* 108). VALIS represents "universal imminent mind" (*Exegesis* 461) which fires Christic "living information" to unlock spiritual remembering, revealing Fat's hyperpersonalized connection to Point Omega (260).

In Chapter 2, Fat explains a vision in which God "had fired a beam of pink light directly at him" (*VALIS* 21). Fat's quest is to find a metaphysical explanation for the experience. This mirrors Dick's life. Much of *VALIS* is a conversation between the two protagonists, Fat and Phil Dick, navigated by the first-person narrator, which is Dick's own voice. This voice embodies Dick's navigation of the two extremes of himself: Fat (spiritually enlightened) and Phil (occluded by matter). Phil initially thinks Fat's vision means he's crazy, but by the end Phil is also invaded by VALIS and begins evolving towards his own Omega Point.

The mechanism whereby the pink beam relays hidden knowledge to Fat is revealed in the Valis movie. The Valis movie demonstrates the noogenic power of VALIS to shape the thinking layer of the planet. This SF movie features an electronics genius named Nicolas Brady. Brady invented a laser machine that produces music out of cognitive information. Fat's pink beam works like Brady's laser. When Brady enters the machine, he is "bathed with laser beams" and music is produced using his mind as a transducer (157).

Music is *VALIS's* symbol for the spiritual energy that shapes thought. Just as Brady's lasers produce spiritual energy causing Christogenesis, so too does Fat's pink beam. When Brady lures the character Lampton into the machine, Lampton's head explodes revealing a computer-like brain. This tells Brady the whole universe is made from information processed by the brain. Fat realizes the movie is an analog of his pink beam vision and that they both reveal the same Christogenic mechanism.

Analogous to the earlier-quoted Goethe passage, in its juxtaposition of the spiritual and material aspects of being human, is that Brady is also unknowingly the President, Ferris Fremont, overseeing "PROJECT VALIS" (161). Fremont is not spiritually evolved and opposes Brady's pursuit of Point Omega. PROJECT VALIS exists to destroy the VALIS satellite, which has been firing beams of energy at Lampton and others. When Lampton's house has energy fired at it, Lampton's eyes explode revealing a "third eye" underneath, which has a "lateral lens" instead of a pupil (159–160). This motif technologizes the psychogenic spiritual faculty Dick refers to in the *Exegesis*. The eye symbolizes the spiritual ability of matter to reflect upon itself, thus enabling the evolution of consciousness. As with Lampton's computer-like brain, this technologizing of human cognition implies the theoretical paradigm laid out in the *Exegesis*, and earlier in *VALIS*, that the universe is a hologram composed of living information. Describing the universe as living information allows Dick to overcome Chardin's problem of how "the cellular revolution should express itself psychically." When Fat states "the phenomenal universe does not exist; it is a hypostasis of the information processed by the mind" he indicates the cellular revolution is simply a psychic revolution because both matter and psyche are composed of the same informational substance (109).

After the movie ends, it is obvious to Fat and Phil that Fat's pink beam vision was not caused by psychological illness but was a function of objective reality. Listing everything in the movie he experienced before seeing it, Fat discovers that VALIS has sent information back in time, pulling it through his mind towards itself, transforming him in a process of Christogenesis. Fat remarks that "the third eye," "the pink light, the 'information transfer … from VALIS… the satellite" from Valis the movie were all in his pink beam vision (169–170). Dick illustrates the collectivizing function of Christogenesis when Fat and Phil meet the real-life Lampton.[4] Lampton belongs to a religion claiming humanity came from the Albemuth Star System. These humans had a third eye that later closed, inducing spiritual amnesia. VALIS re-opens this third eye, causing people to remember their hyperpersonal-collective spiritual link to the cosmos. As he approaches the apex of spiritual evolution through the noogenic power of VALIS, Dick sends Fat and Phil to meet Sophia. She is the "savior VALIS incarnated as a human being" and embodies the Christic manifestation of the Omega Point on Earth (210).

Conclusion

By the publication of *VALIS*, both psychogenesis and noogenesis had been fully realized in Dick's SF *oeuvre*. Christogenesis was partially realized. While St. James and Adams were unable to form a spiritual-collective consciousness, Fat, Phil, Lampton, and others all do so in the religion, The Friends of God. Christogenesis is achieved by those characters who accept Sophia as the manifestation of VALIS on Earth. They unite in The Friends of God to form a hyperpersonalized-collective Omega Point on Earth. Christogenesis is not achieved by those people who remain ignorant of the third eye, which facilitates the psychogenic saving Gnosis of spiritual evolution. Dick's SF *oeuvre* symbolizes—to him—the trajectory of Chardin's theories on Christogenic spiritual (re)evolution. This symbolic trajectory is the literal embodiment of Dick's own psychological development. Fat's Omega Point is Dick's Omega Point. Perhaps in the future, Dick's extensive following will find a way to collectivize this profound psychoanalytic direction.

NOTES

1. See Speaight (1967) for further biographical information on Chardin.
2. See Robinson (1984) for a discussion of Suvin's similar grouping, which Suvin calls "a simple rise, plateau, and falling off in Dick's career."
3. See Heidegger (2010) for being-in-itself.
4. See Burton (2015) for a discussion on personal diversity between Fat's approach to religion, the Lampton's, and Sophia's.

WORKS CITED

The Bible. King James Version. Hendrickson, 2011.
Boon, Marcus. "Between Scanner and Object: Drugs and Ontology in Philip K. Dick's *A Scanner Darkly*," in *The World According to Philip K. Dick*, eds. Alexander Dunst and Stefan Schlensag. Palgrave, 2015.
Burton, James. *The Philosophy of Science Fiction: Henri Bergson and the Fabulations of Philip K. Dick*. Bloomsbury, 2015.
De Chardin, Pierre Teilhard. *The Heart of Matter*. Harcourt Brace Jovanovich, 1979.
_____. *The Phenomenon of Man*. Fontana, 1966.
Dick, Philip K. *Do Androids Dream of Electric Sheep?* Gollancz, 2007.
_____. *The Exegesis of Philip K. Dick*. Ed. P. Jackson and J. Lethem. Houghton, 2011.
_____. *The Penultimate Truth*. Gollancz, 2005.
_____. *A Scanner Darkly*. Vintage, 1991.
_____. *VALIS* Gollancz, 2001.

Heidegger, Martin. *Being and Time*. University of New York Press, 2010.
Jameson, Fredric. *Archaeologies of the Future*. Verso, 2005.
McKee, Gabriel. *Pink Beams of Light from the God in the Gutter: The Science Fictional Religion of Philip K. Dick*. University Press of America. 2004.
Merrell-Wolff, Franklin. *The Philosophy of Consciousness Without an Object*. Julian Press, 1973.
Palmer, Christopher. *Exhilaration and Terror of the Postmodern*. Liverpool University Press, 2007.
Robinson, Kim Stanley. *The Novels of Philip K. Dick*. UMI Research Press, 1984.
Speaight, Robert. *Teilhard De Chardin: Biography*. Collins, 1967.
Stilling, Roger J. "Mystical Healing: Reading Philip K. Dick's VALIS and the Divine Invasion as Metapsychoanalytic Novels," *South Atlantic Review* 56.2, 1991. 91–106.
Suvin, Darko. "P. K. Dick's Opus: Artifice as Refuge and World View," Science-Fiction Studies 5, 1975. 8–21.
Warrick, Patricia. *Mind in Motion*. Southern Illinois University Press, 1987.

Philip Dick, the Earthshaker

Gregg Rickman

In 1948 or 1949 Philip Dick, age approximately twenty, outlined a 25-chapter novel he called *The Earthshaker*. The title character was intended to be a reborn earth deity, and in his drafting of the material, young Philip seems heavily to lean on Norse mythology: one of its characters, an ancient snake, lives in the roots of the world tree, Yiggdrasil. The novel exists only in its outline, two separate drafts of chapters one and two, an additional 35-page fragment, and five pages of notes. In these notes Dick offers the following outline of what would have been a key scene:

> The coming of the Earthshaker is the giving birth by the woman of the unknown animal that escapes in the eating room and transforms them all, as they flee in fear and panic. Running, they fall on to their hands and become animals again. Only the wanderer, outside, escapes, feeling only the cold wind of something rushing past him: the unknown animal escaping. He goes on out afterward, and disappears.[1]

Anyone hearing this who is familiar with Philip Dick's later work will think of his recurring use in his fiction of the great god Pan, or Dionysus. In the short story "The Golden Man," for example, Cris Johnson, a mutant with the cunning of an animal, enjoys a similar escape, rushing past its viewpoint character like a cold wind, just as does the Earthshaker here.

Dick was very familiar with Euripedes' Dionysian play *The Bacchae*; in 1964's *The Unteleported Man*, Rachmael ben Applebaum plans to wile away the years of his solo journey to the Whale's Mouth colony by learning Attic Greek "so he could read the *Bacchae* in the original." By the time Dick came to write his 1970 novel *Our Friends from Frolix 8*, Denny Strong, the distributor of underground literature is, with his "sick strength ... enlarged eyes and tangled hair" a "Dionysus from the gutters of the city..." (41). Dick has begun, in this underrated novel, to portray the disaffected youth of the 1960s as Dionysian figures of revolt.

If Dick ever said anything profound about religion it comes in the 11th chapter of *VALIS*, his novel of 1981, a sustained meditation on the terror as well as the beauty of divine revelation. "But the divine and the terrible are so close to each other," he writes. "God can be good and terrible—not in succession—but at the same time." "The gentle sounds of the choir singing

'Amen, amen' are not to calm the congregation but to pacify the god. When you know this you have penetrated to the innermost core of religion" (197). Dick speaks specifically here of the madness of *enthousiasmos*, of being taken over by God, which by his own account was his own experience in 1974. And he speaks specifically of the Greek god Dionysus as "the one most likely to do this.... And, unfortunately, Dionysus was insane." Taking the mass murder of the innocent at Jonestown, which had just taken place at the time Dick wrote these words, as his example, Dick discusses in *VALIS* this "mass running of panic, inspired by the mad god" as emblematic of God's ability "to thrust himself outward and into the congregation until he becomes them" (197). Divine possession is a form of madness.

We can draw a direct line from the Earthshaker's escape in 1949, and the madness of the Earthshaker's witnesses, who drop to all fours and become as animals, to Dick's depiction of Dionysian madness in *VALIS* in 1981. Dick's further references to Dionysian figures in "The Golden Man" in 1954, *The Unteleported Man* in 1964, and *Our Friends from Frolix 8* in 1970 remind us how aware Dick was of the web of mythology that recurs in all cultures.

My purpose here today is not, however, to catalog motifs drawn from mythology in Philip Dick's fiction, but rather to call attention to the consistency of certain "Earthshaker" themes across his work from the 1940s to the 1980s. One thing that struck me, rereading all of Dick's fiction a couple of years ago, is how much of it flows together from every period of his career. The neglected literary novels, written from roughly 1951 to 1961, are a particularly rich source of material. Unlike many of his science fiction fans, this reader at least finds these novels to be actually very good. Michael Bishop is correct in postulating, in his alternate world novel *Philip K Dick is Dead, Alas*, that if they had been published in the 1950s, as intended, they would have won Dick a substantial literary reputation—even if *Confessions of a Crap Artist* might not have been filmed, as Bishop has it, with Jack Lemmon as Jack Isidore. Like them or not, novels like *Voices from the Street* or *Humpty Dumpty in Oakland* are, if nothing else, very Dickian, saturated with his themes, and the Dick scholar shouldn't ignore them.

I will give two examples of these works' centrality—one merely illustrative, and one important. Dick's reference to Jonestown in *VALIS* reminds us of his lifelong interest in religious cults. In Dick's first published science fiction novel, *Solar Lottery* (1955), we spend a lot of time with the Prestonites, a marginal cult who believe in their dead prophet's revelation of a "Flame Disc" out beyond our solar system. But the Prestonites are anticipated by the cult led by the dynamic preacher Theodore Beckheim in *Voices from the Street*, completed about 1952, who's described in similar terms to the cult leader of *Solar Lottery*: "His great black eyes and massive-ridged brow made him look like some primordial giant, a legend from the distant past" (15). Part One of this early novel ends with Beckheim's seven-page apocalyptic sermon, which is delivered in a hall decorated with a yin-yang symbol that symbol anticipates the Taoist symbolism of *The Man in the High Castle*, written a decade later. Here we have, as with Dick's on-going use of the figure of Dionysus, an eclectic, cross-cultural use of mythologies drawn by this author from across many different cultures.

Thus, my minor example of this "eternal return" of motifs in Philip Dick's work; now to one I find crucial to understanding Philip Dick. My favorite literary novel of Philip Dick is the sublime *Puttering About in a Small Land*. One of my favorite scenes comes in Chapter 12 as the unhappy record repair shop owner Roger Lindahl listens for something in the hum of his intercom system. "Hummmmmmmmmmmmmmmmmmmmmm. How precarious it is. I have to strain. Reach" (148). I draw two connections from this. In *The Man in the High Castle*, Mr. Tagomi also hears a hum over his intercom, and only a hum over his intercom, after he has successfully killed two Nazi agents. But, more obviously, think of a real-life event, Philip Dick during the Valis event listening to the radio and gathering clues to his experience from the tune "Strawberry Fields Forever." In the world of Philip Dick the universe constantly emits a string of signals mixed in with a great deal of noise, and it behooves us to listen to that noise, like Roger Lindahl, and find the signal. "Here she is, the voices said in his ear. They no longer hummed; they spoke" (148).

There's a direct line from searching for patterns in the hum, and Dick's openness to finding clues in the mundane world around us. This certainly includes visual cues, as Dick trusted sound only so far. Dick was, as is well known, an audiophile, accustomed to the careful listening to sound and music (Rickman, *To the High Castle*, 32–3, 94–6, 134–5). As a boy he cut a hole in his record player's speaker so that he could insert his head inside to get the full available surround-sound experience. His novel *Mary and the Giant* (written in about 1955) includes a visit to a party held by Bay Area audiophiles, based on audiophiles he'd met while working at Art Music in Berkeley. In *Eye in the Sky*, published three years later, Jack Hamilton's audiophile room becomes a tomb-world, a black hole, where the dimensions of time and space rotate into each other. During the Valis event he heard his beloved Linda Ronstadt sing over and over again "You're no good." In *The Divine Invasion* Dick transmutes this real life event into a scene where Herb Asher, in his record store, dials into a classic music station with his prime audio system "to calm himself."

> Only a voice issued from the transducers of the system. No music. A whispering voice almost inaudible; he could barely understand the words. What the hell is this? he asked himself. What is it saying?
> "...weary," the voice whispered in its dry, slithery tone. "...and afraid. There is no possibility ... weighed down. Born to lose; you are born to lose. You are no good" [136].

And then Herb Asher hears Linda Ronstadt's "ancient classic" "You're No Good" over and over again, even after he turns off his audio system.

Herb Asher, at the beginning of *The Divine Invasion*, is a curator of information in his dome in a distant star system, his job is to periodically accept "a sequence of high-speed entertainment, audio- and video-taped signals emanating from a slave satellite…: upon storing them he was to run them back at normal and select the material suitable for the overall dome system on his own planet." It was this information "that connects us with home and keeps us human" (15). As such Herb is comparable to other transmitters of popular entertainment, music and in some cases talk, like the disc jockeys Jim Briskin of *The Broken Bubble* and Walt Dangerfield of *Dr. Bloodmoney*. Early versions of this character have chances to demonstrate their integrity—Briskin loses his job at his radio station when he refuses to read the grating advertisements of a sponsor.

Dick's villains, by contrast, manipulate this information stream as a way of ensuring control by an elite: the admen and "Yance-men" of *The Man Who Japed* and *The Penultimate Truth*. As time goes by Dick finds popular entertainment and the mass media intrinsically corrupt; by the mid–1960s another character named Jim Briskin is a television "newsclown" with a trademark "flaming red wig" in two stories ("Stand-By" and "What'll We Do with Ragland Park?") and a novel (*The Crack in Space*). *Our Friends from Frolix 8* is full of withering observations as to how establishment broadcasters skew their reporting to favor the powerful. While the role of an Herb Asher might once have been valorized, as with his heroic disc jockeys Jim Briskin (in his first appearance) and Walt Dangerfield, by *The Divine Invasion* Herb's job is problematic, condemned by the author as a hiding away from life.

A socially conscious reading of Dick's portrayal of the waves of audio and visual information flooding us at all times is certainly possible and is indeed one aspect of his work. But Dick invites us to go deeper. In his world there's the junk signals beamed to us by a false universe—represented by the soupy Broadway tunes endlessly playing for Herb Asher when he falls into a coma—and the real information that struggles to get through. In *Radio Free Albemuth* characters struggle to hide a political message in a pop music recording; the novel's protagonist Philip K. Dick fails and winds up sentenced to pick up trash in an authoritarian police state.

Maybe the trash in the street is a safer place to look. Consider this well-known passage from earlier in *Radio Free Albemuth*.

> There was a beauty in the trash of the alleys which I had never noticed before; my vision seemed sharpened, rather than impaired. As I walked along it seemed to me that the flattened beer cans and papers and weeds and junk mail had been arranged by the wind into patterns; these patterns, when I scrutinized them, lay distributed so as to comprise a visual language [126].

Or as Dick puts it succinctly, in *VALIS*, "The symbols of the divine initially show up at the trash stratum."

This hunt for meaning amid irrelevant noise, for purpose amid the trash, is central to both Philip Dick's fiction and his life. We can track this particular image, the hunt for significance in what is thrown away, back through Philip Dick's writing, all the way back to November 1951 and Dick's first sale as a professional writer, "Roog." In "Roog" the faithful dog barks incessantly, trying to protect the trash in garbage cans from being carried away. The dog perceives the trash as valuable food. He barks to warn his humans, but his humans don't understand him—they can't break the dog's code. If one carefully scans Philip Dick's career, he returns again and again to this sort of pattern recognition—or misrecognition. Jennings, for example, has to recognize the meaning of the seven trinkets in "Paycheck," to reclaim his lost memories and lost life. Ragle Gumm's job in *Time Out of Joint* is solving the newspaper game "Where Will the Little Green Man Be Next," a childish pursuit that is actually Earth's front line of defense against its attackers.

This defines one sort of coding in Philip Dick's work—the perception of meaning out of what seems meaningless—the hum of Roger Lindahl's intercom, the garbage perceived as food by the canine hero of "Roog," the location of the Little Green Man, the god in the trash. Let's call this *decoding*. I'll pass on now to another form of code in Dick's work, his conscious use of *encoding* to pass on messages to his readers. Over the course of his long career Dick secreted messages in his fiction, messages that we by and large still haven't received, because we still haven't cracked Philip Dick's particular encryptions.

By studying and thinking about Philip Dick's work off and on over many years I've located a number of instances of Dick hiding things in his writing. To date no one, to my knowledge, has caught on to these encryptions—I'll pass on a couple of them.

I'll offer two parallel examples from the end and the beginning of Dick's career.

The protagonist of 1981's *The Divine Invasion* is named Herb Asher. Asher is in love with, and becomes involved with, Dick's fictionalized version of Linda Ronstadt, Linda Fox. In reality, a man named Peter Asher was Linda Ronstadt's manager, as Herb Asher takes on managing Linda Fox in Dick's novel. This is of course just a minor biographical detail.

"Asher" is, however, also a Hebrew word, meaning "happy," or "blessed." Dick is thus using a Hebrew word, "Asher," as a character name in his penultimate novel. Let's go back in time three decades. In one of Dick's best-known early stories, "Impostor" (1953), Spence Olham is the protagonist accused of being an android impostor of himself. Olham desperately tries to prove he's really a human only to be proven wrong in the story's deservedly famous trick ending. His last words, looking at the corpse of the real Spence Olham, are "If that's Olham, then I must be..." The story's final line is, indicating the world's destruction, "The blast could be seen in Alpha Centauri."

"Olam" is a Hebrew word that means, in some translations, "world." Dick has cleverly repurposed the word "world" for the name of the character who destroys the world. A similar Hebrew world, meanwhile, "alam," means "to conceal" or "to hide." Dick signals his purpose with his choice of names. That Dick was aware of the subterranean links between his two fictions is signaled by a comment Herb's friend Elias Tate makes to him late in *The Divine Invasion*: Elias tells Herb that he's "a weird alien programmed to blow up the world. You probably have a bomb inside you." This appears to be a direct reference by Dick to his earlier story, where Spence Olham with his encoded Hebrew name *does* have a bomb inside him, programmed to blow up the world, as opposed to Herb Asher with *his* encoded Hebrew name, aimed at saving it.

Thus we see Philip Dick, in 1953 and 1981, encoding a story's meaning with his choice of character names, using a non-English language—in both cases, Hebrew. Philip Dick *decodes* patterns that only he or his characters can see, but he also *encodes* patterns in his fiction that only he knows about—perhaps for his own pleasure, perhaps the way artists Dick liked such as Beethoven and Joyce would encrypt private jokes into their works, perhaps with some greater intent. Now, if we combine these two tendencies—seeing patterns where no one else does, acts of *decoding*, and creating patterns that no one notices, acts of *encoding*, we reach the heart of Philip Dick's working method.

Here are two examples of Dick both encoding and decoding a message.

As mentioned earlier, "Asher" is the Hebrew word for "happy," or "blessed." It's the equivalent of the Latin word "Felix," which also means "happy," or "lucky." Being happy is the same thing in both languages, I guess, although being blessed and being lucky are perhaps two different things.

Be that as it may—in the novel *VALIS* Horselover Fat tells his friends of "the two-word cypher signal KING FELIX" sent out to the world in February 1974. Philip Dick, not for the first time, is being intertextual, as he's referring here to the appearance of those two juxtaposed words in his 1974 novel *Flow My Tears, the Policeman Said*. Felix Buckman is the name of the weeping policeman, and at one point late in *Flow My Tears* the name "Felix" beginning a paragraph appears directly underneath the word "king" ending a sentence—this is "the two-word cypher signal" Dick devoted many pages of his *Exegesis*—his 8000 page commentary on the Valis event—to analyzing.

If "King Felix" was a hidden message Dick encoded in *Flow My Tears*, Dick claimed it was there because he was *told* to put it there, by person or persons unknown. Dick also claimed he didn't remember encoding the message until he saw it printed in his book—he refers to this in his *Exegesis* as "deciphering the message in *Tears*." The King Felix cypher is—in Dick's telling at least—a message Dick sent to himself, a message he *encoded* into his work that he later *decoded*.

As we all know, Philip Dick said he received a vast amount of information in a massive burst from an unknown source, a god or a satellite, in February–March 1974—the so-called Valis event. "Valis" is the name Dick came up for what he called a Vast Active Living Intelligence System.

Four years after the Valis event, in 1978, Dick went thru a period where he called "Valis," the "Vast Living Intelligence system" that had possessed him, "Zebra" instead. "I termed it Zebra because of its ability to camouflage itself," he wrote one correspondent in February 1978. A zebra can hide in the grass of the African veldt without being perceived by the lion that's hunting it. The animal encodes itself as a living bar code, in Dick's reading of how camouflage works, which ties neatly in with something else Dick called Valis, "living information." The god presents himself to us in disguise—encoded.

All this is important to Philip K. Dick, and I can only begin to suggest its significance here. The endless flow of information, sometimes understood, but just as often misperceived, is a central theme of Philip Dick's life and art. He encodes "King Felix" as a cypher into a novel he drafted in 1970, reworked in 1972, published in 1974, rereads in 1974, decodes in 1974. He remembers what he'd once known—anamnesis—but it's the recovered memory of a code unknown, a code he has to decipher and must always wonder if he deciphered correctly.

Jacques Derrida once roamed the halls at nearby UC Irvine, and famously once said: "There is nothing outside the text." I'm sure Jacques Derrida wasn't envisioning the all-encompassing text as a Vast Active Living Intelligence system, but that's how Philip Dick perceived it, whether it was the words of fire that fall from the heavens in *Eye in the Sky*, the soft-drink stand that disappears to be replaced with a slip of paper with the words "soft drink stand" on it in *Time Out of Joint*, or this comment from an *Exegesis* entry of April 1978: "The key here is *pattern* and pattern recognition. Such a person is able to pattern (gestalt) and repattern rapidly, suddenly experiencing a mercurial world. Out of these very many patterns he might possibly *one time* hit on correctly perceived and interpreted authentic traces of objects and processes.... He would literally see it, and its secret life."

If we begin to see Philip Dick's life as a life of pattern recognition we begin to re-see the pattern of Philip Dick's life.

Notes

1. The only copy of Earthshaker was at CSU, Fullerton, and material here is from my notes taken in the 1980s. The estate has since withdrawn the manuscript.

Works Cited

Philip K. Dick. *The Divine Invasion*. Timescape, 1981.
———. *Our Friends from Frolix 8*. 1970. Houghton Mifflin, 2013.
———. *Puttering About in a Small Land*. Academy Chicago, 1985.
———. *Radio Free Albemuth*. HarperCollins, 1985.
———. *VALIS*. 1981. Houghton Mifflin, 2011.
———. *Voices from the Street*. Tor, 2007.
Gregg Rickman. *To the High Castle: Philip K. Dick, a Life 1928–1962* Fragments West, 1989.

Galactic Pot-Healer
A Singular Way Station

Gary Westfahl

I decided to examine *Galactic Pot-Healer* (1969) not only because it is one of my favorite Philip K. Dick novels, but also because I was reasonably confident—correctly, it seems—that none of the other scholars anxious to publish essays on Philip K. Dick would choose to focus their energies on this particular work. Indeed, if one looks for signs of the key quandaries that critics celebrate in Dick's fiction—distinguishing between fantasy and reality, between human and nonhuman, between free will and determination, and so on—*Galactic Pot-Healer* disappointingly addresses them only briefly or halfheartedly before devolving, from the scholar's perspective, into a straightforward science fiction adventure about a man who joins a team of colorful aliens, including "A chitinous multilegged quasiarchnid and a large bivalve with pseudopodia" (91), on a mission to a distant planet.

To epitomize the contrast between the "Philip K. Dick" that scholars prefer to examine, and the actual Philip K. Dick as represented by *Galactic Pot-Healer*, one needs only to contrast the covers of two editions. The 2013 Mariner Books cover—a subdued mosaic of pottery shards—is dignified enough to be owned by a college professor but utterly unrepresentative of the novel's contents, since the book only occasionally deals with the titular topic of pottery. The 1987 Panther Books cover, however, accurately portrays what the novel is actually about—an enormous, one-eyed alien monster attempting to raise an ancient cathedral from a distant planet's ocean (d'Achille; Lofty).

When scholars are obliged to discuss *Galactic Pot-Healer* in comprehensive examinations of Dick's works, a survey of the critical literature suggests two things: first, they say relatively little about the novel, focusing most of their attention on Dick's purported "major" novels while relegating *Galactic Pot-Healer* to the status of a "lesser" work. Second, they regularly assert that *Galactic Pot-Healer* is not really a novel, but rather a "parable" or a "Jungian allegory."[1] The logic behind these statements is clear enough: when Dick describes a dystopian near-future world problematized by the presence of artificial humans, he is obviously writing a genuine science fiction *novel*; when he describes an alien planet inhabited by creatures resembling octopuses and gigantic spiders, however, he must be writing an "allegory."

The perils of characterizing this book as an "allegory" are well illustrated by one of the few extended studies of the novel, Robert Bee's "An Alien God and a Jungian Allegory" (2007). Arguing that the novel "develops into a Jungian allegory," Bee is obliged to complain that another critic has "misread" the novel's conclusion as a happy ending, since "Joe has returned to isolation and failure, the state he was in at the beginning of the novel," having failed to fulfill the Jungian pattern by accepting "the integration of conscious and unconscious" that joining with the Glimmung represents (Bee). But this claim is nonsensical: at the end of the novel, protagonist Joe Fernwright has permanently escaped from Earth's repressive government, constant surveillance, a verbally abusive ex-wife, and a disheartening daily routine of sitting in a cubicle and engaging in pointless word games. Now, on the more relaxed and amenable world of Plowman's Planet, he is free to do whatever he wants, and if that entails making "awful" pots (180), that is surely more pleasurable than anything he was doing on Earth. Thus, one cannot accurately describe Joe's new condition as "the state he was in at the beginning of the novel." A bit more defensibly, Matt Englund's "The Rejected Text: Expectation and Disappointment in *Galactic Pot-Healer*" (2014) interprets the novel as an allegory of another sort, illustrating the value of failure in any effort to be creative; yet this view also seems questionable, since the novel ultimately proves to be a success story—the Glimmung succeeds in raising the sunken cathedral, and Joe succeeds in getting away from his dreary existence on Earth—and those successes largely appear unrelated to their earlier failures.

Still, one can sympathize with these critics' plight, since they undoubtedly felt obliged to characterize *Galactic Pot-Healer* as a typical Philip K. Dick novel, although it is not, and although that therefore required them to force the book into Procrustean beds. Instead, I will argue, *Galactic Pot-Healer* qualifies one of Dick's most poignant and personal works precisely because it is a novel written by a Philip K. Dick who fervently longs to stop being Philip K. Dick, a Philip K. Dick who longs to stop writing Philip K. Dick novels. And the novel can be interpreted as Dick's step-by-step instructions on how he can achieve that goal.

Considering Dick's body of works, one finds nothing unusual in the opening chapters of *Galactic Pot-Healer*—indeed, the material is so typical that it reads more like a parody of a Philip K. Dick novel than an actual Philip K. Dick novel. One readily imagines the dedicated satirist methodically making his way down The Philip K. Dick Checklist: pathetic loser as hero, check; dead-end job, check; dull, stultifying environment, check; repressive government, check; sinister agents monitoring one's every activity, check; annoying ex-wife, check… Needless to say, Joe is bored and depressed by it all, and perhaps Dick himself felt the same way about the very familiar story he had begun.

For Joe and his creator to "escape" from this monotonous gloom (33), they must resolve, or get away from, all of the troubling uncertainties that typically bedevil Dick's heroes and journey toward a different, and more conventional, sort of science-fictional world wherein everything is exactly as it seems, and all one has to do is to be aware of one's surroundings and respond in the appropriate manner.

So, what are the traps of Earth that Joe must evade? First, his life in the "Communal North American Citizens' Republic" (3) of the year 2046 is filled with illusions masquerading as reality: employing the holographic technology of "the Jiffi-view Company of Greater Cleveland" and his mind-altering "psycho-lease" (13), Cleveland resident Joe can be persuaded that he is actually living in a coastal home in beautiful Carmel, California; every night, the government forces citizens to experience an appealing dream; and after Joe is approached by the alien Glimmung to travel to Plowman's Planet and repair the pots in a sunken cathedral, he is disconcerted because the alien keeps taking on different appearances. However, to save money, Joe abandons his false surroundings and calmly accepts his home's true, unappealing appearance; he despises the silly mandatory dreams, calling them "almost worse than being awake" (21), and gets away from them on Plowman's Planet; and the Glimmung's differing guises do not bother him because, somehow, he always recognizes the alien.

There are also forms of artificial intelligence in Fernwright's life, yet unlike the replicants of *Do Androids Dream of Electric Sheep?*, they are clearly and unproblematically inferior to humans. On Earth, the unsympathetic "robo-mechanisms" and "computers" that Joe deals with on a daily basis are dismissed as "bastards" (27). On Plowman's Planet, he is given a robot servant, Willis, who is perfectly content to obey his commands; his only irksome feature is his repetitive insistence that all of Joe's orders must begin with his name, "Willis."

The novel's early chapters repeatedly reference religion: Joe is appalled that citizens accepting his proffered coins seem to regard him as "a kind of supernatural deity" (34); at the spaceport, while awaiting departure, he has brief, unhelpful conversations with robotic representatives of four of Earth's religions—Zen Buddhism, Roman Catholicism, Islam, and Judaism (47–48); among other theological musings, he describes "A man" as "an angel that has become deranged" (46); the others recruited to assist the Glimmung theorize that the alien is a sort of "deity" who has deliberately set out to rescue certain people from their unfulfilling lives (55, 58); the Glimmung is reportedly raising the sunken cathedral in order to revive the planet's ancient religion of worshipping the rival gods Amanita and Borel; and Willis has written a pamphlet discussing Jesus Christ and a related alien deity (105–107) who dies every time a being dies. Yet which, if any, of these religions are real, and how they should affect people's lives, completely vanish as issues in the last part of the novel, as there is only one brief, final reference to the revival of the ancient religion with no indication that the Glimmung or any other characters will ever be involved in practicing this faith.

The issue of predetermination surfaces at least twice: upon meeting an attractive woman, Mali Yojez, Joe suggests that they employ a machine to determine if they will become compatible partners. And on Plowman's Planet, beings called the Kalends promulgate a book with constantly changing texts that apparently predict the future, raising the question of whether Joe, the Glimmung, and the others have free will or are under the Kalends' control. Yet we immediately learn that the SSA machine is not "precognitive," but merely a computer that makes increasingly less accurate extrapolations of the future (62), and the Kalends' ominous predictions are ultimately proven wrong, leading Joe to reassuringly conclude that the beings simply "played the percentages. Generally, in the long run, they were correct. But in given instances—such as this—they were wrong" (167).

When Joe goes underwater to encounter what is apparently his own corpse, and discovers that both the Glimmung and the cathedral have sinister, "Black" counterparts, eager graduate students will pull out their highlighters and mutter, "Aha—the theme of the double!" Yet they will find little more to annotate, inasmuch as the corpse, after briefly urging Fernwright to stay underwater, disappears and never returns, while the Glimmung handily defeats his insidious doppelgänger and raises the correct cathedral with no further references to its dark counterpart.

So, let us summarize how the novel is dealing with some of Dick's most characteristic concerns. Illusions that resemble reality can be avoided or seen through; artificial intelligences can be dismissed as appropriately subordinate to humans; religions may attract adherents but are ultimately unimportant; mechanisms apparently predetermining or controlling human actions are merely calculating the odds; and any doubles that may appear will have no real effects on anyone's life. What we encounter in *Galactic Pot-Healer*, then, is a radically simplified Philip K. Dick world, wherein happiness can be achieved by following a few, commonsensical guidelines.

First, Joe must always be altruistic. When he takes a bag of his "carefully saved-up metal coins" to "Mr. Job" in order to garner a new and better job, he suddenly feels a "strange impulse" to start giving them away to the "hopeless eyes" surrounding him (33), an action that leads first to his arrest but later to his rescue by the Glimmung. He is always nice to his ex-wife, and potential new girlfriend, Mali, even though they regularly make hurtful remarks. When he tells Willis that he once felt "concerned" about a dying spider trapped at the bottom of a cup, he muses that such concern, termed "*caritas*" or charity, "is a factor of intelligence ... a high form of cerebral activity, an ability to perceive something in the environment—to notice and, as the robot had put it, to worry" (109)—virtually defining kindness as an essential human characteristic. Even after the Glimmung fumes at him for disobeying orders and going underwater, Joe immediately asks, "Is there anything we can do? To help him? To get him free" (133)? And while he apparently does nothing meaningful to assist the Glimmung, the alien clearly feels otherwise, for after its triumph it says, "Thank you, Joe Fernwright" (166).

Joe must also be trusting, even when others are not. He first learns of the Glimmung because he always checks his mail tube, improbably hoping to receive an assignment, and when surrounded by strangers awaiting his coins, he sees them "Waiting in a silence made up of trust, as his own earlier waiting at the mail tube had been" (34). After being recruited by the Glimmung, the other craftspeople suspect that the alien does not really want to raise the sunken cathedral, that it is merely a pretext for some alternative motive; but Joe perceives, correctly, that the Glimmung is being completely honest with his employees, after considering and rejecting his own theory that the alien was conspiring with Earth's authorities against him (56). When Mali joins Joe's underwater expedition, she suggests that the Glimmung might have "sent me here ... *to kill you*" (113), but he continues to trust her, correctly, since she harbors no such designs. Mali and the others repeatedly assert that every cryptic bottled message from the Glimmung could be a "forgery" (114), but Joe discerns, correctly, that they are genuine. And at the one time in the novel when he does suspect that someone has an ulterior motive, he proves to be right: he recognizes that Mali urgently wants him to return to the surface because "There's something you don't want me to see," and while she claims that he is merely displaying "Paranoia," he immediately observes the second, black cathedral and tells her, "That's what you didn't want me to see" (121). Joe, in fact, seems an unusual Dick protagonist precisely because he is *not* paranoid, and he is repeatedly rewarded for having an essentially trusting nature.

Finally, Joe must repeatedly assert his own individuality: even at the beginning of the novel, he claims that he is "not like other men" (1), and he mildly rebukes Earth's totalitarian government when the police announce that he is "guilty of a crime against the people": he immediately answers, "The state.... Not the people" (35). On Plowman's Planet, determined to make his own decisions, he ventures underwater not because it had been predicted in the Kalends' book but because, as Willis notes, "You had it in your mind to go below Mare Nostrum before the Kalend showed up and got you to read that passage in the Book" (136). And he sticks to that decision even though both the Glimmung and Mali strongly advise against it. At the end of the novel, when the Glimmung offers his underlings the opportunity to join with him as a group intelligence, Joe is one of two employees who reject the offer in order to remain an independent person; and after a lifelong career of repairing the broken pots made by others, he listens to an alien who urges him to "Be creative. Work against fate" (179) and undertakes, for the first time in his life, to make his very own pot.

The overall message of this novel could not be clearer: even in the strangest of situations, surrounded by the strangest sorts of beings, people should always be kind, trust everyone around them, and rely upon their own good instincts and judgment—and everything will be fine. Joe Fernwright is a benign man who triumphs because he comes to believe, correctly, that he is living in an essentially benign universe. To experienced science fiction readers, then, *Galactic Pot-Healer* can be succinctly characterized as a Philip K. Dick novel that eventually becomes a Clifford D. Simak novel.

Dishearteningly, I feel obliged to briefly describe Simak for contemporary readers who may have never heard of him, even though this largely forgotten author was once esteemed as one of the field's major talents. In an era of increasing urbanization, Simak swam against the tide in celebrating the virtues and values of rural America in gentle, optimistic stories that were often termed "pastoral." His stories' bizarre environments ultimately recall the idyllic rural Wisconsin of Simak's youth; their seemingly unusual inhabitants reveal themselves to be very much like good Wisconsin neighbors, once one makes an effort to understand them; and occasional villains can easily be routed by alliances of the virtuous. His heroes are frequently solitary, like Enoch Wallace in his most famous novel, *Way Station* (1964), but their isolation somehow strengthens their bond with a larger community instead of making them feel strange and alienated. He might be described, then, as the complete antithesis of Philip K. Dick.

As suggested by *Galactic Pot-Healer*, though, I will finally suggest that these two disparate authors had one thing in common: they secretly longed to be each other. Simak, I submit, wanted to be Philip K. Dick, in that he consistently strived to base his stories on an astonishing variety of strange and unsettling premises; however, locked into the mindset of his doggedly placid and untroubled life, he was invariably compelled to make the strange seem familiar, to make the disconcerting seem reassuring—with the exception of the singularly uncharacteristic *The Visitors* (1979), his closest approach to a Dick novel. Dick longed to be Clifford D. Simak, capable of generating colorful and unproblematic adventures filled with nice people properly proceeding toward happy endings, but his turbulent upbringing and prickly personality invariably impelled him in other directions. *Galactic Pot-Healer*, then, represents his closest approach to a Simak novel. However, although he was temporarily successful in dispelling his demons, he ultimately could not bring himself to completely emulate a Clifford D. Simak novel (for if Simak had written the novel, as he could have, he would surely have made Mali a nicer woman, destined to become Joe's supportive companion, and he would have granted him to ability to produce a beautiful pot, not an "awful" one [180]).

As it happens, I can provide no specific evidence that Dick, while writing this novel, had Simak on his mind, although one of the garbled titles of the "Game" Fernwright plays with other bored citizens, "Bogish Persistentisms. By Shaft Tackapple" (9), is officially left unexplained but most likely refers to *The Martian Chronicles* (1951) by Ray Bradbury, another blissfully bucolic author who might be characterized as the antithesis to Philip K. Dick.

So, other scholars may continue to creatively ponder all the unsettling anxieties and obsessions that make Philip K. Dick's works so memorable; but, as always a contrarian, I want to suggest that, at least at times, and perhaps most strongly as he embarked upon his own version of a midlife crisis in 1969, Dick himself would have been delighted to forget all about these vexing matters and enjoy a sojourn in the blissfully uncomplicated world of an author like Clifford D. Simak or Ray Bradbury. Sadly, although the result was a remarkable and widely celebrated body of literature, Philip K. Dick was never able to attain that goal.

NOTES

1. For example, Fredric Jameson, when grouping Dick's output, called *Galactic Pot-Healer* "the best effort" of "a relatively minor Jungian cycle" of novels (349). Stanislaw Lem dismissed the novel as "only negligible," commenting: "Every author is free to produce works of different value; there is no law against a great epic master allowing himself a novel of pure entertainment" (89).

WORKS CITED

Bee, Robert. "An Alien God and a Jungian Allegory." *The Internet Review of Science Fiction*, Apr. 2007, www.irosf.com/q/zine/article/10385.
d'Achille, Gino. 1987, *Galactic Pot-Healer*, by Philip K. Dick, Panther Books, 1987, front cover.
Dick, Philip K. *Galactic Pot-Healer*. Mariner Books/Houghton Mifflin Harcourt, 2013.
Englund, Matt. "The Rejected Text: Expectation and Disappointment in Galactic Pot Healer." *Foundation: The International Review of Science Fiction*, vol. 119, Jan. 2015, 5–15.
Jameson, Fredric. *Archaeologies of the Future*. Verso, 2005.
Lem, Stanislaw. *Microworld*. Ed. Franz Rottensteiner. Harcourt, 1984.
Lofty, Melissa. *Galactic Pot-Healer*, by Philip K. Dick, First Mariner Books, 2013, front cover.

Archaeologies

The Philip K. Dick Society
A Preliminary Archaeology

JONATHAN LETHEM

Keynote, the Philip K. Dick Conference, April 29, 2016

So, this is an informal talk, with show-and-tell materials. I asked David to provide me with a machine, an overhead projector, so I could show you things from this collection, and here it is. I actually really like that this is a machine that seems to be contemplating itself ... which makes it kind of like Electric Ant, Jr.

I'll involve the Electric Ant, Jr., in showing off some things I've excavated from my own holdings. In a sense, I'm bringing coals to Newcastle, since Fullerton has been the ground zero for research and for holdings of the materials that were donated here by the estate, initially, and have lived here for so long. I'll show off some things that may have tantalizingly slipped through the cracks, things that ended up in my drawers instead, by accident.

I'm really telling you a few different stories all at once, and it's going to be difficult for me to make one coherent, chronological sequence out of these. I'll have to do a lot of doubling back, so in order to make that easier or more likely that you'll follow the multiple narratives, I'm just going to announce what they are and let you know.

One part of the story, of course, is a kind of portrait of Paul Williams, to whom we all owe an enormous debt. Our gathering here is the first major gathering of the Philip K. Dick tribe since Paul's death. When I last saw some of you at CSU San Francisco [for the Philip K. Dick Festival 2012], although he was in very bad shape and had been for a long time, Paul was still alive in a nursing home in Encinitas, California.

Williams really is the secret agent, the gatekeeper of Dick's legacy, from the moment of Dick's death until so many others took over: publishers, academics, filmmakers, and a much larger audience of readers than Dick had ever enjoyed during his life. Academics everywhere began to study Dick's work and legacy. New York publishing, Vintage, a division of Random House, began their tremendous program of putting all of Dick's books back into print, a prominence and respectability that he never enjoyed during his lifetime. And we owe something to Hollywood as well, even if there may be some ambivalence about many of the films, for instituting PKD as a pop culture emblem. Through them, Dick became a recognizable name for a certain kind of idea or motif, even for people who weren't literary, or likely ever to read his work, or didn't think of themselves as interested in science fiction as a written form.

All these forces kind of swept in and completed the job that Paul, as the executor of the estate, began. And Paul was working alone—except not alone. Working communally, because that was Paul's native disposition: to make things tribal, to create a collective. To work in concert with other fans, no matter how young, and naive, and willful, and innocent they might be, who came to him and said, "I want to help out." And I was an example of the latter.

The center of this display, and of this description, is the *Philip K. Dick Society Newsletter*. Which many of you here know, because you subscribed to it. Others of you, younger scholars, or academics, or fans, might not have even heard of it. And somewhere in between there might be those among you who faintly recognize the name and think, "Yeah, that's a thing, I've heard of it, but what was it?"

I'm going to make it very evident to you what that was, and how it functioned. It's a portrait of Paul.

It's a description of this process that begins with Dick's death in '82 and culminates, or ends anyway, approximately 10 years later, with the market in a readership for his works exploding, thanks to the Vintage paperbacks and Paul handing off stewardship back to the family, to Laura and Isa principally at that time, and then moving on to other projects in his life.

Paul wanted to focus his efforts on writing about rock and roll again. I'll tell you about that. He also had this mad dream that he was going to switch to Theodore Sturgeon. In fact, he did succeed in getting an entire, massive, authoritative addition of Theodore Sturgeon's complete collected short stories into print from a publisher at Berkeley called North Atlantic Books, in the years after he stopped working with the Philip K. Dick Society.

This is also a personal story for me, because what I did was drop out of college and run away to Berkeley, in a kind of confused pilgrimage. For, when I was in high school, I was obsessed with reading Philip K. Dick's novels. I had this idea that I was going to go and seat myself at the feet of the master. Now, God knows how that would've worked out if I actually set out early enough to find Philip K. Dick while he was alive. To begin with, I was mistaken. From the distance of New York, I didn't know the difference between Northern and Southern California ... so I was pointed towards Berkeley, when he was actually down here already [in Fullerton].

Before I could set out, Dick died. I spotted his obituary in the Village Voice, and was crushed. The residue of my fantasy was that I decided to contact Paul, who'd been announced as the Executor. I think the crucial clue, the thing that helped assemble the ranks of the Philip K. Dick Society—anyway, it worked for me—was that in a Blue Jay edition of *Clans of the Alphane Moon*, or *Dr. Bloodmoney*. Before the title page, there was a little announcement. Those Blue Jay editions were the first posthumous editions of any of Philip K. Dick's novels in the United States. The announcement said that the *Philip K. Dick Society* would be operating from such and such P.O. Box address in Glen Ellen, California. I, and I think many, many other people, on seeing that, sent off a note to Glen Ellen, and it was of course being answered by Paul Williams.

He was the *Philip K. Dick Society*, and he was the one opening the mail.

Now, I don't have the claim of having known Phil, as Paul was always proud to call him. Some of you did know Phil, or at least meet him at a convention. There are others of you who obviously have other kinds of intimate connections to the story, to the publishing of his books, to his life. Nevertheless, this is the place where I myself touch Philip K. Dick's story. By signing up to help Paul with the estate, I end up half accidentally, and very much also willfully, being a kind of official figure in the gentrification, you might call it, of Philip K. Dick.

My story begins with the *Society Newsletter*. Dick's novels were out of print in the United States, with the exception of a Harrison Ford-fronted edition of *Blade Runner* with the words "Do Androids Dream of Electric Sheep" in small type under the words, "Blade Runner." I believe it was the only book in print in the United States. The story culminates with not just the Vintage paperbacks, but with three officially canonical volumes from the Library of America. I'm the editor of those, so I become directly responsible. I'm also largely to blame for bringing the *Exegesis* into print.

But the way my role begins is as Paul's sidekick, helping fold copies of the newsletter and place stamps on the envelopes, preparing the *PKDS Newsletter* for arrival at your doorsteps. That's literary history in the making.

Here's *PKDS Newsletter* number one. This is one of the least graphically interesting items that I'm going to put in front of you, but I'll read a little bit. It says, "Introducing the Philip K Dick Society." This is the first newsletter. Paul always decided he was going put a quote from Dick, as the kind of emblem of whatever the particular issue of the newsletter was going to be. Here he quotes from *Martian Time-Slip*.

Here, he's sort of announcing what he'll do. Quote: "The newsletter will be here every three months, perhaps more often if the body of news or publishable material received so warrants." Paul never kept to that timetable. He was always quite late with it. He continues: "I've had some authors that helped with editing or publishing the newsletter. I fully intend to take advantage of those offers. There is no end to the amount of work that *PKDS* and the estate can generate, so volunteers are most welcome. If you have volunteered, and I'm slow to contact you, rest assured that I will."

Here, on the back of that first issue is a picture, probably the first picture people would have had a chance to see, of Dick's gravestone, in Colorado. There are also some nice family photos. In the first issue you see a picture—kind of the famous picture—of Paul and Phil together.

Paul was, of course, already a famous "zine" guy. He in fact created one of the most important fanzines, or self-published magazines, arguably, in American cultural life: *Crawdaddy*. Along with a few other early, equally homely publications, like *The Little Sandy Review*, and Greg Shaw's *Bomp!* or *Who Put the Bomp*, *Crawdaddy* was the place where rock journalism began.

That sounds like, "OK, big deal," but the fact is, the writers working in this area were trailblazers. Because, the idea that this kind of ephemeral material was worth talking about, and pop records deserved to be written about seriously, was a radical idea. A proposition that's subject to rejection and mockery, initially.

Paul was brazen to announce he was going to create a forum for serious consideration of the newest Beach Boys single, let's say.

This is something he already knew how to do, in other words, to say that something that had been overlooked, or that was regarded as ephemeral or beneath consideration, was actually of an immense importance, even if it was to a kind of select tribe, who are going to attend to it with a seriousness that reflected his own feelings.

That was newsletter number one.

By the second issue, he's begun the pattern where he's always looking for something in the papers—because at that time he was holding a lot of the papers—including what would become the *Exegesis*. Looking for things, letters no one could have read. He's got a self-portrait by Philip Dick from 1968. Then there's a reminiscence by Tim Powers. He was going to the people who were important in the immediate community, to get them on the record. He would do interviews with people.

Quote: "Society members, we now have approximately 225 patrons in the Philip K. Dick Society, and more every day. Which is quite encouraging. Thank you for telling your friends."

People are beginning to respond to this. I think at the peak the subscription list was about 800 people. If you picture that, from the perspective of a completely out-of-print writer, this was a remarkable groundswell of interest.

But at the same time, it's insignificant by any real measures. Certainly no publisher was going to wake up and say, "Oh, my God! There's 800 people who want to buy a copy of this out-of-print book!"

It was a cult. It was a completely self-reinforcing subculture. This was OK. This was comfortable for Paul, and it was the natural state of Phil K. Dick scholarship and fandom at the time, to accept there was a kind of marginality, or exile, or invisibility involved in the pursuit of his books.

Now, younger scholars come of age in an atmosphere where Dick is automatically understood to be important. But consider the state of things at this earlier point. There was only one book you could buy on a new bookstore shelf: that movie tie-in edition of *Do Androids Dream of Electric Sheep?* with the word "Blade Runner" larger than the title. Keep in mind as well, *Blade Runner* wasn't a canonical American film at that time. The movie had been rejected. It had been seen as dull and dour, when people were looking for another *Star Wars*. It had not made a lot of money. No one was particularly bragging about it, and the "director's cut" hadn't been released to begin its rehabilitation.

There were a few titles in print in a kind of marginal way, in editions from England. If you were a bookseller, you could import five or six of Dick's key titles. Fortunately, they were good ones, that were printed in England. Some people had gotten a hold of a portion of the canonical Dick titles. *Flow My Tears* was in print in England at that time. I don't remember what the publisher was, maybe Granada. They were garish paperbacks. Pocket sized paperbacks. There was a *Dr. Bloodmoney* there was a *Stigmata*, but finding outré titles was very difficult. People who were part of this society, a large motivation for people signing up, was simply to write to Paul and say, "Where can I find these books?"

Which again, is a very hard situation to imagine from this vantage: lots and lots of people joined the society simply for the listings from booksellers about the availability of books.

Here's an important newsletter. It says that it's the one that breaks the seal on the *Exegesis*. A scholar named Jay Kinney was given first access and made a survey of the material. Remember, there wasn't some big organization behind this. People might be inclined to write the Philip K. Dick society and address it, "Dear Sir or Madam." As if there was an office building, with a secretary. But this was just Paul coming out of his Glen Ellen driveway every day and dealing with this mail, and dealing with these inquiries.

The *Exegesis* lived in the garage. I saw it there several times. Paul dug out piles of boxes. The security problem wasn't how to deal with the fact that many people thought this was a document of tremendous importance, and that they might come and steal it or publish it. Later, there developed a fantasy about the *Exegesis* as if had been suppressed, or controlled, or hidden in a vault somewhere. The security problem was, what if there was a flood, or a fire? Also, how the hell do you even begin to look at all this stuff? It was so disordered. It was just stuffed randomly into folders. This guy named Jay Kinney did what Paul wasn't quite ready to do and made a first foray. This is, in fact, the first publication of any portion of the Exegesis, apart from the pieces we glimpsed in the pages of *VALIS*.

The third issue of the Society Newsletter is dated April 1984. This photograph is a talismanic photograph for me personally. Dick is wearing a t-shirt that says "Rozz-Tox." Who here knows what Rozz-Tox is? There's a seminal American underground cartoonist named Gary Panter. That t-shirt—and the design is concealed by Dick's folded arms and the woman in the photograph—was a Gary Panter T-shirt. He was an LA based cartoonist associated with a magazine called *Slash*, which was the punk music fanzine that also was the place where the youngest cartoonists in LA went at that time to publish their punk cartoons. These people included Matt Groening, and Gary Panter. I'm probably forgetting some other names.

Gary Panter was, as a young man, a big Philip K. Dick fan. He came out to Fullerton with his girlfriend and a couple other of Dick's admirers from the LA punk scene, and hung out with him one day and gave him that T-shirt, which Phil was proudly photographed in a number of times.

To people like me, I was nineteen at the time that newsletter would have arrived at my doorstep, it was like a bolt from the blue. My three areas of interest were: Philip K. Dick, punk music, and underground cartooning. Here was Philip K. Dick giving it his official seal of approval. I was so turned on by this photograph, trying to account for how he could have been wearing it. It was like a crazy beacon to me.

Many years later I became friends with Gary Panter. He's continued to be a huge Philip K. Dick fan and is extremely erudite. A very interesting reader. When Pamela Jackson and I were in the eleventh hour of the copy edits on the *Exegesis* … this is a confession. There's a lot of weird stuff in that book that doesn't make sense, and it's because of Phil's handwriting. There was no way for me to resolve some of the textual ambiguities, except that I had to resolve them or delete the sequence. Once I got interested in the sequence, if had problem words in it, I had to land on something. So, there are guesses in that book. Inevitably, this happens with archival materials. I talk about it a little bit in the introduction. I give myself a bit of a *mea culpa*. It should be emphasized that if, as a scholar of the *Exegesis*, you are trying to bear down very hard on the interpretation of some completely opaque phrase in that document, it might be that you're just dealing with a typo.

Dick's range of reference was very wide, and some of it was very obscure. So many bizarre, different lexicons: scientific, philosophical, psychological, psychiatric, gnostic gospels. No editor could ever become an expert on all of these different languages, cultural ranges, and references that Phil was drawing on, at great speed, writing in a high fever, night after night. He was drawing on everything he knew. There are so many obscure references in that document; it was our job to track them down and confirm them as much as we could, but there were some that eluded us.

At the eleventh hour, I was looking at some of the most strange references in the book, and we were about to commit to them. There was this one phrase that Dick had used which we, as well as we could resolve from his handwriting, it was in quote marks and it was, "The aging voice of Irwin." What is the reference here? It seemed to be framed as a reference, and it seems so.... I don't know ... filled with implication, that we were like, "There has to be an Irwin. His aging voice must be.... There must be a denominator here, right? That we just don't recognize."

We thought about Professor Irwin Corey, who received the National Book Award on Pynchon's behalf. We thought about finding some obscure scholar named Irwin, whose aging voice would have been influential. We couldn't figure out what it was, but we were about to go to press with, "The aging voice of Irwin." I decided to throw this to some people like Panter, who were great fans of Dick's. It was Gary Panter who said to me, "I think that's 'Ayenbite of Inwyt,' from James Joyce." So, it's a beautiful reference to a very interesting part of "Ulysses" from James Joyce. It was a real save on Gary's part.

I'm going to skip a couple of years of newsletters. Here's newsletter number 13. Dated February 1987.

First of all, how many of you guys have ever seen this poem, "On a Cat Which Fell Three Stories and Survived"? It's a hard poem to come across. It was the front page of the newsletter and it made Last Wave fanzine at some point [Summer, 1984 issue]. It's a gorgeous poem. Dick really was a cat person.

This is the newsletter where I joined the team, so I'm sentimental about it. Let's see, what do I want to point your attention to? I think one of the things happening is, you can begin to see this is an interesting phase of the development in posthumous PKD publications. You have an advertisement from Mark Ziesing, who was a heroic small-press publisher who brought out *The Man Whose Teeth Were All Exactly Alike*, and I think *The Dark-Haired Girl*. You see that one of the variant editions of *The Unteleported Man* has just been published in England. That *Radio Free Albemuth*, at that point, had been rescued, and it's Hartwell who's really responsible for picking that up. Arbor House was doing it [January 1986], and there was going to be this announcement that there'd be a mass book in paperback [by Arbor House/SFBC in June 1986]. You got other small presses who collaborated on his *Ubik* screenplay [published as by Corroboree, June 1985]. The posthumous material and the mainstream books had begun to trickle out.

This was a very odd period in his publication profile, in the certain sense in that his major works, the defining works that had had an audience at some point, the 60s novels and early 70s novels, were still all almost all out of print.

What you could get, if you relied upon a very crafty new bookstore, one that could order presses like this, where you can get all the arcane stuff ... you can get the works that hadn't been published during his lifetime.

The letters were coming into print in a very extensive massive edition, and things like *The Dark-Haired Girl* were soon to appear, with curiosities like the children's book, *Nick and the Glimmung*, soon available. You could read *Nick and the Glimmung* but you couldn't get a copy of *Now Wait for Last Year*.

Maybe you could find *The Man in the High Castle* in a used bookstore. It was one of the easiest books to find that way, but it wasn't in print. Which is a very strange inversion effect that happened as the *Philip K. Dick Society* energies helped propagate this excitement about the legacy.

This legacy took the form initially of exploring the unpublished works. You can always make an argument to your publisher that "Hey, this has never been published before, so people might buy it." As opposed to, "Bring back into print this book that never sold in the first place."

Let's keep going through the Newsletters. Here we are in August 1987. There's been an opera based on *VALIS* which takes up a lot of attention at this time. *Total Recall* is a rumor at this point—a film in development based on "We Can Remember It for You Wholesale" with some impressive names involved. Mel Gibson might be the star. Bruce Beresford to direct. The newsletter was tracking the slow emergence of his works into various realms: republications, film projects, and scholarly reference. It was also clocking references in the popular culture which were very few and far between.

Nowadays, you can't turn around without having someone claim that their work is influenced by Philip K. Dick, because it's a very hip thing to say. But at that time, to see anyone mention him, all of a sudden, it was a bolt out of the blue. Sonic Youth one day announced that one their songs had Philip K. Dick influence. This was electrifying.

This was galvanizing, because it seemed to say that our guy was not going to disappear, that he had some currency or relevancy that would translate outside of our little army of *PKDS* members. Meanwhile, here in this issue, is my first published critical writing. Again, offloading the kind of work that he just wasn't willing to do himself, Paul noticed that *Zap Gun* was about seventy-five pages longer in the manuscript edition than the book was. He said, "Well, the society members will be interested in this. Somebody's got to read through both of them and figure out what's different." So, I went through the manuscript and compared it to the book. In some ways it turned out to be a very dull result.

Because, first of all, that was an example, I think, of a book written, even for Dick, at top speed, with cursory attention. Dick was riffing. The ideas are typically brilliant, but his commitment to the resolution, or the characters, or the fulfillment of the themes is almost zero.

Because he wrote, I guess, on amphetamines, and when you're writing fast you sometimes don't remember to stop, every chapter kind of went on after itself. The characters would talk about what had happened. He was trying to finish a book. He was watching the pages stack up and he liked that. He would let the characters just kind of re-hash. It was almost like "Last week on *Zap Gun*." There was too much of this rehash material. When the book had finally been sent in, and of course it was like a five hundred-page manuscript, some editor said, "Well, that's not a good paperback length," and they'd cut about three pages off the end of every chapter. Mostly for the better. In any case, this article was my first critical or scholarly effort, and Paul published it in the Newsletter. In the next issue, I reviewed *The Dark-Haired Girl*. Likely my second critical writing ever.

I should describe the atmosphere of the mailing parties of the *PKDS* newsletter. Paul would come down to Berkeley and run this thing off at a place called Krishna Copy, on the corner of Telegraph Avenue and Dwight Way. He would come to my house, with his tiny car stuffed with boxes. And we would spend hours and hours stuffing envelopes, folding these things which were getting thicker and thicker, into letter-sized envelopes. It was crucial, he never made a newsletter that was longer than twenty pages, because he had to be able to get it into a letter-sized envelope in order to afford the bulk mailing to send it out.

Then, we had to put all the mailing labels which he'd printed out onto the envelopes, and put them into numerical order according to zip code, because that was how you presented a tray of fanzines to the post office in order to qualify for bulk mailing.

This was a ritual that connected to his days of doing *Crawdaddy*. Paul knew how to do it. He could do it stoned out of his mind. We were always very much stoned out of our minds. We would just sit there and get paper cuts, and he would bring the latest Bob Dylan bootleg, which was usually a cassette in those days. And we'd put it on my stereo which had a cassette player, and we would listen and talk awhile. And he would reminisce all the way through it or describe the Paul Williams exegesis on Bob Dylan, while the thing was playing at top volume. My wife at the time would always be very far away from home on the days that we had mailing parties.

There would be other volunteers who would come and converge on our house. John Fairchild was a staunch mailing party guy. There was this other pair, who I keep hoping will turn up at one of these gatherings and say hello, who were almost always part of the mailing parties. They lived, I think it was in Santa Cruz, and they had a band called *The Pink Beam Experience*. They had a whole, not just a record, but a whole band that was conceived around the pink beam events. Their only LP, or the only one I ever had which they gave to me, was on translucent pink vinyl.

We would all convene to mail the thing. Paul always would thank the people who participated in the mailing party, you can see it here. Managing editor Andy Watson. Whitman Reynolds. Thanks also to, now, Suzy Shaw and Greg Shaw, and I want you to notice those names. The great southern California equivalent to Paul Williams was Greg Shaw, who started the magazine *Bomp!* He was as much a founding father of rock criticism as Paul was. He had a record label doing power pop and psycho-punk or whatever ... '60s punk, "Nuggets"-style music. And so, for this particular day, with no fanfare whatsoever, Greg Shaw and his wife showed up at my house and helped with the mailing party. Later on, I figured out what an amazing figure he was.

This is dated, so here we have issue 22, 23, dated December 1989. This is a time when I think things were sort of on a verge. Since we last spoke in April, a lot of news has accumulated. Two long-anticipated Dick biographies, one already in the stores, and the other due in December or January. *Total Recall* is about to come out. You can feel the change, the kind of phase transition, that this is probably the peak where we have 800 subscribers. There's a bibliography, there's others from other countries. The world seems to be awakening in a dramatic fashion, to PKD's writing. Media attention. This is an interesting hallmark, I think: a full-page feature on PKD in *The Village Voice Literary Supplement* by Erik Davis.

I mean, Erik Davis has turned out to be an important figure, but at this time I think he was unknown to Paul. He hadn't announced himself to Paul, so he was kind of coming from outside the Philip K. Dick subculture, such as it was. A terrifically interesting moment, because the Village Voice was influential. It still wasn't the New York Times, but it was the beginning of this saturation of references from within an intellectual, literary, hipster, academic realm, which leads to the status Dick holds today.

In fact, Erik was eventually to become a really, really important part of the *Exegesis* editorial team. Really, in a sense, his name should be on the cover. As an expert on religious mysticism and psychedelia, he caught all sorts of mistakes, and he understood the implications of certain references.

Here's the first piece that I'm actually proud of. I wrote a piece for the society newsletter. It was in 1990, still years before I would really be publishing much of anything anywhere else.

I guess in this year, 1990, I had one or two short stories in science fiction magazines. I was knocking on the door myself. Here, in the *Newsletter*, I wrote a piece comparing Dick's work to other writers, pushing it outside the science fiction context, for comparisons. I put it in contrast to Flann O'Brien's *The Third Policeman*, and a recent novel—at the time a recent novel—by Lawrence Shainberg, called *Memories of Amnesia*. I talked about Lewis Carroll, as well, as maybe a kind of a common denominator for all these works. There was an attitude towards the fantastical that was reflected in all of them.

This is me rehearsing my future role as a bridge between Philip K. Dick and a literary culture that thinks it isn't interested in science fiction, talking about it in terms of other things that I like that I think help make his extraordinary distinctions legible to that resistant audience. Now, the fact that I was doing it, of course, for the *Philip K. Dick Society Newsletter* means that it wasn't achieving any purpose. Not yet. But, it was a dry run for my gentrification project, right?

Another huge moment—and recognized as such by its being fully reprinted in the same year, in the December *Newsletter* in 1990—was when the *LA Weekly* put Philip K. Dick on the cover. The piece was written by Steve Erickson, one of the major surrealist novelists and major LA novelists of our time, and one whose work is powerfully influenced by Dick's.

This was long and beautiful study of Dick's work, making extraordinary claims for it, in a very, very prominent place, of even greater importance than Eric Davis' piece, because it was the cover of the *LA Weekly*. Dick's face was suddenly on the front of a free weekly.... This is something that's hard to remember: the prominence of the free weeklies in our cultural life at one point. It was a dominant place to encounter culture. That's not true anymore, of course. The Internet has definitely eaten their lunch, but, again, it's just another moment, a tick on the clock towards the world that we're in now.

Stories in the press. I kept a large pile of press clippings about Philip K. Dick as he emerged into the light. Here's a front page piece in *The New York Times*. Paul, though, was livid, as perhaps any one of us would have been, the day we saw that. In a sense, it was the day when he was taken from our secret care, and, for better or worse, graduated into a different kind of context. He was both exalted and patronized. Even if people inserted little disclaimers about how they didn't take science fiction seriously, or that they thought he was a little bit crazy, or whatever. He was still being celebrated, and talked about.

There was no denying anymore that he was someone who'd done something that had to be contended with. Though it might be in fits and starts, he was going to be making his progress into the American canon as much as, say, other kinds of vernacular of American art have done: the comedy of Lenny Bruce, or rock and roll itself, or comic books, AKA "the graphic novel." It was like you couldn't keep it in the dungeon anymore. Accompanying that, of course, was a renewed commercial interest in publishing him, and so you have Vintage, putting all the books back into print.

Here's a great item. One of the things I want to focus on—switching my focus a little bit—is on unpublished pieces of Dick's writing that appeared in the *Society Newsletter*. To me, they're part of his published works; I forget that other people don't know them.

For instance, he was asked by some fanzine to review *The Divine Invasion* under a pseudonym. This is a review that Dick wrote of his own novel as by Chipdip K. Kill. Which I think is a name for him that he didn't make up himself. It was given to him by John Sladek, an SF writer who wrote parodies of other SF writers, and anagrammized their names. So, here's Dick re-appropriating the name Chipdip K. Kill and writing a merciless review of *Divine Invasion*.

"The same old jokers never die, they just write pompous novels."

And, the ending of the review says, "Phil Dick has tried everything but homosexuality, and that's probably where he should have begun."

Paul notes here that the fanzine that solicited the self-sabotaging review from him never managed to publish it. Its only publication was in the *Society Newsletter*. Along with the *Newsletters* themselves, subscribers would be recipients occasionally of these pamphlets that Paul would create of unpublished items. Of course, this was really Paul's way of fulfilling his commitment to the subscribers without having to write a whole newsletter. The pamphlets were really Paul's way of bailing out. It was much easier than writing and editing a whole newsletter. I was part of inflicting these on people—and I suspect the subscribers were ambivalent about them. There might be both excitement and yet a sense of being cheated. Because the tone of the newsletter was so involving. He made such a community by the way he talked to the subscribers; you really looked forward to this as a kind of broadcast. It was sort of like being in *Dr. Bloodmoney* and having the satellite pass over your house, and you could tune in for a while.

Suddenly the whole world was about Philip K. Dick for a little while. Reading him in those *Newsletters*. It was such an extraordinary example of how Paul had accomplished something like he did with *Crawdaddy*; he declared by force of will that a community of like-minded people existed, and so therefore they did. Rock and roll wasn't just music on the radio. It made a community, and I, Paul, am going to tell you what this community feels like, by writing.

Here's another pamphlet, a very odd item, but a very polished piece of writing. It's called *Warning: We Are Your Police*, and it's an outline for an episode of a TV show called *The Invaders*. For some reason, at that moment Dick had an idea for an episode of an existing TV show, and he sent it to his agent, and they of course failed to get any attention for it. So then, it just went back into his papers. This one is an essay about "Schizophrenia and the Book of Changes" which had run in a fanzine. The title is *Nazism and the High Castle*. Here's another, the outline he wrote to sell *Our Friends from Frolix 8* to his publisher, which of course diverges enormously from the published book.

Now, here's the last issue of the *Newsletter*, the farewell and the hand-off. It even includes Laura writing a thank you note as they take over. The 30th and final issue of the *Philip K. Dick Society Newsletter*, dated December 1992. By this time, Vintage had put most of the books into print. It's really a different world than it was 10 years previous.

Now, I'm going to show you even more stuff—beyond the *Newsletters*. In the years that I was working with Paul, and sometimes going up to Glen Ellen, we would make erratic delvings into files.

Paul would sometimes just pull stuff out, and photocopy it, and puzzle over it. Perhaps he was considering it for the newsletter. Oh, wait, first: this is the first letter I ever received from Paul, dated 1985. I forgot about this. When I was nineteen, I made my move to make contact with him by proposing that I was going to adapt *Confessions of a Crap Artist* for film. Paul refers me to Dick's agent, very politely. It wasn't until I came out to Berkeley that I kind of sidled up to him. I should tell that story too.

The way I met Paul first in person was, I went to something called Ser-Con One, at the time a very important science fiction convention, held in the Claremont hotel in Berkeley, on the Berkeley-Oakland border. It was my first ever science fiction convention. An amazing one to attend because of who'd gathered there. Terry Carr was still alive. William Gibson and Bruce Sterling were just emerging. They were there. Delany was there. It was a great gathering, and made very comfortable by the extraordinarily lavish parties that the Scientologists were throwing at that time. They somehow had this idea that they were going to win us all over by buying everyone free drinks. Everyone was laughing at them. I remember somebody older ... someone famous, from L. Ron Hubbard's generation, who recalled L. Ron as a young man—he told a story at the bar, recalling those days. He said, "I remember when L. Ron used to say to us, 'I'm going to start a religion,' and we would say to him, 'Oh, God! You go and do that L. Ron, just get out of our faces!'"

So, when I first laid eyes on Paul Williams, he was there at this gathering that I was interested in, or trying to identify with, but I had never been part of before. Of course, I already knew his special relationship with Philip K. Dick, and I was interested in meeting him. He was wearing a Meat Puppets t-shirt, and it was sort of like seeing Dick wearing the Rozz-Tox t-shirt. Everything coming together. I thought: "I'm home." Everything I care about can fit together. It's allowed to be in the same place...

Another story out of the garage: one day where Paul was digging in a box and was, "Oh, you'll want to see this," and he handed me Phil's own personal copy of the *I Ching*, which was, first of all, very worn and swollen. It was almost like a book that had been in a shipwreck and then been dried out, it was so sweaty with use. Inside it were all these paper slips, because any time Phil made an inquiry of his *I Ching*, he'd write down what the inquiry was, and leave it on the page that the coins had told him to interpret as the answer. Some were extremely specific, and very recognizable references from one of his novels, like, "Should I go and buy some Nembutals for X tonight, or should I tell her I can't?" He'd gone to the *I Ching* to make this inquiry.

Here's an angry letter to a SF fanzine. In middle of a controversy around whether Stanislaw Lem should be allowed into the membership of SFWA, Dick is defending his actions—he was paranoid about Lem, and wanted to accuse him of treachery—and, at the same time, trying to differentiate his protests from those of Philip José Farmer, who he feels was an unbearable reactionary. But of course, the reason Dick is having to split this hair, about how he's not a reactionary and Philip José Farmer is, that I believe the circumstances were such that what Phil did was participate in the black-balling of Lem at that time.

Okay. Let me get back slightly to the culture of the membership and the culture of the Philip K. Dick society itself. It seems a little strange, but what happened here is that I inherited someone else's—another subscriber's—collection. I'd like to show it to you. Partly, I just want you to see this, to behold that I'm not the only person who preserved these things in a binder. They were precious objects. They were like a kind of a religious transmission, a thing you held onto. And in fact, this other subscriber, a woman named Angela who gifted me with these materials, treated hers even more reverently than I did. They're very neatly bound up, a full run of the *Newsletter* from beginning to end, and all the extras. But, she also included all of the stray material that she associated with the Society; just as I have my own stray materials, she included hers.

So you see that, like me, she clipped Erik Davis' piece. At the time…. It's so commonplace to see references to him now, but, back then just to open the *Village Voice* one day and see a full page devoted to Philip K. Dick, you'd think: "Finally."

Here is Angela's first inquiry to Paul. Actually it's a draft. I think she's trying to figure out what she wants to write to him. "Angela Wyman, Philip K. Dick society. Dear Sir/Madam, please tell me information regarding your society membership. My interest in your society is sparked by fruitless search for the following books: *Galactic Pot-Healer*, *The Ganymede Takeover*, *The Crack in Space*. If you can help me in this matter, I would appreciate it."

It's hard to remember, in our current culture of plenitude, of overabundance, that to be a fan used to be all about *scarcity*. Whether you were a hound in a record store looking for a song that you'd read about, or heard on the radio once, or read Greil Marcus describing in one of his books … you couldn't just go listen to a clip on YouTube.

Similarly, you might be consumed with fascination for Philip K. Dick, and be unable to get your hands on the material. So many of the inquiries to Paul had to do with this kind of thing. It was a kind of mantra. I heard these titles. I've seen the list of the whole list of titles on other books by PKD. You might think: "Oh, God, he wrote so many. I only have four. What am I going to do?" Paul would respond by sending out information on booksellers, and then everyone in the society would correspond with these booksellers, and try to buy these items, and here's the Gyphon Bookshop, which is a bookstore in Manhattan, on Broadway.

It's still there. I used to work there. It was a specialist in a couple of things: Oz, and Oz books, and science fiction. They would sell to these fans, the books that they couldn't find. They were good at finding things. Angela had been buying books from Gryphon, probably in the period when I was working there. Small world, this *PKDS*.

Then you have this guy, who's very important in my personal history. Gerry Kleier was a bookseller in Berkeley. He was an independent operator doing his own book scouting, but he also worked at Pegasus Books on Solano Avenue and gave me my first job. Gerry was a dealer Paul would refer people in the society to, because he was so good at finding Philip K. Dick books, and had made such a particular effort in that regard. In fact, the reason I got my job at Pegasus was because I went and dropped the name Philip K. Dick to Gerry Kleier. Again, wheels within wheels.

Someone earlier spoke of Phil's generosity with his manuscripts, giving them to people. He was also given to autograph lots and lots of things for his friends, providing them with stacks of things to sell if they needed things to sell. And so, I ended up, because he'd autographed all of Joe's stuff, and it was mountains of it, and Joe sold it to Gerry Kleier, and as result I ended up with a couple of really interesting items. Here's one.

This circles back to Paul. Dick's association with *Rolling Stone*, of course, was entirely through Paul Williams. Paul was the bridge between that "official" counter culture realm for Dick. Part of what made him among hippies, truthfully, is that Paul wrote that big article in *Rolling Stone*. Then, all his publishers started quoting it. "The best science fiction mind on this or any other planet," was on every edition of 1970s paperback Philip K. Dick, credited to *Rolling Stone*. That kind of created this aura. One of the residual results of this was that when *Rolling Stone* started this new magazine, called *The College Papers*, they invited Dick to contribute a story. Or perhaps Dick sent the story to *Rolling Stone*, at Paul's encouragement—even though they weren't typically publishing fiction. I think it's one of his really great short stories. A very, very funny one, "The Exit Door Leads In." Here's the page, with the autograph to Joe. It's kind of a hideous illustration. It's hard to make it out. And, they misspelled his name, which happens more than once. It's misspelled in the credits in the Schwarzenegger film, as well.

Let me switch gears. I have some other things I could throw under the magic machine here, but ... instead, let me talk very briefly and personally again about my own experience of those days. One of the interesting things was that I was a New York kid, and my sense of what California was like came as much out of Phillip K. Dick's novels, as it did out of Chandler's novels, or out of Hollywood movies, or watching *Adam 12* on television, or anything else. I only lived in a kind of a fantasy idea of what California consisted of, but I really wanted to live in Berkeley specifically because of Philip K. Dick.

The apartment I was just describing, this little, tiny apartment in the flats, where we did the mailing parties, where Paul and Greg Shaw and the Pink Beam Experience came and hung out and sent you subscribers these newsletters, it was only three blocks from the Francisco Street House, where Dick had lived and wrote so many of his earliest stories and novels.

It was also just one block in the other direction from the intersection of University and San Pablo, which is the place where we see the bomb fall in the opening scenes of *Dr. Bloodmoney*. And, it was only a block away from the Lucky Dog Pet Shop, which was still in operation there.

I was living—I never did succeed in meeting my hero—but I was really living in his back pocket there, in a sense. I was writing my first stories and novels there, just a stone's throw away from the house.

But, I had a strange, kind of ill-fated, pair of attempts to shore up that connection. The first was that I went into the Lucky Dog Pet Shop one day. I said, "Do you know how important this place is?" And, I explained there was this very important writer who'd written about the place, and it had become kind of an emblem for him.

The woman at the counter said, "You know what's funny is someone once came in before and mentioned this. I was very interested, and they promised to show me the essay that had been written, that they'd mentioned. I was waiting to see it, but it never came."

I said, "Oh, don't worry, I'll photocopy it and bring it in for you." So, I went home and I reread the Lucky Dog Pet Shop essay, and of course the woman at the counter is described as such an authoritarian monster. It just broke my heart. I ended up reproducing her bafflement because I never went back, and never showed her the essay. It'll have to remain a mystery to her.

The other part of the story is, I had this idea that I would go and bliss-out in front of the Francisco Street house, that it was going to be a kind of special place for me. The day that I first decided I was going to go and do that, I got there and it's this totally vacant neighborhood. I mean, just quiet, midweek…

By the standards of a New York City kid, it was the suburbs. I mean, the Berkeley flats aren't really the suburbs but, with the space between the houses, and sparse parked cars, and nothing going on for miles around, it's pretty placid.

On this particular day I set up across the street from the house, and a security guard came over and started hassling me because there was some freshly poured concrete and he'd been hired to protect it so there wouldn't be any footprints or, "Jonathan loves Shelley," or anything written in the concrete.

And I told him, "I'm just looking at that house over there..."

He was totally distrustful.

It was such a Phil Dickian moment, because I was trying to do the most innocuous possible thing: stand on a street and look at a house, and yet a security guard had come over and confronted me, and dislodged me from my position.

My goal of going over and having my moment of Zen contemplation in front of the Francisco Street house remained this weird, irritating, unfulfilled mission. So I went back another day. And, shades of the short story, "Roog," there was a dog.

This dog saw me standing there. You know how dogs don't like things to be a little bit not quite right? Like, if you're just walking down the street, you're fine, should you stop, the dog thinks, "why did he stop?" The dog began barking at me, maniacally, running across the street, chasing me off. It was like he'd been given the assignment by the security guard.

So, I was foiled a second time, this time just by a dog. Clearly, the dog was the reincarnation of the garbageman-chasing-dog from Dick's story "Roog," right? So, I had this thwarted relationship to the Philip K. Dick neighborhood.

Let me stop there, or pause just once more to honor Paul. For those of you who had any kind of contact with Paul, even if it was just through reading, you know that he was intimate by his nature. Reading the newsletters meant you had a relationship with him. Because he created one.

We're gathered here at a remarkable moment. Obviously, there are people in the room who knew Phil personally. We're the living witnesses to the creation of a bridge through time: a time when a very eccentric writer who lived and wrote, for the most part, under a kind of ignominious disregard, to the point at which that same person is unmistakably—not just because I kind of tricked someone into putting him into the Library of America but *unmistakably*—by a very general accord, considered one of the most important American writers of the 20th century.

We are the living witnesses, and also participants. For those newsletter subscribers among you, you are in a sense living participants in this absolutely unrepeatable and specific action, of raising Phil Dick into the pantheon, an action initiated by Paul Williams when he conceived the first issue of that newsletter.

Audience Member: I was wondering, has there been a collection of the *PKD Society Newsletters*?

Lethem: No. It would seem a natural thing now for someone to do, to help publish the entire run of the newsletter. But, of course, the copyrights might be quite difficult to assemble and clear. Paul was very open-source in his way of doing things and, of course, the stakes were very low back then. So he just published the unpublished Philip K. Dick materials with impunity, but also things written by other people, all of whom might not all automatically consent to reprint rights.

Audience Member: I contacted Paul about publishing his newsletters and he said, "OK." So, then I put the first one on Total Dick-Head, and within a day he called and said that he misspoke, because of all the different authors that were in play there, and he can't get clearance.

Audience Member: What advice to you have for those of us who would like to start our own PKD fanzines, and what sort of thing would you like to see in fan scholarship in the future?

Lethem: Well, the particular circumstances I've been describing, someone like Paul Williams being made executor of an estate, and the vacuum that he filled, the particular energy surrounding that project—none of that could ever be reproduced. At this point we're all just sort of ticks on a gigantic elephant, right? There's scholarship. There is a reputation. There's a gigantic enterprise that's being collectively participated in, even by people who wouldn't dream of coming to a conference like this, but have written essays or books of importance or interest on the subject of Dick's work.

Back at the time that the society was in operation, nearly anyone who cared about Philip K. Dick was a subscriber to the *Newsletter*—a unique and unrepeatable trick.

Of course, I'm a great believer.

One of the things that was beautiful about Paul, or about his friend Greg Shaw, was that in an atmosphere where someone might have conceived of professionalizing, or becoming rich and famous like, say Jann Wenner, who started *Rolling Stone*, they saw the value in remaining amateur—the power of being a permanent fan. For them, the liaison between a professional artist and a member of their audience was not a thing to be monetized or try to shift to a professional basis. Instead, it was fluid and arose from personal impulse.

It was communal in its basic premises. That's the value of the fan atmosphere, is that it is fundamentally communal.

Audience Member: And ultimately in love with the material.

Lethem: Yes. And in love, right.

Audience Member: I have a quick question. We heard, he typed stories very quickly. The *Exegesis*, he handwrote?

Lethem: There were sections he reworked by typewriter. Some of the most finished, interesting, and satisfying sequences he reworked. Maybe there were some he originated on the typewriter. Not many. I think it was mostly handwriting. Remember, he didn't think of it categorically as akin to his novels. He wasn't planning to publish. It was a personal voyage into understanding. He was writing to himself.

Audience Member: Can you say something about how Lawrence Sutin became involved, and maybe a little bit about Sutin's first selections from the *Exegesis*, and how that got put together?

Lethem: I can try. Whereas Jay Kinney's initial foray was something I was very familiar with, because I was right there, by the time of Sutin I was a little further away. I don't actually know how access was given to Sutin. What I can comfortably guess is, in that time, when scholarship was still wanting, and Paul was still the one opening his garage to those who seemed scrupulous enough to share with, that Sutin, as the biographer, was given free range to involve himself in these materials.

I think Sutin himself explains that at first he read it in passing, then realized how remarkable this material was. He began compulsively reading it. It was only because he had done a biography that he ended up looking at it. Then he thought, "I can make some crucial interventions here."

His eye was great. Pamela and I had to throw up our hands at a certain point. As enormous as the material was, Sutin had gotten to so many of the most approachable and persuasive sequences. There was no question of excluding what he identified. We had to put the majority of Sutin's selections inside our volume, because it was so good, the stuff he'd identified.

Sometimes, though, he'd cut it off short. In places we take the Sutin passage and we carry it on, beyond where he stopped. The nature of the *Exegesis* is that Dick was writing past the point of no return. There would be five amazing pages, ten more fairly compelling pages, and then five pages of Dick recording his failure to bring the point home. He'd be writing and more or less admitting it: "I'm falling asleep, attenuating, repeating myself, I hate my life, I should go to sleep and never do this again." Some of those needed to be included to get the point. Nearly every passage stops being compelling at a certain point. Sutin's interventions tended to be shorter than ours, because we had more space to work with...

Audience Member: As someone who wasn't around at the time of the development of the fandom in the early '90s, there was one document that was always precious to me, for a whole range of interviews with fans, journalists, as well as cultural figures. That's the *BBC* documentary, *Philip K. Dick, a Day in the Afterlife*, that also includes interviews with Paul Williams, which I thought was very nice.

With that connection with the *BBC* ... and also, he's great. I mean, he was with Elvis Costello, and Terry Gilliam, and all this. It's a great document of that period. I was wondering if there were other documentaries or kind of connections? Also, when you think about the *BBC*, the UK fandom, or the fandom in other countries, how was that?

Lethem: Paul was good at making bridges to the international fandom, and it's reflected in the *Newsletters*.

I myself didn't know about that *BBC* documentary until quite a lot later. I don't know why. It just didn't reach my radar. You mentioned Elvis Costello. One of the ways the construction of the reputation as we now know it was signaled, was by these fellow artists in other art forms, making explicit tribute in various ways. There were several such moments. Elvis Costello cited him in a liner note. That was when Costello's things were all put on CDs. He wrote these long annotations, and he talks about Philip K. Dick in the annotations for one of his own CDs. There was the opera of *VALIS*. And there was a theater group, that did a very interesting adaptation of *Flow My Tears*. In San Francisco there were things I don't.... Steven Flack and I were ... you were there that night. That was the Philip K. Dick Night at DNA Lounge, an elaborate tribute to him one night, at what at the time was one of the prominent night clubs in San Francisco.

Audience Member: When was that?

Lethem: Oh, I'm going to guess that was '88 or '89.

Audience Member: What about Crumb?

Lethem: Right. Robert Crumb's cartoon was another flare in the darkness. There were these moments, you know?

We think a lot about the English language stuff. Of course, famously the French had kept him in print when we had failed to. There was also the film adaptation of *Confessions of a Crap Artist*, which was titled *Barjo*. The very book I wanted to adapt, I guess, when I was in college.

Paul Williams appears briefly in that film actually. He's in a scene. These funny little bridges were being built into the culture in different ways...

Here's a tiny... I'll become vain again, I'll give you another anecdote about myself. When I finally published my first novel, the *Society Newsletter* didn't exist anymore. But, there was this next kind of newsletter, *Radio Free PKD*. Which Paul had happily handed off, and it ran for a little a while. I followed Dick's example. I reviewed my own novel negatively under an anagram of my own name in the pages of *Radio Free PKD*. My anagram for myself was Pot No Mental Jet.

Audience Member: A name I'd like to mention, David G. Hartwell. He died...

Lethem: Oh, of course.

Audience Member: I'm not in the position to know, but some have credited him with basically being there at the creation as an adviser to Paul Williams.

Lethem: Yes. In the sense that this is partly a biographical tribute to Paul Williams, it is really my oversight not to have brought Dave Hartwell's name into it much earlier. Because, they go back all the way to the creation of *Crawdaddy*, and they helped catalyze one another's careers, such as they were. They shared the mutual obsessions with rock and roll and science fiction.

In a funny way, it's almost like they divvied them up between the two of them. Paul went careening off into *Crawdaddy* for a while. While Hartwell became such an important editor in the SF field. So, Hartwell was important specifically to Philip K. Dick's [reputation], keeping the flame lit during the most difficult time. And, yes, he was always there for Paul. In every sense…

Great. Now food and drink have been mentioned. That might be a clue as to where we should all adjourn.

PKD at California State University, Fullerton

A Question-and-Answer Session with Nicole Vandever and Paige Patterson

TIM POWERS *and* JAMES BLAYLOCK

Moderated by Nicole Vandever and Paige Patterson, April 29, 2016, the Philip K. Dick Conference, CSUF

Vandever: Some background on our university in case you don't know. As many of you do know our university has a unique history of science fiction.

Professor Willis McNelly, a professor of modernism and science fiction here at CSUF in the '70s, worked really hard to collect various manuscripts for our university to give the likes of Frank Herbert's *Dune* and Ray Bradbury's *Fahrenheit 451* a home in our Special Collections, which has just been growing and is really awesome and you should check it out.

Included in that effort is not only various manuscripts and letters of Philip K. Dick, but in a sense Dick himself. Philip K. Dick had fallen on hard times living in Northern California, and asked McNelly if he might find a home in Fullerton. McNelly found Dick a place to stay here. Literally here … we could walk to some of his apartments in like twenty minutes from this very location, which I think is really cool.

A home was made for Dick in Orange County, which is also the location of *A Scanner Darkly*, and it's CSUF where he would become a part of the academic life of a few students. Two of these students have so kindly come back today to share their own experience as students, writers, and friends of Philip K. Dick here at CSUF. Paige, did you want to introduce our writers?

Patterson: On my far left, your far right, we have Tim Powers. He is a science fiction and fantasy author, and alum of CSUF. His works have been translated into numerous languages. Perhaps one of his most popular work, *Anubis Gates*, won him the Philip K. Dick Award, and his later works would win him two Locus Fantasy awards and three World Fantasy awards.

Right here, we have James Blaylock, also an alum of CSUF. He is the author of fantasy and steampunk and supernatural fiction. Blaylock has won the World Fantasy Award twice, and has written numerous books, many of which feature California and Victorian London as the setting.

Vandever: We'll start off with some general questions. What was it like for both of you, learning from classes, from Philip K. Dick, from each other at CSUF? What was your relationship like, if you could recreate it here for our imaginations, specifically if you wanted to bring up the creation of "William Ashbless." I think that was a great story.

Powers: I don't know that we went to a lot of classes.

Out front of what used to be the Commons, there used to be a tree where there's cement now, and we set up a table and chairs out there, and pretty much spent the day there. We would usually go the first day of class to get the mid-term and finals schedule and then go to class on those days, so you really only had to attend class twice a semester. Of course, we were English Lit majors—if we were Physics or something, it would be more serious.

We met Phil Dick through, as you say, Willis McNelly. Phil was in Canada and totally at the end of his rope. He had gone up to Canada to be guest of honor at a convention, and when the convention ended, he just didn't go home.

He simply stayed on, because his house in Northern California had been blown up and the police had told him he wasn't welcome, and so he figured he really had nothing to go back to there. He wrote to Dr. McNelly and said, "I got nowhere to go," and McNelly read that letter to his class. Two of the girls in the class said, "Well, we just lost a roommate, he could come stay with us."

McNelly relayed this to Phil Dick, and Phil said, "OK," and got on an airplane.

I knew the two girls and they said, "Do you want to come to the airport and meet Philip K. Dick?" Luckily, I had not read much of his work or I wouldn't have been able to speak, but I went along and we picked him up.

It turned out that they had only a couch for him to sleep on and wanted him to pay for all the groceries, and so very shortly he moved in with a guy who had just been divorced, right over here on Quartz Lane.

At that point, he was only like two blocks from the college. It was a relatively quiet period for him, living by the college, having a relationship with the college through the manuscripts and magazines that eventually the college did get from him, and talking in McNelly's classes from time to time.

Vandever: Did you take classes he spoke in?

Blaylock: I had a science fiction class with Willis McNelly, I think when I was around nineteen years old, which would have made me a junior, let's say. I had no idea of the existence of Philip K. Dick at the time. In fact, I had no idea before I signed up for the class that such a thing as modern science fiction existed, which I know is going to sound just a little bit strange.

I had grown up reading H.G. Wells and Jules Verne and Conan Doyle, and other ancient writers of nineteenth and early twentieth century science fiction. When I was through with their books, I stopped reading SF entirely. I signed up for Will McNelly's class and we got the reading list of a dozen or so books that included *Dune, Double Star, Childhood's End*, and *Earth Abides*—this long list of absolutely wonderful books, and I said, "Where have I been? How did this get past me?" At that time Phil was writing letters to Dr. McNelly, who read them in class.

I didn't actually meet Tim until 1972, when I was graduating. Going around in my mind was the question, "What am I going to do about graduate school?" because there was no way on earth I was going to go out into the hard world at that point. I was accepted at Riverside in UC San Diego into what would have been MA or Ph.D. programs. Tim and me were hanging out a lot by then, and my writing life was waking up, so to speak. I had a couple of friends at school who I surfed with all the time, and I thought, "You know what? To heck with those other schools, I'll stay at Cal State Fullerton because I have a lot of friends here." I don't know whether I'd advise students these days that that's a good reason to pick a graduate school, but it worked out really pretty well for me, and in the next couple of years I determined that I wanted to find a way to stay at the University forever, and so I became a teacher.

I did not meet Philip Dick, however, until 1975, when Tim introduced me to him, which meant that I'd been out of Cal State a year by that time. The first book of Phil's that I read was *Dr. Bloodmoney*, which I followed in time with all of his novels, deciding that one after another was my "favorite."

Patterson: Can you tell us a bit more about how you became interested in talking with Philip K. Dick? Could you talk a little bit more about that? How you shared interests with him?

Powers: I had grown up reading science fiction. Sort of opposite of Blaylock, I had not really read Jules Verne and Arthur Conan Doyle. But I mentioned that I had not read Philip Dick's stuff appreciably before meeting him, which was fortunate because I have met writers whose stuff I grew up on and when I do meet them I can never even speak. I have to kind of spit and stammer and sweat, and shake their hand and rush away. I don't think they're even flattered. I think they just wonder, "What was wrong with that guy?"

But luckily, with Phil, I was able to talk more—I was aware of his name like John Brunner, say, but little more than that. Then gradually I started—since here he was!—reading his books and cumulatively appreciating, "this is actual genius. This is probably the only genius you will ever actually know well."

It was fascinating to... He was in a dormant period when he flew down here. He had had all kinds of terrible adventures in Northern California, and then in Canada he attempted suicide and so forth, and so, for the first year or so of being in Fullerton, he really wasn't writing.

He was hoping to get royalty checks. Really none of the New York people, the science fiction world, knew where he was. It was fascinating to see him come out of that with books like *Flow My Tears, the Policeman Said* and *We Can Build You* being reissued or coming out for the first time in book form.

It was, for Blaylock and I—and for K.W. Jeter too, a friend of ours who was in the picture—it was educational to see the life of an actual, professional, freelance writer, and that it was mostly being broke. In fact, I think the Phil Dick estate probably still owes me about 40 bucks.

He was always, like, "Powers, can you loan me 20 bucks?" "I already loaned you 20 bucks." "Well, can you loan me another 20 bucks?" "OK, here we go." It certainly took away any of the aspects of glamour we might have thought that career path had... But at the same time, it made it look achievable.

He's got no car, no money, neither do I. This could work.

Blaylock: When I was hanging around with Phil, we didn't talk about writing much. At the time I was writing what would probably become my first published short story or two, so I was really an amateur. I didn't really want to suggest that I wanted to talk shop too much. Also, we were so busy talking about cats, and music, and food, and I don't know…

Powers: What's wrong with our cars.

Blaylock: Yeah. There was always something wrong with our cars. That took a lot of time up. Although, I did come away with a lot of useful stuff. I remember the very first night that I met Phil, who was living on Commonwealth at that time, right across the street from school.

Powers: Yeah, I think it was just a few blocks that way.

Blaylock: We sat talking until, maybe two in the morning, and I remember there was a bottle of Zinfandel that we polished off. There might have been two.

He convinced us pretty thoroughly that the Soviets had a madness ray that was impervious to the horizon, and that it was now angled through the earth toward Los Angeles and that we would wake up in the morning and everybody would be out of their minds, dancing around in the street and howling.

This struck me as terrible news and was pretty typical of conversations with Phil. The next day we'd be talking to Phil, and he'd laugh and say, "I really had you guys going last night."

When you were talking to him, you could not tell whether he believed it to the point of abject fear, or whether he was just throwing out something because he had these two young gullible guys on hand and could hose us with some kind of story. I never forgot that madness ray. I loved the idea. I'm glad that the Soviets are not pointing it at my head anymore.

Powers: Yeah, that was a bad day.

Blaylock: Recently in a Steampunk book, several years ago, I decided that my evil guy would have a madness ray and be threatening London, in that exact same way. I stole it wholesale from Phil.

Powers: Do you remember the night he convinced us...?

Again, Blaylock and I were over there late at night with a bottle of Zinfandel, and Phil convinced us—he slid around and leaned forward to tell us this secret—he told us that archaeological evidence indicated that in San Diego, fossils showed that prehistoric man had one eye and two noses apiece. That these were the original Cyclops, and very scary creatures.

He convinced us that the world had not seen the last of these creatures. I remember Blaylock and I driving home in absolute terror. I was keeping a journal in those days, so I was able to see what day it was he told us this story.

And then recently I was looking at his *Collected Letters*, and in one of his letters, a week before he told us that story, he told some correspondent, "I read the thing you sent me about the prehistoric man with the two noses and the one eye—what a bunch of nonsense!"

I think, "You wouldn't know that was his opinion when he was telling us about it." I think my wife remembers real well, too, how he would sometimes, late at night, lean forward and say, "My researches have revealed ... ."

He was researching all these Neo-Platonist, pre-Socratic, obscure Gnostic scholars. He'd say, "My researches have uncovered a fact which has only been known to twelve people in the history of the world ... each of whom died within twenty-four hours of learning this fact, and I want to tell it to you."

I'd be like, "No. I'm not listening. Shut up." I think this is why a lot of interviewers, and people with a hasty look at Phil Dick, conclude that he was crazy. They hear these things once, and the come away with, "that guy's nuts." They don't go back the next day, to see him ridicule the idea.

Blaylock: I remember the night that we were there, the infamous Cyclops that they apparently dug up in a ditch that was being excavated near San Diego.

Powers: Yeah, San Diego.

Blaylock: But the government had suppressed...

Powers: Of course they did.

Blaylock: ...the find. Yeah. That's why I love the government so much, they suppress all these cool things that you later hear about. Suppressed things are particularly fun simply because they're suppressed.

Also, I remember being stricken with fear when he was telling us that only twelve people had learned this terrible business, and that Ambrose Bierce had been one of those twelve people. The official story is that late in life he wandered into the Mexican desert and died, but actually he was taken out by the infamous organization that was orchestrating the Cyclops thing. I think it had to do with KGB also, didn't it?

Powers: How could it not?

Vandever: Thank you. That actually, perfectly, leads into another question we wanted to ask. Philip K. Dick wrote an essay called, "How to Build a

Universe That Doesn't Fall Apart Two Days Later," and had the following to say about science fiction: "Science fiction writers, I'm sorry to say, really do not know anything. We can't talk about science, because our knowledge of it is limited and unofficial, and usually our fiction is dreadful."

In terms of these ideas about science fiction and reality, I'd like to ask, as writers of science fiction, conspiracy theories, supernatural occurrences, all of that ... when you have these worlds that you've created, how do you make what you write real and believable, even though, inherently it's not, these elements are not?

If it weren't real on some level, we'd just throw the book out the window at some point. How do you make it real and believable?

Powers: I find that the trick is to picture it very thoroughly. Like I frequently postulate some sort of secret conspiracy that's been going on for a long time in history.

What I do is I look at actual history and try to find enigmatic or inexplicable or irrational events, and say, "against what supernatural back story would those not be irrational? Against what sort of back story would they in fact make total sense?"

Then it's like being a cold case detective. You look for clues. I'm convinced that I could read a biography of Beatrix Potter and, if it was a very thick biography, and I approached it with this kind of honorary paranoid squint that I adopt when I do research, I bet I could find a lot of stuff in the life of Beatrix Potter that would make you think, "Ah-ha, here we have evidence of..." God knows what. Something supernatural!

I wouldn't do that, just because I like Beatrix Potter and it would be unkind to find weird meanings behind Peter Rabbit and Mrs. Tiggy-Winkle and all. But I do think it's real important that you trick the reader into thinking it's happening in a real place, ideally, this here very world, to real people in a real time.

The more you can staple your fantastic elements to stuff the reader's familiar with, the easier it's going to be to get the reader over that speed bump of incredulity. Because, as you say, always the risk is when you're writing science fiction or fantasy that the reader is going to say, "Wait a sec, this is all crap." Which, of course, it is.

But yeah, you want to make the theater flats and the backdrops as convincing as possible to try to stave off that realization on the part of the reader.

Speaking of Phil Dick, he was very good at that in... I think of books like *Now Wait for Last Year* or *Dr. Bloodmoney* which have worlds very different from our own, post-apocalyptic and so forth. But by showing us the day-to-day life of ordinary little people trying to run a cigar store or something, those mundane details in the foreground tend to validate the weirdness in the big background.

They always had worried about their rent. Phil Dick's characters are always worried about their jobs and their rent.

Blaylock: Everything Tim said is right on the money. I actually go about it two different ways. In the books that I've written that had to do with California and had some sort of fantastic theme, I tend to write only about places I know absolutely well. I was born in Long Beach. I grew up in Anaheim. I've lived in Orange County all my life as did my father and my grandfather for a good part of his.

Once I decide I'm going to set a piece somewhere, whether it's in my own neighborhood or the beach or up in the canyons of the Santa Ana Mountains, the question comes to mind, "if some fantastic thing were to happen here in this place, given the people who live in this place and the kind of weather that we have in this place, and what it looks like, etc., what would it be?" That narrows things down a lot.

I wrote a book called, *All the Bells on Earth* that is actually pretty claustrophobic. It's set not only in my neighborhood in Old Towne, Orange, but within a four-square-block area. I think somebody gets three blocks out of the neighborhood at one point in the book, but they come straight back again.

I was impressed by that everyday aspect of Phil's books, too—to have average characters, working stiffs, whoever it might happen to be, going about their business, except that something strange is going on that draws them in, until they're up to their ears in the supernatural. In *Bells* it was a vaguely satanic thing that was happening in the neighborhood. My character, despite his own best efforts to avoid it, got drawn into it, and had to deal with it to his peril.

When I write Steampunk stories, I go about it a different way. I made a conscious decision back in about 1985 that if I would write a book set during the Victorian era, when science was largely imaginary and there were still lost cities in the jungle.... Even in the early twentieth century, when *The Lost World* came out, the Conan Doyle film, people believed in what they were seeing on the screen, that there were dinosaurs living in South America on a big plateau.

I figured, if it's 1875, the sky's the limit. If I needed a madness ray, then I'd put in a madness ray. Everybody believed in rays back then. Heaven knows what they didn't believe in. That was an open door to work the novel in any way I wanted to work it. Sometimes it required a lowball sense of humor. Sometimes, if the plot was particularly serious, then I'd cut the humor and tell a straight story. But mixing in imaginary science. I simply had to make it plausible. Often it was plausible, because I said, "1875."

Powers: You said, "Lord Kelvin."

Blaylock: Lord Kelvin helped, although he was an imaginary Lord Kelvin. And it always worked to add a machine. The word "machine" is...

Powers: How plausible do you want it?

Patterson: With the genres of science fiction, fantasy, why do you choose to write about a place like Fullerton? Is it simply because it is familiar? Or do you ever find yourself having to step outside of your comfort zone? How do you go about doing that?

You sort of answered it already, but I'm more focused on the aspects of Fullerton and what it means to you. Because Philip K. Dick wrote a lot of works that revolved around this area. Do you think that influenced your writing at all?

Blaylock: Well, real quick I'll say, "Yeah, I think it influenced my writing." I'm not sure that I ever slip over the city line into Fullerton. I usually stick to Orange. I have to say in answer to your question, I'm often happy staying within my comfort zone, which means close to home. I tend to write about people I know in the places I know in my own experiences of the world. I'm willing to believe that other people have other experiences that I don't understand well enough to write about them myself, so I'm quite happy to stay in my own neighborhood so to speak.

Maybe this is because I've lived for so many years in this area, but I've always found Orange County to be an interesting place. I've seen some very strange things here. There's something about it that strikes me as being right on the edge of the borderland. I think that comes through in my fiction. People say, "well, here's Blaylock creating this Orange County that doesn't exist." I want to deny that, and say that the Orange County that I create when I write is the Orange County that I live in.

If you live in a different Orange County than I do, that's fine and dandy. Maybe there's something Phil Dickian in that, that we all live in a slightly different universe.

Powers: Yeah. I've written a number of short stories that take place in Orange County, largely because, for twenty years, my wife and I lived in Santa Ana ... and so I don't need to research Orange County very much. Or if I do, I can just drive around and look at it. I don't, in the case of a short story, want to have to invest in becoming an expert in eighteenth-century Austria.

In novels, I do generally go further afield. I've had novels in Los Angeles and San Francisco and Las Vegas, but most of them have been set in England, Germany, Russia, etc. Though I do try to emphasize that it is this world, it's not some alternate Germany, alternate Los Angeles. It's this one you could get on the phone right now, because I do want as much as possible to solicit, seduce, trick the reader's credulity. If I say, "no, it's an alternate Los Angeles," I've instantly ceded a whole lot of ground when it comes to credibility.

Thinking of, "Have I used Cal State Fullerton much?" In one of my books [*The Anubis Gates*], the protagonist was a literature professor at Cal State Fullerton. He soon gets marooned in 1810 London, but at least he started at Cal State Fullerton.

Blaylock: One thing I'll say just about writing Steampunk and, God knows, the sort of historical things that Tim writes, is that there's a lot of work in them. I probably spend four to six months doing research in order to be able to start writing with the knowledge that I can make the story plausible.

While I'm writing, attempting not to reproduce Victorian language, because if I try to write like Charles Dickens or something like that, (A), I couldn't do it and, (B), I might not have any readers. But to try to contrive a language that is plausibly Victorian, I suppose, but still sounds like me, requires constant attention to big dictionaries that tell me whether I'm using an Americanism or not, or when a word came into popular use—whether the word "dirigible" is OK at a particular date, for example. I can't tell you how many times I've twirled around in my chair to open that dictionary.

Earlier, when I was suggesting that I wrote Steampunk because I could get away with making things up, that was only half true. Some things, and not just language, require accuracy, and if you lace a piece with historical people and events, it adds to the reality of the thing.

Powers: I think your science in the Steampunk stuff is more plausible than you say.

Blaylock: Me, too.

Powers: Not a lot more, but ... more, yeah. You talk about Newton and Kelvin...

Blaylock: Oh, yeah.

Powers: ...and the behavior of gases under pressure. Science fiction is supposed to be not quite accurate science.

Blaylock: Actually, what I do is I think, "OK, I want to have a madness ray. I want it to involve, perhaps, a big precious stone." I don't know how to make any of that sensible at all. I call Powers on the phone and say, "I want to put in a madness ray involving a gigantic emerald." He says, "Think in these terms," and I furiously take notes...

Vandever: You said that you write what you know. Philip K. Dick had a more touching way of saying that.

He said, "I want to write about people I love and put them into a fictional world spun out of my own mind, not the world we actually have, because the world we actually have does not meet my standards."

You mentioned his ideas. They were kind of ephemeral and they would change day to day. But he had these visions of the world. He was, in some ways, amazed by the world; in some ways, not happy with it. He was definitely an outsider, and that kind of comes into his work, the outsider, the other.

My question is "what is the other?"

Powers: I think, personally, the value of writing science fiction fantasy ... people sometimes have asked me, "why don't you write a real novel sometime?" Meaning mainstream. I think if I was to try to write something about a handicapped boy coming of age in Pittsburgh—mainstream, that is—it wouldn't be chapter two before he started getting phone calls from his dead grandfather.

It would just seem inevitable. It's always seemed to me that writing mainstream fiction would be like being given a palette of colors to paint with, but not blue. Or a composer being told to compose a symphony, "but not those three keys." It seems like an arbitrary and artificial restriction to, say, "write a story about people with their emotions and crises and all the adventures they have but not this kind."

I would say, "well, what if I want to use blue in my canvas? I want to use those keys in a composition I write. What's wrong with them?" They'd say, "Well, they don't exist. They aren't real, the science fictional fantasy things. Unlike the pickup trucks and the credit cards and the Big Macs, those things aren't real."

I would say, "Who cares? Everybody still has the circuitry in their heads to respond to it." I know people that say, "I'm not scared of ghosts or vampires. I'm scared of nuclear war and urban gangs." I think, "Sure, it's noon, there's a lot of people around, say that." But you know if that person was the only person in an empty house at 3:00 a.m. and they heard something dragging downstairs, they're not going to say, "I bet that's an urban gang member!" They know exactly what it is. It's a werewolf.

Since the circuitry does still exist in our heads to resonate to this type of story, I think, why deprive that circuitry of a chance to resonate?

Blaylock: I don't know if this answers the question, but every once in a while, you come across a story and think, "I didn't know that could be done with words." Sometimes it changes entirely the way you view storytelling and how you want to write, or whatever it might happen to be. That happened when I was in Will McNelly's class and read *The Left Hand of Darkness* by Ursula Le Guin.

I don't know that the themes in the book could have been dealt with in that way, except as science fiction. I've always admired science fiction and fantasy because writers, if they're good enough, they can do that…

Vandever: We have one more question. Then we're going to open up for everyone else's questions. Kind of a closing thought. Obviously, Philip K. Dick's body of work is still relevant, still important. That's why we're all here. It continues to be translated, adapted into various medias, discussed critically, enthusiastically.

As friends of his who have watched his works become so important in the SF canon, what do you think his legacy is? How has he influenced science fiction writing, or society in general?

Blaylock: I'm not positive how Phil's work influenced science fiction writing. I'm not a science fiction scholar by any means. I know how it influenced me, but I've already talked about that. I was a little bit amazed when it dawned on me that Hollywood was buying up his stories and novels for large sums of money at an astonishing clip when much of it was too strange to be filmable, or so I thought. Obviously, he's had a big effect on the world, and as is generally the case, it might be years from now before we know quite how big that effect was.

Powers: I think he had a real big effect on science fiction since say, 1980. I think before Phil Dick in the science fiction field you didn't see as much of the high-tech low-life. The shabby future where huge developments have happened, enormous technological advances, but a scrabbling, shabby type of life is going on nevertheless.

I think of the huge expansive space travel in *A Maze of Death*, but the characters are what? Squabbling about the ice cream or something. In *Now Wait for the Last Year*, a character who builds very sophisticated brains for some kind of spacecraft or something, some of the brains are slightly defective, but instead of throwing them in the trash, he puts them on little carts so they can scoot around. In the city you'd see these things backing into alleys as you made noise approaching. I remember at one point, in a heavy rain, one of the little creatures has backed its cart into a box to get out of the rain. That picture of the kind of seamy deteriorated aspects of an otherwise glamorous future show up in cyberpunk, certainly William Gibson's *Neuromancer*, all the way up to books like Paolo Bacigalupi's *The Windup Girl*, which certainly has that ostensibly advanced future, but if you look more closely, you see the sad stories.

Of course, you see that in the movie, *Blade Runner*, which had not a lot to do with Phil Dick's actual book, but you see the huge impressive pyramids, while down on the street level there are lots of weird little noodle stalls and torches.

Vandever: Thank you for everything. We're going to open it up now to questions from everyone. There's already one, cool.

Powers: Talk really loud.

Audience Member: As friends, drinking buddies, and writing students, I wonder what was the experience of seeing yourselves reflected perhaps as composite characters but nonetheless depicted in a book like *VALIS*?

Powers: Phil Dick's book, *VALIS*, was largely autobiography. In fact, the first half of the book is simply autobiography—and then the savior is reborn as a little girl, and it becomes science fiction fantasy. Yeah, there is a character in there that was based on me, David, the Roman Catholic young man.

I remember reading it and there is one part where the Phil Dick character says to me in the midst of some crisis, "Could you not tell us what C.S. Lewis would say about this situation? Could you please do us that one favor?"

I told him, "I don't always quote C.S. Lewis!" In another place, when the savior has been reborn as a little girl, it says, "David," that's me, "had zoned out into some sort of comatose state. The Catholic Church had taught him how to do this, how to withdraw when confronted with evidence that threatened his faith."

I said, "Phil, what the hell is that? What is this Catholic Church zombie-out business? Where did you get that crap?" I remember he said, "Hee, hee, hee, hee, hee."

Actually, it was a lot of fun. There were a couple of real-life characters that he also used in that book who probably didn't have such a good time reading the book. I was overall pleased to… You're nervous reading it, "what are you going to say next? Don't go crazy. Come on, man." It was fun.

Of course, K.W. Jeter was also a character in that. He was the character, Kevin, who kept wanting to confront God with the fact of his dead cat. The fact that his dead cat disproved all of God's claims to omniscience and omnibenevolence.

I remember Phil said that at the last judgment Jeter was going to whip out his dead cat from under his coat: "it would be stiff as a board, he could hold it up by the tail and say, 'Never mind judging me, how do you explain this dead cat?'"

Audience Member: I was just curious about whether or not Philip K. Dick talked about, because you mentioned that he was doing research, did he talk much about philosophy and his readings in those areas? It does show up in quite a bit of his work.

In like, *A Scanner Darkly*, he has some pretty interesting reflections on the notions of personal identity, consciousness, things that define the philosophical tradition and I'm wondering did he talk much about that stuff?

Blaylock: Yeah, he would. It was certainly no secret that he read philosophy. I can't remember him really carrying on a whole lot about it when I hung out with him. He was usually too busy telling wild stories.

Powers: Also, he always assumed you were as erudite as he was. He'd say, "You remember what Plotinus said about this." "Oh, yeah, remind me?"

He would come up with these… He was researching every damn thing, Kabbalah, what have you. He would come up with these, especially late at night, astonishing theories. I remember he, at one point, said he had concluded that the Holy Spirit lives in retrograde time, like Merlin in *The Once and Future King*.

The Holy Spirit knows, that is, remembers, the entire future, but has no idea about what, to us, is the past. He's moving the other way and for one long evening Phil had me half-convinced that it was true.

Then, of course, next day, I'd say, "Phil, I've been thinking about that business about the Holy Spirit." And he'd say, "That was a bunch of nonsense, Powers, I mean what the…? I can't believe you'd take that seriously."

I remember one time he called me up and said, "Powers, yesterday my research researchers indicated to me that I have the power to forgive sins." I said, "No kidding. Who have you absolved?" He said, "Well, nobody. You weren't at home, and Jeter got all huffy and said he didn't want his sins forgiven, so I just forgave my cat's sins."

Audience Member: From your perspective, being friends with Phil, what were some of his favorite science fiction novels, or short stories, or writers?

Powers: Good question. He liked Clark Ashton Smith, I recall. He had at least one of the old Arkham House collections of Clark Ashton Smith. He was crazy about A.E. Van Vogt, *The World of Null-A*, *The Weapon Shop*... Do you recall another case?

Blaylock: Maybe J.G. Ballard?

Powers: Yes. J.G. Ballard, yes.

Blaylock: Which isn't surprising. And he was a big fan of *The House at Pooh Corner*.

Powers: Yes.

Blaylock: It's only a little bit science fiction, maybe the part about factors and making a suction pump.

Power: He was a big fan of the Pooh books, that's true.

Blaylock: Yeah, in fact he convinced me that book was one of the ten great books.

Powers: Which I think it is.

Blaylock: Well I hadn't read it, and I went home and read it, and I thought, "oh my gosh, he's right." I don't think he was kidding with that one.

Powers: No, when he would quote the bit about "the place at the top of the forest where a boy and his bear would always be playing," he was practically in tears.

Blaylock: Yeah.

Powers: As anybody with a heart would be.

I can't think of any others... There were a lot of science fiction writers he liked. He was great pals with Norman Spinrad. He thought very highly of Robert Heinlein, partly because Heinlein loaned him money one time when he was really broke. Which he admired Heinlein for doing, because politically, they were at odds. I'll think of some later. But certainly Clark Ashton Smith and Van Vogt...

Audience Member: What did he have to say to you, if anything, about The Lem Affair and his problems with Stanislaw Lem?

Powers: Yeah, yeah, background on that. In the mid '70s, I guess, Science Fiction Writers of America decided to give an honorary membership to Stanislaw Lem, ostensibly because Lem wouldn't be able to pay for a membership because the only money he had was Polish zlotys. They said, "Lem, unlike the rest of us, gets to be a member honorarily."

There was one other, I think J.R.R. Tolkien had been made an honorary member. As soon as this happened, Lem wrote an article saying that all American science fiction writers were frauds and hacks and had no value, and just couldn't state emphatically enough how worthless their work was.

Everybody in the SFWA, Science Fiction Writers of America, said, "How come we're giving this guy an honorary free membership when he thinks we're all a bunch of losers?" Everybody said, "Yeah, how come we are?"

Philip José Farmer and Phil Dick said, "We quit if you're going to give a free ride to this guy, who thinks we're all a bunch of clowns." I remember Jerry Pournelle was President of *SFWA* at the time and he said, "Good point. Let the guy buy his own damn membership if he wants."

They told Lem, "You can be a member but you've got to pay, like everybody else." Lem said, "Why would I want to hang out with a bunch of losers like you anyway?" Lem stopped being a member of *SFWA* and it was largely Philip K. Dick and Philip José Farmer who led the 'Ditch Lem' movement.

Blaylock: I think I'm on their side. Why should he get a free ride?

Audience Member: Although Lem did say that Dick was the one exception.

Powers: A little louder.

Audience Member: Lem said that Dick was the one exception to the losers.

Powers: True.

Audience Member: But that wasn't my question. To what extent did you see the paranoia that a lot of people ascribed to Phil, that he was paranoid often, sometimes, or never?

Powers: Phil as a paranoid author?

Audience Member: Paranoid person. That came up in the Lem business. Not related to Lem, just ... that'd be when he thought that Lem might have been in cahoots with the KGB or something... I know people say that Phil was paranoid and I was wondering...

Powers: I think Lem was in cahoots with the KGB.

I bet we could both come up with examples of Phil having paranoid reflexes. But to a large extent I think his paranoid reflexes were valid. Maybe at that point it's not paranoia anymore. When he was living in Northern California where he had a whole lot of his most affecting experiences, somebody really did blow his house up in the weirdest possible way.

He came home one day after the police had told him that if he didn't leave town he could expect a bullet in the back or worse. Leaving him wondering, "what's worse?" He came home one day and every window in his house was busted in, and under each window were heavy duty army-type boot prints and stacks of plastic bags, sealable plastic bags.

When he went in, I've seen photos of all this, every open container of perishable food was missing. If he had two boxes of Cheerios and one had been opened, the opened one was gone, as if because of exposure to something. His locked filing cabinet had been exploded open, packed first with wet towels, to muffle the sound.

One of the very few things stolen was a page of Latin he had written while under the influence of LSD, even though he wasn't consciously able to read or write Latin. That may have been the whole purpose of the break-in. I'm talking a little paranoid myself here.

But enough weird stuff had happened to him that I think his reflex was not unjustified. In the '70s he had become the hero of a fair number of Marxist behind-the-Iron-Curtain writers and Western writers of a very Marxist slant, like Darko Suvin. It was not unreasonable I think for him to be a little ill at ease at being so heavily endorsed by this particular crowd.

We are now post-Cold War so it's not all that easy to put ourselves into that perspective. I think I would have been a little uneasy too.

I remember getting letters from readers in Russia and they would arrive very looked-over and with a lot of evidence that the government was aware we were getting letters from behind The Iron Curtain. I'm thinking, "I don't know this guy, what are you looking at me for? I'm a Republican, come on."

Blaylock: My memory of the '60s is that they were a paranoid time. Contemporary writers were writing paranoid books and I think lots of people wrote stories about their fears. Also, I've got the original *Rolling Stone* article about the break-in in Phil's place. It's a great article. I think it posits like seven different explanations.

Powers: Paul Williams.

Blaylock: Pardon?

Powers: The interviews with Paul Williams?

Blaylock: Yes. They were really good. Space aliens on one hand, the Army, the Black Panthers.

Powers: They had the CIA, military groups living in the hills around the Bay Area.

Blaylock: He was not paranoid to such an extent that he was focused on one group and was certain he had the answer. I think he was playing with the idea that there were potentially many answers and actually developing an interest, maybe even a "writerly" interest in what had happened to him as well as being fearful that it could end badly.

Powers: That's true. In fact you do want to keep in mind that, when these things would occur to him he would be thinking partly, "I wonder if this is some sort of trouble that I should be aware of?" But also at least as strongly, "I wonder how this would fit into a book. I wonder how you could put a science fictional spin on this."

His *Exegesis*, which is non-fiction philosophical ramblings, a lot of it sounds crazy until you read the whole context and realize, "OK, he's stopped doing philosophical extrapolation by this paragraph. Clearly he has begun outlining a possible novel." You don't want to start taking this as him saying, "I believe this is true." It's more, "Look, he's shifted into novel outlining."

In fact, one thing I do want to say before this all shuts down, there's a sort of caricature picture of Phil Dick that you get, from just hasty cultural references, of him being a drug-addled crazy hermit who believed all these mystical William Blake type things.

Actually, while that's a handy sketch, it's not at all a realistic picture, it's a caricature. In fact, as you'd know from reading *VALIS*, he was the most humorous and skeptical guy you could imagine. Also, probably the funniest guy I've ever known and very generous and kind.

I remember we used to say that you could call him up and say, "Phil, I've been evicted. I need 400 bucks and somebody to help me move my couch." He'd say, "OK, I'll be right over—oh—who is this?"

Audience Member: Just following-up on the Paul Williams interview. When you were talking about the way he would come up with these weird stories, and then take them back. I knew Paul Williams briefly in Encinitas, where he lived at the end of his life.

I had a copy of "Only Apparently Real," which was the collection of those interviews he did in *Rolling Stone*. He's spewing out all those different theories about what had happened to his house in Marin.

What's wonderful is it all ends when Paul asks him, "Are you actually paranoid?" Then Dick goes into this long explanation, and then he ends with all these different theories, then he says, "I realize all this was supposed to describe why I wasn't paranoid... So all you had to do was ask that cop I was avoiding about the guy walking on his hands and knees across the street."

It was jokey at the end of this whole thing. Spitting out all these things he comes up with this punch line. You think about the two Phil Dicks, Horselover Fat and Phil Dick in *VALIS*: there's the crazy half. Then there's the completely rational half, the Phil Dick character who's describing Horselover Fat as crazy.

Powers: He was always way quicker to make fun of his paranoid theories than we would be. He'd explain why the CIA is probably across the parking lot right now, with a sniper scope on a rifle. We'd be thinking, "oh my God, we'd better run down the stairs crouching."

Before we could ever find flaws in his conspiracy theory, he would've smashed it to bits, himself, "Well, no, that wouldn't work because of this and, blah, blah, it's ludicrous." "Oh, I guess it... I kind of liked it, but I guess you're right."

PKD Goes to the Movies

A Panel Discussion

Daniel Gilbertson,
Gary Westfahl *and* Paul Sammon

The Philip K. Dick Conference, April 30, 2016

Westfahl: As I understand the improvised format, we'll each begin by making a statement. Then we will discuss matters amongst ourselves for a while, and then probably about half way through we'll open things up for input from the audience.

Having said that, I actually did not prepare a statement. I did that yesterday. What I did prepare, though, was a list of what I believe to be the five possible topics that might be addressed by a panel entitled "Philip K. Dick Goes to the Movies."

The first one and I think the one you're expecting us to talk about would be to discuss the various films and television programs that are officially based on Philip K. Dick's stories, such as *Blade Runner*.

There is the second topic: other films that are not officially Dick adaptations but seem to be borrowing a bit from Dick or that are influenced by Dick. I believe that Daniel will have some words to say about that.

The third and fourth topics can be dealt with briefly, if at all. The third question would be, "Was Philip K. Dick influenced by the movies? Did movies have an impact on his work?" As far as I can tell the answer is, not really. Someone else may have something to say.

He also did a little bit of writing for the movies as a fourth topic. One example I know of is the published *Ubik* screenplay, though again, other films might be relevant to what Philip K. Dick wrote for the movies.

A final topic, and this might be a nice way to end the panel, would be to talk about what works by Philip K. Dick should become movies or television programs. Having said that, I think I will now turn the microphone over to Daniel who has some prepared remarks, then we'll let Paul have something to say.

Gilbertson: Thank you Gary. I'd like to begin by thanking Cal State Fullerton for their gracious hospitality...

Our topic is "Phil goes to the movies." My question is, who pays for his ticket when he gets there? Had Phil lived longer, he would of course have gone to the movies many times for free. He'd have been invited to screenings and premieres to see his name up there on the silver screen—no ticket required. The man would have relished every moment.

What about those movies that Phil had a hand in but which he would have had to stand in line to buy a ticket to see? Movies that the man "only" inspired.

I would like to suggest that if all the movies Phil had a hand in were openly acknowledged, there could be no doubt that he deserves the title of "Hollywood's Greatest Science Fiction Writer." In support of this statement, let me add one to the list that's often overlooked.

It's been hinted at by many over the years, including *Robopocalypse* author Daniel H. Wilson. Noting that "Second Variety" had just been voted "Favorite Philip K. Dick short story" on philipkdick.com, Wilson wrote:

"'Second Variety' is... OK, have you ever seen *The Terminator*? You know that part at the very beginning—it's this apocalyptic future, and there are these humanoid cyborgs with red glowing eyes marching over a field of human skulls, spraying everything down with these Gatling guns, and the humans are being chased around like rats? Then of course it cuts to Los Angeles and you're thinking, 'Damn, I wanted to see that movie.' Well, this is that movie. 'Second Variety' is what I just described almost exactly. I don't know the complete provenance, but there's no way that 'Second Variety' didn't have some impact on the whole Terminator world." [*Ed.*: The quote can be found on the website *Five Books* at https://fivebooks.com/best-books/best-books-robotics-daniel-wilson/ as part of an interview, "The Best Books on Robotics: recommended by Daniel H. Wilson," conducted by Sophie Roell, with no date attached.]

OK, Daniel, here's your complete provenance. For me, like many in this theater, it all began with imprinting on Phil's writings at an early age. Around 1960, I read "Second Variety," a short story he'd penned some seven years earlier.

It was a powerful anti-nuke statement based, as I learned later, on grim tales of World War I trench warfare that Phil had heard at his father's knee. Fast forward twenty years to Hollywood's Sunset Gower Studios. I was a freshly minted development person at Capitol Pictures. Good product was very hard to find, especially when you were working for a tiny shoe-string operation.

In 1979, eager to create a classic science fiction movie franchise, I convinced my employer to option "Second Variety." Back then, this tale was not as familiar as it sounds to today's audiences. Self-designing, autonomous killing machines called claws—a military project gone wrong—hunt the remnants of humanity in a post-nuclear war setting. The more sophisticated claws mimic people in order to infiltrate the bunkers where the humans are sheltering.

One morning, I happily skipped the office and drove down to meet the great man. In a typical Dickian plot reversal, instead of the lavish home I'd imagined, I found a cramped third-floor apartment in an unimpressive building that was going condo. Phil's main worry was finding enough money to buy his conapt.

My employer, Virginia Palance, Jack's ex, was no fan of science fiction. To gain her interest, I had updated Phil's 1953 story. I called the movie *C*L*A*W* with asterisks just like *M*A*S*H*. Claws meant "Cybernetic Learning Anti-personnel Weapons." My treatment extended Phil's story in several directions including an upbeat third act, which set us up nicely for the movie's first sequel.

Phil had written this sequel, "Jon's World," two weeks after he'd penned "Second Variety." In it, Phil sends his hero back in time to change history by preventing the claws being invented.

In short order, I was able to present Virginia with what I presciently termed a multi-billion dollar film franchise with infinite story combinations. Forget James Bond, this was to be the biggest movie franchise ever, a forever franchise.

Virginia loved *C*L*A*W* so much that she exercised her option to buy "Second Variety." Phil delightedly applied this windfall toward buying his conapt. Although I offered to write the screenplay, again on my own time, just as with the treatment, Virginia insisted that I interview writers to adapt Phil's short story.

I took her request as an opportunity to find emerging new talent. One interviewee was James Cameron, at that time a fledgling art director. During our first meeting, we laughed out loud when, after hearing my pitch, Cameron predicted, "I'm going to direct this movie." I made a prediction of my own: whoever directed *C*L*A*W* would be first in line to direct the sequel to *Alien*.

Sadly, as interest in my little movie project grew, Virginia became increasingly involved. Meddlesome isn't too strong a word.

She insisted on a big-name writer, without any corresponding increase in my meager development budget. I knew Dan O'Bannon through H.R. Giger, who had introduced us when he took me to the Academy screening of *Alien*. I convinced O'Bannon to adapt Phil's story for Writer's Guild minimums.

Initially, I thought this was a great coup. Virginia, who loved to hang on to the purse strings, was absolutely delighted. This was all because I had yet to meet Paul Sammon, who can tell us more than one horror story about O'Bannon's shortcomings. These included a chronic inability to deliver pages on time.

To make a *very* long story short, he pulled the same stunt on me. I wound up doing most of the writing myself. True to Phil's source material, the finished screenplay described a non-stop, intelligent, action film replete with ironic twists and an ending that left the door open, not just for a sequel, but also an entire series.

I was pleased when everyone embraced this screenplay, but the verdict that really counted was Phil's: "A winning script.... Sensational ending, better than my original story. The last line has tremendous punch, Daniel. I read it, emitted a shriek, and fell over backwards."

Outside readers and development folks also loved the script: "This ingenious and nakedly unpretentious shocker has tightness, suspense, and drive." "It's a story with ideas and it moves like a rocket." MCA Universal's Carl Foreman sent me a letter in which he said, "This is really a marvelously imaginative script."

H.R. Giger had recently won an Oscar for his design work on *Alien*. I sent the script to him in Zurich. He kindly offered to design the non-human claws. Cinematographers, composers, and established A-list directors lined up to express interest in *C*L*A*W*: Dick Lester, Richard Donner, Phil Kaufman and a relative newcomer, Joe Dante.

The list of would-be investors grew at a similar pace. Executives from companies like MGM, Orion, AVCO Embassy, and Hemdale became my new best friends, eager to share the booty.

However, not for the first time, it was a letter from Phil that really made my day: *C*L*A*W* is "shaping up to be something wonderful ... to capture the sense of wonder that all too many science-fiction movies strive for but ultimately lack." Phil went on to reference how involved he'd been at every stage and concluded, "This is going to be a film I can take pride in."

I drew up plans to release *C*L*A*W* on May 25, 1982, the same release date as *Star Wars* in '77 and *Alien* in '79. I then got busy with the paid TV rights, promotional merchandising, science fiction fandom, casting, and the like.

Capital Pictures' attorney predicted that *C*L*A*W* would do eighty million dollars in sales. To celebrate, Virginia threw a big party at the Vine Street Brown Derby Restaurant. To my delight, Phil attended with Maer Wilson, who is here with us today.

I was eagerly anticipating launching my Hollywood career into the stratosphere with this project and Phil's wonderfully cinematic, robotic guys and girls. Sadly, Capital Pictures rewarded my efforts with a painful projectectomy.

Overnight, my Hollywood dream of being the first to adapt a Philip K. Dick story for the big screen faded to black.

Let me conclude by noting, once again, that if all the movies Phil had a hand in were openly acknowledged, there could be no doubt that he deserves the title: "Hollywood's Greatest Science Fiction Writer." Thank you ... and thank you, Phil.

Sammon: Thank you, Daniel. And thank you Gary, for moderating. What Daniel just said rings true, at least regarding the experiences I had during the thirty-year period I worked within the industry. As well as my ongoing, forty-year writing career, authoring film books, anthologies, novels and other fiction and non-fiction texts. End of shameless self-promotion *(laughs)*.

I have also worked on roughly one hundred movies, and was fortunate enough to enter the Industry during a period when Hollywood—and when I say Hollywood, I mean major studios—was unaware of the base audience for the science fiction, horror, fantasy genres.

After *Star Wars* upended everything in 1977, there was a mad scramble to replicate the economic success of that film. Of course, the people who were in charge of the studios and the story departments and production departments and so forth, hadn't a clue. They weren't readers; Hollywood people, on the whole, don't read much of anything, other than emails, trade publications and scripts. So, in the late Seventies they didn't know anything about SF.

That ignorance allowed an opening for people like me, who were familiar with all manner of genre films and movies in general and film history and how things worked within the Industry—or, at least, how I arrogantly assumed they worked. And I was heavily steeped in science fiction. For instance, I'd first read "The Father-Thing" in 1959. That was the first Philip K. Dick short story I read, in *The Magazine of Fantasy and Science Fiction*, I think.

I was raised in a family atmosphere that emphasized literature. Which was surprising because my parents came from poor Pennsylvanian families with nominal educational backgrounds; my father's father was a coal miner, and my mom's dad was a truck driver. But for some wonderful reason my parents were also passionate autodidacts, and voracious readers, and by the time they died, I would certainly say they were college material. My dad was in Mensa! My parents also forced me, in a sense, to appreciate the pleasure of reading, and through that pleasure to expand my educational and intellectual horizons. For instance, I was reading Emerson and Melville long before high school; my dad, bless his heart, who was a fantastic raconteur, used to read the poetry of Poe to my younger brother and I as bedtime stories. At the same time, I was reading the first issues of *The Fantastic Four* and *The Hulk* and lots of DC Comics and scrounging up old horror comics like *The Vault of Horror*, and watching *The Crawling Eye* on TV, or seeing the first release of a 1954 double bill of *Them!* and *Riders to the Stars* in a Tokyo theater when I was four years old. The first two movies I remember seeing, by the way.

Riders to the Stars ... (laughs). Bad science in that one. Or perhaps I should say, um, early ignorance of science. I vividly recall a shot of a dead astronaut floating past another spacecraft whose captain was looking outside his ship using a World War II submarine periscope! ... The visor on the corpse's helmet has blown out. Behind it, instead of a face, is a skull.

I'm four years old, right? A blank slate. This is one of my first movies—I thought I was watching a documentary! I shrieked at the top of my lungs, jumped out of my seat, ran up the aisle and out of the theater and immediately got lost. In Tokyo. And my mother, who taken me to this show, couldn't find me. She was frantic. Turns out I was just a couple of blocks down, having an ice cream cone with a Tokyo policeman in his little corner kiosk.

So. Seeing *Them!* and *Riders* during their initial release, which both had elements of science fiction and horror, made such an impact on me that I immediately became a science fiction and horror film fan. But who knows. If I'd seen *Singing in the Rain* first, I might have turned into a junior Bob Fosse.

In any event, I've recounted these stories to explain how I came to have a lifelong knowledge of, and passion for, the textual and the cinematic. That passion isn't limited to genre. My tastes are actually catholic, quite eclectic; they range from everyone like James Joyce and M.R. James and Jean Ray to George Saunders and Phil Dick to the most obscure, esoteric art films and blatantly commercial Hollywood product.

I was lucky enough to be available during a period in Hollywood where, as a freelance writer during the Seventies, I'd already been doing numerous pieces for everything from *Cinefantastique* magazine to the *Los Angeles Times*. Mostly, I was furiously writing to help support my wife and myself. Then a filmic window of opportunity opened.... [A] friend of mine, Mick Garris, started working at New Line Cinema. He said, "Paul, we know more about this genre stuff than half of the people working in the studios. I've got a job working that angle. You should get a job, too." I said, "Mick, I don't have any connections, I don't know how to do this." Mick then talked to someone, who turned out to be Gordon Armstrong, a vice-president of theatrical publicity at Universal Pictures.

Gordon called me in 1980. He'd done a little homework. He brought up the fact that I had done publicity work for Disney on *The Black Hole* and been one of the first people to bring to the San Diego Comic Convention a clip of an upcoming science fiction film. This was in 1978, right? So I was way ahead of that curve. To make a long story short, Gordon offered me a job as a studio publicist. I then started working on a single title, quickly moved up to juggling a lot of different films, genre and non-genre. From about 1978 until roughly 2005, I was either a junior and/or quasi-senior executive with various studios, or I was crewing and actually working on a number of films, or was putting together dozens of behind-the-scenes featurettes and EPKs—

Electronic Press Kits—before I eventually began co-producing TV shows and series.... Some of the theatrical films I worked on included *Conan the Barbarian*, with Schwarzenegger, *Conan the Destroyer*, *Return of the Living Dead*, David Lynch's *Dune* and *Blue Velvet*, *Manhunter*, *F/X*, *Robocop*, *Robocop 2*, in which I have a bit part as a narcotics detective and for which I was the Computer Graphics Supervisor, and *Starship Troopers*, in which I appear for all of ten seconds as a guy who pushes a cow into a pen holding a captured Warrior Bug, which immediately tears the cow apart.

On to Phil Dick. One of my great passions, as I indicated, was SF literature. I inhaled the works of golden age science fiction writers like Theodore Sturgeon, Robert Heinlein, Richard Matheson, Harlan Ellison, Fritz Leiber, Ray Bradbury, Issac Asimov, Alfred Bester, etc. Most of whom I eventually met. They were available to me as soon as my wife and I moved to Los Angeles from San Diego. One way I met my icons was by crashing cocktail parties at various Cons before I became a pro myself. That helped (*laughs*). I'd stick my hand out to someone and say, "I'm Paul! Who are you?" They'd say, "Gene Rodenberry." I'd go, "Oh! Oh! *Star Trek*!" They'd smile. Then I'd ask, "Why was the third season so awful?" (*laughs*). But I guess I did that in a gentle way, because I can still remember Roddenberry replying, "Because I wasn't the producer anymore." Which is true. He'd kind of let go of the reins, and Fred Freiberger became notorious for ruining that third season.

By the end of the 1970s I'd built up a vault of knowledge and a few contacts and a growing love for what I was doing. I was also just getting up a head of steam, professionally speaking, when 1980 rolled around. It was then that another opportunity presented itself—I'd heard that what would eventually be called *Blade Runner* was being scripted and prepped for shooting. Which leads to another sidebar. I first met Philip K. Dick in 1973, right here, at this University. He was here to do a short talk. His topic concerned the human and the not human, the simulacra, as well as the whole idea that behind the real world lurks another. Which interestingly enough—Phil and I used to talk about quantum mechanics back in 1977, before wave particle duality and quantum entanglement became the empirical *soups de jour*. Phil was telling me about Niels Bohr, Max Planck, and quantum foam; I was saying that, to my limited knowledge, Einstein had only finally and reluctantly agreed with all this after years of trying to poke holes in the whole notion of quantum physics. That's one topic I recall we discussed, anyway.

Phil was another autodidact, you know. He read omnivorously. Everything, everything. He was either reading, writing, or trying to find a girlfriend (*laughs*), with all due respect. As for the man, I found him to be exactly the opposite of the myth that is now out there. Phil was not some crazed, strung out, hallucinating, drugged out.... He was kind, he was warm, he was very funny. But he was also human. And to be human is to be flawed. He had a temper, for one. He also loved to talk. Then again, so do I. So that was a match made in ... well, somewhere.

Over the years we talked about his mother, too. Because although the situation was reversed, we actually came from similar familial backgrounds. I had a somewhat emotionally—well, not cold, because he could blow very hot, but my father didn't really know how to talk to me or father me, while my mom was warm and supportive. Reverse that and I think you can imagine what Phil told me his own parents were like. Anyway, Phil began talking about his mom, once we reached a certain level of trust. I think that that maternal relationship very much influenced Phil's own romantic interests. That's a personal observation, though. Who knows? Perhaps Phil was looking for a mother, in a sense. But that's just me. I'm sure some of you on this panel and out in the audience understand this topic far better than I.

I did use to go to Phil's apartment, the same one Daniel was talking about, and this was a few years before *Blade Runner* was a blip on the horizon. That was because I'd kept my reporter's nose to the ground. For example, I was aware that in 1975 an adapted *Electric Sheep* script had been written. One that had been dumbed down and that Phil disdained. "Maxwell Smart meets androids," as Phil put it. He described it as a bad sitcom. Horrible.

Then I found out that Robert Mulligan, the man who'd directed *To Kill a Mockingbird*, was involved in another adaption of *Do Androids Dream of Electric Sheep?* Which at this point was called *Dangerous Days*. That had been written by a New York-based actor and screenwriter called Hampton Fancher...

As for my involvement, somewhere around late '79 or early 1980 Phil and I talked and he said, "Hey, you know, it kind of looks like a *Sheep* movie might happen." I said, "Well, fantastic." I also said, "Look, I've been doing some work for the studios, maybe I should see if I can get something going for myself around this, because I loved the book so much and know what happened before when your other options fell through and blah blah blah... If nothing else, I'll see if I can get some word out." Long story short, I wound up...

Wait. Jesus. Here. This is the book that got me on this panel today *(holds up a book)*. This is *Future Noir: The Making of Blade Runner*. It essentially took me four years to write. It's been in continuous print for twenty years, it's in its thirteenth printing, and it's been sold to numerous foreign territories. Japan, the UK, Italy, Spain, Korea... I guess I did something right.

Honestly, though, I have to be humble about *Future Noir's* success. Because I was writing about someone else's product. I do think that I performed a fairly good job with my book. People seem to love and buy *Future* because it's exceptionally detailed and, more importantly, readable. But bottom line, I was the Boswell to Dr. Johnson's—Ridley Scott's—haunting, astonishingly crafted film. Also, I find *Blade Runner* to be such an amazing echo of so many core phildickian concerns, without being faithful to the novel itself. For *Blade Runner* is very unfaithful to *Electric Sheep*, in many ways. Yet Scott's film replicates the tonal qualities of Phil's fiction: the claustrophobia, the emotional constriction, the whole idea of what is real and what is not real. What does it mean to be human? What does it mean to not be human? And *BR* is drenched in melancholy; also, very concerned with death. Death and decay. Phil was afraid of death, you know…

I'm sure many of you know that Phil had, in the early '70s, gone through a period where he was living, well, almost on the street, metaphorically speaking. He was having strangers come in all the time and ripping him off. Anyway, I had an affinity with him there too, because at the time we first met in '73, I was entering a very "street" phase of my own life. We could talk honestly about that sort of lifestyle. I think that's one of the reasons he trusted me to whatever extent he did. Not to the same extent as someone like Tim Powers, of course, who knew Phil far better than I and was a much closer friend. Still, Phil did occasionally open up to me. About life, family, death, intellectual concerns, philosophical byways, all the things that fascinated him. He also loved to joke around. I say all this just, again, to reemphasize that the Philip K. Dick I knew was nothing like the PKD myth that's out there now. Phil did not have a third eye in his forehead. He did not walk around with mystic waves radiating off a scrambled brain. Phil was just a guy. Immensely talented, sure. Unique, definitely. Formidably curious and intelligent. But also ordinary. Sweet, kind, warm. Fun.

Another thing. Someone said earlier, or asked, how influenced was Phil by films? Well, I remember getting a phone call about two o'clock in the morning one night. Phil liked to do late-night phone calls sometimes, when he was up writing. "Hey, Paul," he says, "You go to all these movies." I go, "Yeah. Who is this?" And he goes, "Oh, It's Phil." I go, "Oh, OK," trying to wake up, since I'd been sound asleep. Phil says, "Did you ever see *3 Women*? The Robert Altman film?" I said, "Yeah, I love that movie." He says, "Yeah, I just saw it again. They had it at some art theater. Wow! What a great film! One hundred and twenty minutes about three women!"

Then I think I mentioned that *Women* reminded me of Bergman's *Persona*, where an actress metaphorically vampirizes a nurse's personality. Phil goes, "Oh yeah!," and we were off.

So yes, Phil Dick did see films and he did love them. But I think Phil's value-set and mindset and themes and concerns were there internally, from the beginning, and then emerged through his fiction. You can see, from the very beginnings of his writing, such as "Roog," that first short story, a phildickian through-line. Narratively, metaphorically, philosophically, in all the work he did. Interestingly enough, I once asked him why he wrote so much, why he was so prolific. He replied, "Well, I had five wives and I have a lot of alimony to pay off." I thought he was kidding. He was not kidding. Another myth punctured. Yes, Phil was prolific. He loved to write. He also had alimony payments! But Phil certainly had a mind that was just incredibly, incredibly concerned about the different types and aspects of being a human being. I mentioned that we loved to talk philosophy. I have a philosophical bent that I hide from most people, unless they're receptive to that. Phil was. We would just go on and on about the human condition. Partly, perhaps, because Phil lived in a rough neighborhood. A very rough neighborhood…

As for *Blade Runner*, we will talk later in the Q&A about *Blade Runner* and so on. But just to let you know, I was there from the moment that Ridley Scott was hired. I was there through all of pre-production. I was there through the entire shoot. I was there through all the special effects stuff. At the same time, I was working a day job at Universal Pictures. So, for almost a year I was living on two to three hours of sleep a day. I'm not exaggerating. And here's the thing—I did it on caffeine, not cocaine!

I'll pass on to Gary now.

Westfahl: I thought one question to toss out to the panel and perhaps in Paul's case the answer is obvious: the best Philip K. Dick adaption perhaps followed by the worst Philip K. Dick adaption.

In the first category, my surprising nominee as the best adaptation of a Dick story, not the best movie of his, would be *A Scanner Darkly*. It is remarkably faithful to the novel and its animation, I think, works especially well to convey what it is like to live in a constantly drug-influenced world. And the striking scene for me created a great contrast, was of a scene in the film *Naked Lunch*, where the William S. Burroughs character encounters a giant insect at the bar. And done as live action, it's very jarring. You think, "Great special effects, what a great insect," but it just doesn't seem to fit in with the rest of his experiences.

In *A Scanner Darkly*, when Keanu Reeves encounters some giant insects, because they're animated like everybody else in this land, it's like, "Oh, yes." The mailman comes, his girlfriend comes, the giant insect comes, it's all one of a piece. I think that's a remarkably effective Philip K. Dick adaptation. I'll ask the other panelists for a favorite Dick movie.

Gilbertson: I'd probably make it a dead heat between *Blade Runner* and *Scanner*. Certainly the worst one would be *Next*.

Sammon: I guess I'd have to agree. Obviously, I have a certain bias towards *Blade Runner*. But as far as a faithful adaptation, yes, *A Scanner Darkly*. Although I did find *Darkly's* animation off-putting as opposed to…. I understood what Linklater—who's a fine, fine filmmaker—was after. I love Linklater, I think he's a wonderful director. But for me, I saw *Scanner's* animation as more of a stunt. It was lovely to watch, but dramatically, all that animation threw me out of the picture. Everything that you see in *A Scanner Darkly* was filmed live action first. Then they rotoscoped, the term is—it used to be done by hand but now they can do it by software—where they place animation over the live action to replace the latter. Yeah, *Scanner* was definitely a textually faithful, moving film, despite my reservations. Still, I kept thinking, "Gosh, I wish I could stop being distracted by this psychedelia; I'd rather watch a live-action version of this." And I love psychedelia!

Still, *Blade Runner* remains, to me, not only the first but best PKD adaptation, at least cinematically. *Next*, on the other hand, is way down there; it did have a pretty cool nuclear devastation scene. But there are so many bad Philip K. Dick adaptations littering the bottom of the barrel it's hard for me to poke through them.

Westfahl: My hands-down candidate is *Total Recall*.

Gilbertson: Which one?

Westfahl: The original one, not that the remake is that much better. Watching *Total Recall* is so frustrating because you can see at the basis of it was a really good script and a few fragments of it remain before Arnold Schwarzenegger became involved.

I've described it as a good twenty-minute adaptation of the story "We Can Remember It for You Wholesale" padded out by ninety minutes of Arnold Schwarzenegger killing people. It's not only that the violence is so ubiquitous and repetitive but I think it's also so alien for Philip K. Dick, who so many people have emphasized was such a gentle person.

There's actually very little violence in his stories. In the original "Wholesale" story, when they tell Quail, "Gosh, I think we're going to have to kill you," he talks them out of it. But of course, in the movie they just start shooting at him and he starts shooting back and it goes on for another ninety minutes. I find that a very disheartening movie to watch.

Sammon: Just a bit of back story. *Total Recall* was originally going to be directed by David Cronenberg, based on Dan O'Bannon's and Ronnie Shusett's script. It was going to be a Dino De Laurentiis production. They worked on that for eight months, while David did a rewrite. But ultimately it did not fly. As many shows do, it ultimately collapsed. There are always reasons why, money or conflicting schedules or power plays and/or other things. *Total Recall* certainly would have been a completely different film if David Cronenberg had directed and rewritten it.... But the 1990 *Recall* that ultimately came out was not totally beholden to Arnold Schwarzenegger. It's more Paul Verhoeven's movie. Believe me, Paul might make some pragmatic allowances for star power, but Verhoeven movies are Verhoeven movies!

Again, I have first-hand knowledge of this. I worked with Paul on *Robocop*, and then I worked with him on *Starship Troopers*. I've written extensively about his work as well, including doing the licensed *Making of Starship*

Troopers book. Verhoeven has a strong, intelligent, unique personality. He loves to critique. He loves to provoke. He loves to push…

Back to *Total Recall*. Paul Verhoeven was the one pushing that cart. He was at the height of his career in 1990. Arnold was at the height of his career as well and, yes, they did turn it into a slaughter-fest. However, the Dickian concept of "Is this a dream or is it a reality?" was maintained throughout *Total Recall*. Paul loved that notion. Although, again, for a science fiction film, *Total Recall's* science was absurd. Take that scene where Arnold and the female lead are ejected, unprotected, into the Martian atmosphere near the end of the film. Their eyes start to bulge and they go through all these protracted near-death spasms and prolonged prosthetic effects before returning to normal. That's so silly. I told Paul later, "You know, I understand dramatic license, but Jesus, that was nonsense. This is not what's going to happen. They'd be dead very quickly. Their hearts would freeze." It's like being hard-vacuumed. I don't know if you know that.

Audience Member: Instant decompression.

Sammon: Yeah, except it's not explosive, it's implosive. Sub-zero as well. If you read … you can go online and find out exactly what would happen to you if you jumped out of a space shuttle clad only in your underwear. Hard SF literature has been writing about what would really happen in that situation, too. For decades. But in any event, *Total Recall*, in terms of its high body count, was calculated to provoke. Not just the violence—the entire film was calculated to provoke. That's why there's a mutant woman with three breasts.

Paul just loved that kind of stuff. Again, though, I said to Paul, "You know, *Total Recall's* ending and a lot of the other material was silly." He says, "Yeah, yeah, yeah, I know, I know, I know. But filmmakers deliberately play dramatic tricks to keep audiences in their seats." Then he said, "But, really, what in that movie was real? What was a dream?" So, Paul loved the phildickian aspect of that movie's "reality."

Westfahl: Two other prominent Dick adaptations that I would call mediocre—they're not the best, they're not the worst—would be *Minority Report* and *The Adjustment Bureau*. I've written lengthy reviews of them that you can find online.

What they show to me is that the difference between Philip K. Dick and Hollywood is that Philip K. Dick could come up with strange ideas and embrace them and adjust to them and I think that's true of the two stories that inspired those films. Hire psychics to predict who's going to commit a crime and arrest them before? It can work fine. Every so often strange people come along and readjust reality? Hey, I can live with that. When they take these ideas and make them into film, Hollywood's thinking, "Oh my Gosh, this is against freedom. This is against free will. Precog is evil and must be replaced.

The adjustment team must be overcome so that Matt Damon can do whatever he wants to do."

They become this very conventional morality tale of "the status quo must be maintained," whereas Philip K. Dick was perfectly willing to accept the fact that, hey, the status quo is going to be changed some day. Maybe we would think it's weird but maybe it'll be just fine for the people in the future. Hollywood can't deal with that.

Gilbertson: Very good point. It's interesting how many elements of Phil's writing Hollywood has difficulty with, mostly because they need a chase. That's what they're always looking for: an excuse for a good chase because if your film isn't fast-paced then it's not going to be a success.

Obviously, you can't stop to have philosophical ruminations in the middle of a chase. Every movie that's successful is, in essence, a chase movie. Really, in a sense we haven't moved very far from the old black and white movies where they chased through LA falling off fire trucks. When they do slow the chase down, it's just basically an excuse to reinforce the importance of the family, because that's a very safe wicket to defend. Of course, this is the reason I don't watch much prime-time television. Every program is, in essence, a reaffirmation of the family that is presumed to be watching that TV program.

Which is fine. I don't object to that at all. I just find it overly repetitive. Of course, one of the great joys of reading Phil is that there's very little repetition. You really have to pay attention. You have to wonder.

Sammon: I actually have a slightly different reaction to both *Minority Report* and *Bureau*. I thought *The Adjustment Bureau* worked in the sense that there was a true romantic chemistry between the leads. I looked at it as simply a romance with … yes, it had the chase elements. Yes, it had Terence Stamp as this "tweaker of the real." But I thought as a medium-budget film that was pitched at a mainstream audience, it worked rather well.

And *Minority Report*, I actually have high regard for. I think that it is not, of course—other than the Precogs and some of the elements that are in Dick's original short story—in any way a faithful adaptation. But there is an overall vibe throughout that film which I felt was very phildickian. One of the touches I loved was this street character who helps Tom Cruise out at one point, this shady guy who's wearing sunglasses. He apparently can see pretty well. But then he takes his glasses off and he has no eyes. I thought, "Wow. Somebody's actually read Philip K. Dick."

I understand that *Minority Report* divides a lot of PKD fans. Civilian audiences, though, love it. I actually kind of warmed up to it too, when I first saw it. Is it a rigorous Dick adaptation? No. Is it about 30–70? Yeah. Is it a Steven Spielberg film? 100 percent…

Westfahl: Perhaps it's time to see if anyone in the audience would have a question or comment. You'll have to shout but please go ahead.

Audience Member: I'd like to hear the panel's opinion of Ridley Scott's Amazon series based on *Man in the High Castle*, bearing in mind that Daniel says he doesn't watch television.

Westfahl: I haven't seen it either.

Sammon: Can you hear me? All right, fine. When I last spoke to Ridley … I'm writing a piece on *The Counselor* at the moment, the film Ridley did that's based on Cormac McCarthy's first produced motion picture screenplay. The film that no one has seen *(laughs)*…

In any event, Ridley asked me what I thought of *The Man in the High Castle*, because I had seen it *(the first season)*. Defaulting to my usual blunt self with Ridley, I said, "Well, it's faithful insofar as it incorporates Dick's basic idea of a street-level view of this alternate history," with the Japanese and the Germans winning World War II. I also said, "But it's not phildickian enough. It doesn't have enough weird or challenging edges to it."

To me, at least so far, *Castle* is basically a thriller/chase/espionage type of thing. I also said to Ridley, "It does improve as it goes along. But to my way of thinking, you sort of missed an opportunity here. Because you could have added more of Dick's skewed perspective."

Ridley stares at me. Then he goes, "You know what I thought the biggest mistake was?" I said, "What?" He said, "I wanted to direct the pilot, but then we had a re-write and I couldn't do it. I'm sort of sorry that I couldn't do it, because I think that would have changed the tone." So that's *The Man in the High Castle* from my point of view.

Westfahl: That, in a sense, is an iteration of the same old story. They go to Philip K. Dick because he's so strange and then in the process of adapting him they make it less and less strange. By the time it hits the theaters, it's just another action movie. I'm not surprised at all to hear that's what happened to that series. Someone else?…

Audience Member: Since you mentioned the director's cut, does the panel have an opinion about the two versions of *Blade Runner*?

Sammon: Let me go first on that. There are actually approximately seven versions. I've seen them all. The least-known was something that was done on CBS (television network), which was the first network to broadcast *BR* as a movie of the week. In that version, there are alternate scenes and what they call TV dialogue, which is cleansed of all of the cursing and so forth. A couple of scenes are also gone from that variety.

More backstory. While I was around *Blade Runner*, I made a few friends from the British contingent who were involved in making the film. *BR* had a British director, a British producer—Michael Deeley, whom I will always thank for opening the door to this film for me—and Katy Haber, a wonderful British production executive. Plus a great English associate producer named Ivor Powell. Ivor is the nephew of Dilys Powell, who used to be the film critic for *The Guardian* newspaper for many, many years. Then there was Terry Rawlings, *Blade Runner*'s editor, who is also English. For some reason I and the *BR* Brits got along like a house on fire. Those friendships helped me see variants of the film before *Blade Runner*'s initial release.

For instance, Terry would literally show me freshly edited *BR* scenes on a Moviola. Now, back then editors had access to what they called flatbeds, horizontal editing tables where you'd put a big reel on one side and a take-up reel on the other. The footage would run through a splicer and magnifier and backlit screen. Horizontally. The reels lay down flat. But the old Moviolas were upright, vertical devices. You may have seen these in photos or in older films and newsreels. Where there are upper footage reels and lower take-up reels and editors hold their foot down on a pedal, pushing it like an old sewing machine, as they watch the footage on a little green-metal surrounded screen about this big *(indicates a screen about three inches across)*. Moviolas were Hollywood's de facto editing device for decades; the first ones used by the Industry on a common basis, in fact.

Anyway. I saw portions of about four or five cuts of *Blade Runner* on a Moviola. Rawlings would ask me, "Hey, I've put a scene together, do you want to see some of it?" I'd say, "Sure." And this would be around one o'clock in the morning, or sometimes during the day, with just the two of us sitting there, watching. Fascinated. Having said that, and having seen virtually every *BR* variant, for years my particular favorite was what I identify in my book as the Workprint.

The Workprint was a cut they screened as a sneak preview in Denver and Dallas in 1982, while gathering audience reactions before Warner Brothers released *Blade Runner*. It's quite different from other versions of the film; for example, the Workprint has only one bit of narration, near the climax. Deckard and Roy Batty are on the rooftop. Roy's dying. Out of nowhere Deckard says, in voiceover, "I watched him die all night. It was a long, slow thing, and he fought it all the way." Then Deckard's voiceover went on for a few more sentences. But that was it. And for many years, I preferred that particular version: the Workprint. Until 2007's Final Cut.

I was around when the Final Cut was being done by Charles de Lauzirika and Ridley, by the way. I helped them color-correct a scene. Charlie, who was the producer and motive force behind the Final Cut, and who did a fantastic job, is younger than I. He hadn't been on the *Blade Runner* set, like I had. He called me and said, "You know, we've got a color problem with a scene. Ridley can't remember exactly what the lighting was like. Do you remember?" I replied, "Well, let me come down and see." I drive down from the forest in Altadena where we once lived to the Warner Brothers lot. I drive on, find the post-production stage where they're restoring the Final Cut—I think it was their big re-recording stage, although I could be wrong on that—and Charlie has a scene up on the screen. I go, "Oh, cool! Deckard discovering Pris under the veil! Yeah. I remember that. It was lit pinkish-red. Rose. Rose-colored." Charlie says thanks, Ridley tweaks it himself, and the scene is back to what it originally looked like. I was shown around the various editing suites and other departments where they were doing The Final Cut at various times as well. That was gracious of Charlie. So I had a tiny bit of input into that Final Cut. *Future Noir* was certainly lying around as a guidebook throughout the Final Cut's restoration, too.

As for my favorite version of *Blade Runner*, today it's The Final Cut. I did vacillate between the Workprint and the Final Cut at one point, but now it's the Final Cut. Incidentally, I loathed the original Theatrical Cut. Loathed it with a passion. I thought the tacked-on happy ending was completely antithetical to what had preceded it, and as for the voiceover, which was meant to echo a hardboiled 1940s *film noir*, that narration was dreadful! Badly, badly written.

There is a myth that Harrison Ford intentionally read the lines of that voiceover in a monotone, in order to sabotage the original theatrical cut's narration. That's not true. Harrison is much too much of a professional to pull a stunt like that. He read what was given to him. And what was given to him was literally coming off of a typewriter outside the recording booth and handed to him, hot off the platen. The original cut's narration was pounded out—an appropriate phrase—by Roland Kibbee, a guy who used to work for Burt Lancaster and Ben Hecht's production company. Kibbee then became a TV writer…

In any event, I hated the original theatrical release. The voiceovers are terrible, that bogus happy ending was added at the last moment, there's no unicorn daydream suggesting Deckard might be a replicant, etc., etc., etc. But the Workprint, ahh. That is available on multiple DVD sets. If anyone has the so-called Briefcase Set, that's the best one to get to see various versions of *Blade Runner*. It's a five DVD set. I did the audio commentary for the Workprint on that one. Some edited telephone interviews I conducted with Phil Dick are included in the Briefcase too. And I'm all over Charlie's *Dangerous Days*, the excellent documentary he did concerning *BR*. I had a mustache back then, though. People hardly recognize me now. I also had scalp hair back then!

On to the Final Cut. That version is the closest to what Ridley originally wanted. People ask, "Why are there so many different versions of *BR*?" The reason lies not at the feet of avarice—"Let's release as many versions of this film as possible to keep the cash flow going." They were due to Ridley's schedule. He has never, ever stopped working. He's *always* working. Partially because, in my estimation…. Ridley suffers from depression, you know. He has talked about this openly. He's called it, like Winston Churchill called it, the black dog that is forever nipping at his heels. That's one reason Ridley never stops, to outrun the black dog. He's a hurricane. Always moving forward. And for many years he had no interest in his legacy. Not at all. You could not get him to talk about *Blade Runner*. Well, except to me, perhaps. Ridley's always been focused on what's in front of him. And every one of the various versions of *BR* that came out before The Final Cut, which was also a bit of a nightmare, were the results of long, hard fought behind-the-scenes battles.

All these variants started appearing in 1990, really, at least publicly, when there was an accidental screening of the Workprint at a 70mm film festival in Los Angeles. The festival organizers thought they were going to be screening a regular 70mm version of the Theatrical Cut. But suddenly people were watching a version of *Blade Runner* they'd never seen before—it was the Workprint! Which in turn jump-started the release of the so-called "Director's Cut," which really isn't. I could go on and on about this but I've already sucked out the air; we don't have the time. The complete details are in here (*holds up* Future Noir *again*).

Anyway, to condense, *BR* kept morphing until 2007, twenty-five years after its initial release. In 2007 Charlie de Lauzirika and his associate Paul Prischman tracked down all of the elements of the film and sat and talked to people like me and other people who were concretely and creatively involved in the film and put together the version that Ridley always intended. Charlie even tweaked or re-shot a couple of scenes, such as pasting Joanna Cassidy's face over an obvious stunt woman during Zhora's death scene. Joanna, incidentally, fit into the same Zhora costume that she wore 25 years earlier. And she wore that during the Final Cut's digital greenscreen reshoots. Cassidy is another terrific *Blade* Runner person, by the way. She's a great friend of mine, a wonderful person. No shit, ok? I'm not blowing Hollywood pixie dust here. Joanna's a huge film buff. We go to the movies together. She's one of my movie buddies.

Back to The Final Cut. Between 2006 and 2007 Ridley finally was able to concentrate for about a month on restoring *Blade Runner*, after years of not really having the time to do otherwise. He said, "Ok. Here. This is the version I've always wanted, and intended." Incidentally, when you see the Final Cut, you should keep in mind that what you're seeing is not a film. The Final Cut was restored and distributed digitally. So what you're viewing, at home or in a theater, is usually a digital version. At the moment, there are very few celluloid versions of the Final Cut. Because studios have more or less gone completely digital. They're also throwing their original celluloid prints away. Or losing them. Studios have been forever supposedly archiving their back catalogs and then misplacing them. It's getting more and more difficult to see 35 millimeter films. DCP, or Digital Cinema Projection, is king these days…

Anyway, to wrap this up, there's your long, long story about the tangled history behind the varying versions of *Blade Runner*. Personally speaking, as someone who has been so deeply involved for such a long time with this film, I'd rank my favorites, top to bottom, as The Final Cut, the Workprint, The Directors Cut, The International Cut, and the Theatrical Cut. Did I just confuse everyone even more? (*laughs*)

Westfahl: OK, someone else?

Gilbertson: Just before we leave that, Gary, Karl Wessel told me a wonderful quote yesterday about *Blade Runner*, something Phil had said. When he read the script originally, Phil said it should be called, *Eat Lead and Die, Andy.* (Laughter)

Dick's SoCal Dream

JONATHAN LETHEM *in Conversation*
with SAMUEL SOUSA

The Philip K. Dick Conference, April 30, 2016

Sousa: We're going to be talking about Philip K. Dick today, and then maybe branching out a little bit more into Southern California and science fiction within the realm of Southern California.

My first question for you, since we're talking about PKD, is a three-parter. The second part of all three is the why, but here's the three-parter. What's your favorite PKD book? What's the one PKD book, if you could, you would wish you had written? What is the one PKD book you would want to be in?

Lethem: Best one to live in? That's great. I've fought over and over not to have to pick one absolute favorite, but then again I have *Ubik* tattooed on my arm, so I think I probably made my life alliance with *Ubik*.

Really, I would prefer to be allowed to say [six]: *Ubik, Stigmata, Martian Time-Slip, VALIS, Scanner,* and then the [sixth] spot open.... There are a lot of them that I love. But *Ubik* is at the summit, and then maybe just below it, *Scanner, Stigmata,* and *VALIS*.

VALIS maybe changed my life the most, in some ways. It was the first book I read when it was new. I was his fan while he was alive for a chunk of time, but I was reading old books that he'd written long ago. That book came out in '81, and I read it in '81. This emanation from the present of Philip K. Dick's brain, and just the difference in that book and the way he had changed into this other writer, and the way in which that book—now I see it as a very strong bridge to a kind of autobiographical fiction that I often write, and read a lot of by other writers.

I think that book is very emblematic for me. Finally, *Ubik* and *VALIS*. Maybe VALIS is the one I most would have liked to have written, although it's also the one I'd probably have been least qualified to write, among my favorites.

I almost think that I could be audacious enough to think I could have come up with *Ubik* and maybe executed parts of it even better because it's so slovenly in some ways. Other things about it I find intimidating and awesome and probably I couldn't have done.

VALIS requires the arcane obsessions that drove him hard at that time, and I don't have those, so I probably couldn't have written *VALIS*. To put together all that Gnosticism and make it drive the characters and the content of the book in the way that it does is unimaginable to me.

But I guess I could do an analogous project where a gravedigger is into old Funkadelic records … and that information could drive the book. If, instead of *Fortress of Solitude*, I'd written a book about a character driven insane by the suspicion that a certain musician appears on a certain track on a Parliament Funkadelic record from 1971, but he can't prove it, and he goes into another world… Maybe I could have done that.

Sousa: Want to write that down?

Lethem: Yeah. That'd be good. That'd be good. To live in is a very different problem. Do I get to be… I don't think I'd want to be the protagonist in very many of his books, but I might like to stand to one side and survive the mess.

Sousa: Why would you avoid that protagonist role?

Lethem: Well, I think one of the things I most admire about his writing is that the narratives are so conceptually extraordinary. The reality breakdowns, the paranoia, the metaphysics are so intense. But that makes him sound like a writer like Borges or something.

At the same time, what makes him really special is that the subject, the character undergoing these reality breakdowns, is so emotionally labile. So helpless. So at their mercy, and that seems extraordinary for the reader. It seems very, very challenging to be that person.

Because the beauty—the humor and the emotion and the sadness and the intensity, the real human aspect of his books—is that he comes up with these conceptual things and then, for the characters, everything actually depends upon them. They're not a sport, they're life itself.

That's not really a way to live, day to day. I might opt for one of the early absurdist ones. Maybe it would be best to live in the right part of *Clans of the Alphane Moon*. I could probably hang out with the hebephrenics and just spin records and smoke dope.

Be a hebephrenic, why not? That's OK. I found my people. You had a question?

Audience Member: The topic today is Dick's SoCal Dream. I'm just wondering what role you think Southern California … what effect Southern California had on PKD's writing, especially the last decade while he was here in Southern California?

Lethem: I'm going to take your question and I'm going to back up and do some frameworks, including explaining our difference in relating to the subject matter.

I'm from New York City and my understanding of and interest in California was cultivated by ... it was mediated. I knew both Southern and Northern California because of the Beat Generation, reading Jack Kerouac, reading Philip K. Dick, reading Dashiell Hammett and Raymond Chandler. Watching movies, seeing it in the backdrops, seeing it as the subject, watching a Robert Altman film like *The Long Goodbye*.

It was endlessly a series of images and ideas, notions. It was anything but a real place for me. One of the reasons that I was interested in having this conversation with Sam, apart from the fact that he and I just like to talk, is that he's the ultimate opposite. He's totally rooted in this place, knows it from the ground up.

Now he studies Californian culture, he thinks about it, and he's a devotee, as I am, of some of the people who've mediated it, like say Nathanael West, we share a love for Nathanael West, but all of those mediated experiences for Sam are laid on top of innate, rooted, local knowledge ... somatic knowledge of this place.

That sets up us, and where I'm starting from.

When I tried to understand California or think about California, initially I was a very, very avid consumer of a lot of those things I just mentioned, Raymond Chandler and Philip K. Dick and Hollywood films, long before I got to come out here. Even though I got to come out here when I was nineteen, I'd already developed such an exaggerated sense of what this place meant and what it was for and what was interesting about it.

A lot of what I'd absorbed was really wrong because, of course, it was a sensorium, it was images, it was a simulacrum. It was a fiction, and this is a real place. But a lot of it was right because one of the things that strikes me about California, having arrived here, is that it is a place made up partly of reality and fantasy, fictions.

It's a place very deeply informed by utopian concepts, of the idea of the American self-reinvention kind of meets its western edge here, right around "Go West, young man." It's a place where history has been expunged. Europe is very far away and instead you get to, ostensibly, start fresh and make a utopian dream here, and self-invent. Now this has lots and lots of positive and negative results.

It's also a very dystopian place, precisely because those ideas are insupportable, and in their collapse, in their unsustainability, you get all sorts of disasters. You get people like in Nathanael West's *Day of the Locust*, who come here from the Dust Bowl, essentially, with a dream that they're all going to be in the movies and they end up just staring through a screen at a magical world that they can't enter.

Sousa: It makes me actually think ... probably the book I identify most with what you're saying, especially the idea of the west and hitting that edge, is *They Shoot Horses, Don't They?*, which quite literally takes the most nagging, or negative, character in the book out onto the edge of a pier, into the middle of the ocean, and kills her.

Lethem: It's like, could there be another place outside of this? No, actually. One of the things that always fascinated me was learning—I don't know if this statistic holds true anymore, but there was a point at which the greatest number of per capita of suicides in the United States was the Bay Area, which seems really paradoxical because isn't this a place…

First of all, the weather is temperate, it's marvelous. People come there to fulfill themselves, but it's precisely, I think, that if you're living in a bleak place, if you're living in Pittsburgh or the Dust Bowl or North Dakota, if your life is shitty, you can project that and be confirmed that the environment tells you, "Well, of course it is." Right? It's a condition of reality.

But if you go to a place where everyone is avidly selling themselves and their environment as "We've reached it! We're fine, we're great! You can do whatever you want here, total freedom! It's wonderful," then any bleakness you discover must be … you must be the problem. So you kill the problem.

You can't kill North Dakota or Pittsburgh, but if you're in the Bay Area and everyone is living the dream and telling you that all the time, then if you're bummed out, you're the sore point. That was a theory of mine.

I'm still backing up in a way, to set up an adequate answer to your question. For me, a lot of what I responded to in Philip K. Dick's vision of California, because remember, I was young enough I wasn't reading the LA books yet. He published *A Scanner Darkly* when I… Whatever, I guess I would have been sixteen, fifteen, but I didn't find him right away.

I was reading about *Dr. Bloodmoney*, I was reading about the Rim, and San Francisco in his books. Again and again, I was reading about Oakland and Berkeley, even without really completely putting the geography together. Some of this connected to what was already a lot of fantasy for me because I had read a lot of the Beats and I had this idea that the Beat Generation was still a living thing.

Well, if you go to North Beach, there are poets, it is still a concept there. My parents were hippies, so even just the residue of Haight-Ashbury, the idea of the Bay Area as a place for alternative culture, for specifically anti-New York … the Old World hierarchies, the Ivy League crap, Columbia University that Ginsberg had fled. This whole sense that the Bay Area was a place to get free of that kind of thing was very powerful for me, so when I discovered Dick's novels and I identified with them and I saw these signifiers, that seemed to connect and feed me.

One of things is that, from the distance of New York, Southern California by contrast is presented to you a little bit like the Annie Hall-Woody

Allen moment. The flat, grotesque, superficial car culture, writers going there to have their lives ruined by Hollywood.

You get a certain amount of that, having lived in the Bay Area for a while, the Bay Area also digs caricaturing Southern California that way, too. Since I went from New York to the Bay Area, both in my imagination and then in my life—I lived in Berkeley and Oakland for ten years in my twenties when I was becoming a writer, and I didn't come down here at all.

I had that weirdly, doubly reinforced. Even as I was discovering California and finding out the ways in which it was a real place and not just a fantasy, LA remained to me this very bad cartoon. I understood it very poorly and I thought it was all one thing, and that one thing was contemptible.

What's interesting, too, if you see early references to Southern California in Dick's writing, he'll participate to some extent. I can't remember which novel it was, but … it's glimpsed in the backdrop of some book as being only a place where there's just a permanent race riot and it's gotten taken over, it's one big race riot.

You also find early references, mostly to, in a way, the simulacrum culture down here, like Disney's Lincoln robot, who actually is a very sympathetic and marvelously humane character because Dick loved that kind of paradox. But his identifications are with emblems like Disneyland, or a race riot. He's not dealing with this as a real cultural geography.

When he ends up here, it's not just, of course, that his life has changed. The culture has also changed. Through the sixties, especially in the science fiction demi-monde, into the seventies, although it begins to curdle in the seventies, but you can still feel it in a way, when you go back to Berkeley, that you're entering a bubble where the counterculture was never completely…

Sousa: Dissolved.

Lethem: Dissolved, right.

But in Dick's life, and in the culture, things were different by the time he's writing something like *VALIS*. *A Scanner Darkly*, of course, is the pivotal book because it's the one that says, "This world that I've been a part of is exposed in this landscape."

There's something about this landscape and the way people are living in isolation in these apartments that's obviously a transmission about his own experience of how his life has changed. It's relatively barren, he waits for visitors, and he's in this spatiality.

There's no downtown, there's no Tupper & Reed, there's no university as an emblem of the authority he hates, but the intellectual life that he cravenly admires. There's just the highways and the apartments, and it's like, "What is going on?" and "Who am I?" It's me and my record collection in a room, and then we take drugs and we pass out.

It's a really different cultural geography for him. It's one, I think, that mirrors the exposure of the ideals of a communitarian counterculture existence which would.... Even as he's a writer who is so alone and classic and unique and strange and distrustful of affiliations, in his Bay Area writing, he is nevertheless still subscribing in a certain way to an ideal of community, and a lot of those books are about the challenges, the fractures, or the violations of tribal identities, kinds of freaks of various natures.

Dr. Bloodmoney obviously being the outstanding example of how he turns dystopia into an opportunity for people to form a new kind of tribalism or a new collective identity. Even in the horrible Martian books, the networks, the systems of human beings are trying to sustain some form of community in a challenged, radical circumstance.

The psychics in *Ubik*, they're like a tribe. Down here, he begins to deal with this inevitable fragmentation and isolation.

Audience Member: What year does he come to Southern California?
Lethem: Well, the move is, what, it's in '70...
Sousa: '72, I think.
Lethem: '72? Yeah.
Sousa: ... so how much of that do you think is comparable to the sort of a collapse of the '60s? ... How much do you think the collapse of that dream influenced the worlds that he crafted?

You're talking about isolation, and that's really what you're seeing in the sixties—the shortcomings of civil rights, the shortcomings of the hippie movement, counter-culture, the anti-war protests, feminism—all of these things that were going to bring us a utopia and, for whatever reason, were battered out of existence.

How much of that do you think affects the writing he does?

Lethem: ... Dick was always of his time, but always set himself apart from it. I think these things were very influential on him, but *unlike* some other writers. You could pick a science-fiction writer like Theodore Sturgeon or a literary writer like Richard Brautigan. You could say, there are some writers, who, despite being very unique sensibilities, were able to identify fully, and say, "This is all... I'm part of this counter-culture."

I don't think Dick ever had an unambivalent relationship to the sixties, because he was prone to seeing new authoritarianisms or perverse ideological pitfalls opening up, even in idealistic or utopian scenes.

Also, I think you could even just say he was an instinctive contrarian or dissident. He was a dissident against anything, and everything, like "What do you got?" Kind of like Marlon Brando in *The Wild One*. But of course he was also a product of and a participant in these things, at other levels. I think he had deep affiliations with just the idea of...

You could hear him writing about this in certain places, where he starts to only want to hang out with young people, because, at a certain level, he's identifying with a "never trust anyone over thirty" kind of concept, even though he himself is a little old in the tooth.

Sousa: I'm over thirty, and I can't blame him.

Lethem: He's got this sort of permanent "the kids are all right," even when of course the kids are not all right. He wants to be around them because he feels like there's something that they're suffering or seeing, that they have access to a sacred reality just by being on the outside of institutional authority.

Yes, I think that of course it was costly to him, as it was costly to so many people, to see those kinds of Utopianisms fragment at the end of the seventies...

Sousa: We were talking before this about Art Spiegelman or Gary Panter and *Slash* magazine, that dissident attitude, and that's why they are identifying with him. Do you think there's something inherent about it? I guess what I would say is that there seems almost to be something inherent about…

The primary goal, the primary focus of Southern California seems to be the individual, and any kind of encroachment on that is cause for unrest, whether emotional or physical violence. So we were talking about *Slash*, which was an early punk magazine, and so many people associated with that were making a pilgrimage to see the PKD…

Lethem: … coming to find him.

Sousa: Yes. But then also just expanding that world out thinking about *Black Flag* or *X*, these punk bands. Because Southern California punk was so distinct, it seems to me that maybe there's a draw there. Maybe it wasn't what drew him here but a connection he found.

Lethem: Yes. We've talked about this in other contexts. It's so funny. We are also a generational… We talk across the generational divide, as well as the geographical one.

I identify with punk. A version of punk came along to galvanize me at a crucial time in my coming of age, as it did for you in yours, but they're two different punks. Mine was the New York, very decadent, arty—Ramones, Patti Smith, Talking Heads.

Even though it set itself up as a counter-culture by contrast to something like SoCal pop, it's quite privileged and it has a bohemian privilege to it. It's immediately surrounding itself with things like connections to Paul Verlaine.

Kids identified with it, but it's not really a blue-collar, pure indigenous thing. It's kind of fancy, and it was much more strongly connected to the hierarchy of preceding rock and roll. Patti Smith comes out of Bob Dylan and says so. There isn't that much of a returning it to the lower classes, even though that fantasy is in there somewhat.

Sousa: Even though she comes from that. If you're going to pick someone like Smith, she comes out of the working class, for example.

Lethem: Right, she does, but there's still this royalty in the way that that kind of punk is formulated, which has to do with New York City. It has to do with at least the ease of connection both in time and space to the record industry.

Whereas the L.A. punk that galvanized you growing up really was a kind of exile culture. You have a few things in the background that succeeded, kind of succeeded, like *X*.

Sousa: Even that's minimal.

Lethem: Even that's minimal. Mostly it had this lineage of cult bands—the *Screamers*, and so forth—that are just really only for the people who saw it. You had to be at the show.

The truth is, you could buy a Patti Smith record. Yeah, it's a great bragging point if you went and saw them at CBGBs once, but it's also true that they'd continue and you could see them at the same New Jersey theater and it was really just a rock show.

But the *Screamers*, it was like a secret occurrence. It was really avant-garde, very blue-collar avant-garde. I do think that Dick is a good emblem for that permanently dissident, non-affiliated kind of cultural expression.

Now, of course, Art Spiegelman actually gentrified himself quite nicely. He's got Pulitzer Prizes, on the cover of The New Yorker all the time.

But the atmosphere around *Slash* magazine, the kinds of things that were uprising, and the fact that they were looking for … to me this connects very strongly also to another underground. Not a music underground, but the *Zap* comic, the cartoonists Robert Williams and Robert Crumb and Spain Rodriguez—those guys, who were essentially non-assimilable.

Crumb, eventually, sort of, he's in museums and stuff, but for the most part they were true dissidents, and their work contains a strong grain of skeptical amusement about the sixties counter-culture. It doesn't tend to subscribe to it fully.

I think that Dick's relationship to hippiedom, in some ways, it seems to be similar to the *Zap Comix* guys. It was like, "Yes, but … a lot of freaky stuff is great, but I don't want to start signing up for your new revolution. Or maybe you forgot this other old stuff is good, don't forget to do stuff and fantasize about it."

Sousa: It's almost like they don't want to play for any teams. This fits better into Southern California, the sense of individual self-reinvention.

Lethem: I'm going to go on another tangent. This is where I wish Erik Davis had shown up to talk with us about SoCal indigenous mystical traditions. In a weird way, there's a lineage from the Aimee Semple McPherson stuff, the Nathanael West era apocalyptic religion and what you find in *VALIS*, and that is that, as the sixties fragmented, there was so much disaffiliation and so much isolation and disappointment… I really owe it to Erik for identifying this for me, helping me believe that it was a thing… The girl who shows up at the door wearing the thing is not in a vacuum in *VALIS*, wearing the fish symbol. That in Southern California culture specifically, one of the places the hippie dream went to hide when it was unsustainable, politically or in other places, was in Christian freaks. That that was a place where there could still be a tribalism. That there was a very powerful movement of some of the idealism and some of the sense of crowd identification or affiliation or identity that took some of the elements of the sixties counter-culture, but switched them from being political or drug-cultural or based in rock and roll culture and moved them instead into mystic Christianity, specifically like putting the fish on your car and going door to door and being a Jesus freak.

And that that was something that Dick was also catching the scent of and seeing. This idea that emerges in the late books that's there going to be an underground and it's going to be a Christian underground is a residual idealism that I think connects to the way… You talk about Southern California being fundamentally about the individual, but I think things are always themselves and their opposites.

When you come into this environment—this is to go back to my big generalization about California being the final destination of the American dream of self-reinvention and leaving behind all the old orders of hierarchies, old religions—then you're in a vacuum and the individual is in a panic, "Who do I follow? What do I do?"

That's why we get L. Ron Hubbard and Aimee Semple McPherson and Jim Jones. You get people stepping into that vacuum, sweeping up the energy of all these atomized individuals and saying, "Here's the new thing. Yeah, we threw off the shackles of the old, but I'll be your new leader, don't worry." Because the isolation that comes with the possibility of self-reinvention is also terrifying.

Sousa: It makes me think about Chuck Smith—I think, if I got his name correct, he was the founder of Calvary Chapel—who was doing just that in Costa Mesa, right down the road from Santa Ana, in the seventies. This idea of taking, of creating a church, a Christian church of Calvary Chapel…

I'm sure if you're from Southern California, you will certainly be aware it's a chain of churches around the Southland. A very, very large church, broad membership, but also a very, at this point, a very right-wing, very almost what you could predict as being sort of Christian.

Anyway, when he starts the church, it's a freaks' church. That's his goal, that everybody can come in with long hair, with sandals. Anything goes here. Take that utopian ideal that you were getting from rock and roll, from the counter-culture and mold it into your Christian faith.

Now if you look at that, it's become something much more conservative, much more right-wing, but it seems like… There's a vacuum and you can't instantly connect to that definition of what you're going to be; there's a vacuum that can't be rectified.

Lethem: Another result is to participate in a mob or a riot, which is what Nathanael West is portraying at the end of *The Day of the Locust*, is that there's, in that vacuum, just a collective identity of tearing down like lemmings, or lemmings marching into the sea or destroying the temple.

I want you to talk about what you, as a witness to California punk... that whole era, what was your route to connecting coming of age in that music scene, in skateboarding, in the instinctive attractions of that culture to a local version of the literary? Because you have a very interesting image of.... You're very conscious of small press publications and local authors. There almost is a corresponding literacy in this area that you've turned me on to.

There were some things I was aware of, like Aaron Cometbus, the great Berkeley-Oakland zinester, though I think he's living in New York right now—a documentarian of Berkeley's and Oakland's counter-cultural life, of the Gilman Street Project and so forth.

How do you trace your own awareness from skateboarding to Philip K. Dick?

Sousa: I probably have a pretty typical mid-thirties avenue into punk, which was *Green Day*. But almost instantly, and I can even go back before that and say I always identified with stuff that was outside of whatever was in my immediate culture. I grew up in Chino Hills, very conservative, white, very run-of-the-mill, small-town Southern California. And so early on, late eighties—I had an older brother who gave me all the access to this stuff—when gangster rap culture [was] happening in its early form, there was an immediate response to me because it's something so different. Something so exciting and so against everything else that I could see with my eyes, like everything that's visually happening.

For example, this isn't Southern California, but on the *Public Enemy* album, *Fear of a Black Planet*, there's a song called "Burn, Hollywood, Burn" that's about the fact that there's a lack of black actors and black characters in the mainstream movies. And this was the song I probably identified with most as a kid. It's totally absurd. I wasn't in the industry, I wasn't a part of it or anything like that, I'm not black, but there was a desire in me to just identify with being outside things.

Just to give you how dedicated to not being on the team and trying to be an individual I was, even when I went to Catholic high school, that was a choice. I went to Catholic high school for two years. It was like, "I got to get away from all the people I grew up with and meet a new set of folks in a new environment." It failed miserably; I couldn't have felt more alone than being in Catholic high school.

When I got into punk, I already skated, and there's just this outsider sort of counter-culture that you can access at various levels. You can be from Huntington Beach. You can just touch a tip of the iceberg, maybe listen to a few punk bands. Or you can go to a surf show, where there are bands playing. Same thing with skating. But you could also dive deeper in and follow any kind of avenues there were—there were blues punk bands and crust punk bands, there were street punk bands—any kind of avenue you wanted to go there.

Probably the thing I take most from punk is a sense that, for lack of a better term, that nihilism can work. That allowing people to live and exist in their own realities with a certain amount of respect can work.

I remember there's a great zine called *Fire Is Metaphor*, and the last line in it is, "Nihilism works." Basically, the idea is that if you allow people just to be themselves, you can find a sort of currency with which everybody can make their lives work. I don't know that that is actually plausible on a grand scale, but it's an attractive outsider idea.

It was definitely something that attracted me because I felt like when I came into the punk community I could be whatever, go down whatever avenue. I also know and have said multiple times, I don't want to join anyone's team. I don't want to be on anyone's team. I keep my team small.

The next step then was to go down these avenues of zine culture. You access places like Rhino Records or, when I was growing up, Fullerton was the spot for Bionic Records over on Chapman and State College, which was the best place to go. Both these shops had great zine selections and all kinds of obscure music and curiosities to get into.

I have to say that still exists here in Fullerton in two different ways. With Black Hole Records downtown, which is very much dedicated to that early eighties, almost that cross where Black Flag meets Christian Death—that kind of macabre punk. Then also with Burger Records, which is down State College and is much more of a rock and roll freak thing. I don't say that negatively, I just mean they have long hair and the place smells like dope every time you go. They're committed to aesthetics. Both places, as well as the other record stores mentioned, all had this zine selection, all had this culture to access.

It's interesting to have come of age in what seems like, and I know it's not totally what it seems like to a certain degree, the last little bit of that searching, because now I can get zines from anywhere, all over the country.

All I have to do is get online, find the zine distributor, and access whatever looks most interesting, whether I'm getting it online, digitally, or I'm ordering a copy. Whereas before, I got every new issue of Cometbus because I determined the distributor.

Lethem: There used to be a thing called "Factsheet Five," which a lot of people who were in concurrence with the *Philip K. Dicks Society* environment

… [followed]. It was run by a guy named… Mike Gunderloy… He was the Internet before there was any Internet. He would just list every zine in America and give you their address. He fostered a culture of swapping zines. He would say the best way to get the zines is to make one yourself and to swap them with another.

It was a remarkable example of something I think you and I are both interested in, which is the black hole, the gulf that exists between what's scanned and digitized because either corporations or boomer-age fans with resources at the helm of cultural projects have digitized them and reissued them now [and what's not digitized].

When the Internet starts there's a gulf. There's a dead spot or a blind spot. That's where a lot of the zines that you and I care about and grew up with are still dwelling. You google them and you can't get barely any reference whatsoever. There isn't evidence of them. Ironically because they're too near, they're too close to the beginning of the Internet.

Sousa: I'm always surprised when I google something and it seems not to exist. I somehow feel like my memory is wrong. I'm getting the title of the album or the band wrong. When you're talking about zine culture that you can find, when you do that, you do that alone. I mean you were talking earlier about the *PKD Newsletter*, but even that is going to be … not only is it a small, very specific group or setting, it's going to be a small group that is assembled.

Most zines are done by one person and it takes time and work to photocopy everything, staple everything together. What's interesting about, and different from say, like, Calvary Chapel or the underground community, is that there are people who in the underground are trying to retain a sense of individualism.

They want to retain the liberty that comes with it. They're checking to make sure it embraces something that really feels like their own, but they're also desperate for community. That's why they go to shows and they slam into each other.

They're desperate to feel that physical connection that someone else exists in a manner of speaking, sort of marinating in this stew of loneliness and self-determination.

Lethem: Let me circle around in this weird way to the part where we began, with this framework of California as real and then [not] at the same time…

When you and I first met, you were talking about rewriting a Nathaniel West novel. I come, as I said, from this California is the myth of the idea and the image of the catastrophe of the utopia, all these things before it's a real place for me.

I then come and see it and I begin to work out, conjugate on the ground, the somatic experience with all this baggage. What's it like for you coming up from inside Chino Hills, when you hit people writing in various ways, contending with the utopia and dystopia? The whole West, how do you conjugate that…?

Sousa: Oh, I connect with it… We had a conversation in one of the courses I teach last week about the fact that people in the Mid-West don't necessarily always have fences around their property.

It was kind of this thing where students couldn't wrap their head around, "well, how do you know where you're property line is?," you're not going to worry about it. If you drive outside of Chicago and you're heading west, you've just been on the highway, out towards DeKalb, you go by past miles, and miles, and miles of track homes, where there are no fences. Nobody is concerned about the property. Here, it's extinct. You're not just putting up a fence or wrought iron fence. You're most often putting up brick walls. Or you're putting up a…

Lethem: Cinder block walls.

Sousa: Right. Cinder block walls. Thank you. It is the same thing with the cars. Mass transit has grown here only really over the last decade. It's become more and more accessible, so it's not Chicago. It's not like New York. It's not like the Bay Area.

Lethem: Yeah. It's not built into the concept of the city.

Sousa: No.

Lethem: It's right on top of it.

Sousa: In fact, you know that from the way history … it was actively fought against. There was—what was that—The Good Earth Foundation? Which was Ford, Standard Oil, and Firestone Tires that fought to actively end the rail system, in Los Angeles.

When they succeeded in that, they created a real … individualism, at that point, was woven into the fabric. Especially, because…

Lethem: It became infrastructural.

Sousa: Right. Because, especially, ten-fifteen years later, as the suburbs just expanded in the post-war era. That's exactly what it is. Everyone is going to become the individualist. Now, look there are sincere moments of attempts at utopia… In *City of Quartz* [Ed.: *Excavating the Future in Los Angeles* (1990) by Mike Davis], he writes about, I think it's Llano Del Rio and this idea that people are setting up this circle of utopia out here in the West. I just think that is a space where that's impossible. It's impossible, I think, to ultimately forge…

Lethem: Something like Victoria Gardens is a nightmare vision. I don't know how many have been to that place, but it's a place where the post office and the library are incorporated into the mall. The mall has swallowed the town.

Sousa: Yeah. That actually also happened to Chino Hills, and its base would be Irvine Spectrum or the Block, here in Orange, where they created these outdoor malls, ostensibly to function like downtown areas. What they've done now, and really, it's kind of really interesting to see, if you go to the Shoppes in Chino Hills or to Victoria Gardens, they have relocated all of the city services to the mall. Even in Chino Hills, the fire department, the sheriff's department, City Hall, the county library, it's all located across from the Barnes and Noble. It's all located across from the Vans store and Trader Joe's.

They've incorporated, with like you're saying, the bureaucracy into the commerce. What's even great, even better about this place, is that they've tried to design them like small towns. When you go to Victoria Gardens, it's not like it's just an outdoor mall, you can literally drive through. There are streets, and stop signs, and crosswalks, and parking spaces where you go to.

Lethem: It's sort of like going to Lego Land getting in one of the Lego cars. It's like a little pretend car. Your car becomes like a pretend car in a pretend town…

Sousa: Just after I read Baudrillard's *Simulation and Simulacra* I went to Victoria Gardens for the first time, and you become just aware of everything. Almost everything he's saying is exactly true. It's becoming a map for a small-town experience.

It's a simulation rather than reality. I was aware of the way things were really commercialized here, and I think that was part of what drove me. Just to look for something else, anything else I could find. Dos Lagos is coming to mind, too. That's another place where the city hall is at the mall. It's nice that you want to try to this… It's very, very, very, earnest, wholesome idea to want to be able to create that kind of downtown atmosphere. It's nice that you are trying to do that for your city and kind of, hopefully, give your city that small town feel.

Jonathan and I both live in Claremont. Claremont naturally has that feel.

Lethem: It's a simulacrum of a small, college town in New England.

Sousa: Yeah. For something in Southern California there's nothing similar to it. It's such an anomaly that it seems natural. Whereas now with these towns, you talk about the fact that every three exits there's a Kohl's and a TGI Chili's Applebee's. It just becomes like the map gets regenerated.

Lethem: It's like the background in *The Flintstones* where you see this tree and the rock. I suspect that we should open this up to questions. I know we'll keep talking.

Audience Member: Could either of you speak to the specific places that Dick lived, Fullerton and Santa Ana? What did it mean to be in those places in the seventies, that are particular from the rest of Southern California?

Lethem: It's a question for you, more than for me. Apart from the fact that we are occupying some of that ground right this minute, I know them essentially through his fiction.... What I know about, apart from once visiting the Nixon Museum twenty years ago, having some Vietnamese food, I think about these areas through his letters.

Sousa: I don't know that I can speak specifically about that, but what I find fascinating both about the late seventies and Santa Ana and Fullerton is the paranoid response. I feel like that comes through in *A Scanner Darkly*, that kind of paranoia that's there.

If you think about the band The Middle Class, who are coming out of Santa Ana in '77, '78, often referred to as the first hardcore record, it's got that same kind of detachment from the mainstream, where people are looking at the status quo and wanting to get away from that.

If you look at what's going on here in Fullerton, you've got Social Distortion, Agent Orange, Adolescents, Black Hole Records, it's the same type of thing. People are looking into getting away from the status quo. Or even if you fast forward, and the guy's name is going to escape me now, but his first name is Steve.

He was the guy who, about a decade, decade-and-a-half ago, was elected to city council in Santa Ana. It was done on a fluke. It was a write-in campaign. I can't speak extensively, but here's a guy who his first claim to fame was that in the '80s he was arrested for shoplifting from Albertson's.

At that point, he wrote a book in which he believed that the Bank of California, Albertson's and, I want to say, McDonald Douglas were in a conspiracy with the government to control minds. This guy, eventually, about fifteen, twenty years later, gets elected to city council.

It's totally worth your time if you look him up on YouTube, you can watch him use the city council platform as just a way for himself to vent about mind control, about corporate conspiracy, about gun control. At one point, he brings his gun to the city council to talk about how safe it is that he can bring a gun to the city council.

There inherently is in Southern California, whether Dick specifically was attracted to it or not, a paranoia that is in his work, a sort of cynicism and paranoia about the system.

Lethem: It's funny, it popped into my head, just the atmosphere also of that film *Repo Man*. "Ordinary fucking people, I hate 'em." The sense of the completely anodyne reality, that the only thing you can do is abreact and freak out, like the characters in *A Scanner Darkly*.

Sousa: I have my own question for you now. Do you think there's any connection between Philip K. Dick and *They Live*, and what that connection is?

Lethem: There's a very literal connection which you probably don't know. The guy who wrote the short story that was the basis for "They Live," Ray Nelson, who's still around in the Berkeley area or the Bay Area, collaborated with Philip K. Dick on that—and was one of the two writers who ever collaborated on a full-length novel with Dick—so there's a traceable link.

Obviously, *They Live* is like a super distillation of a really simple Philip K. Dick idea, in a way made more viable by eliminating some of the kinds of elaborations or paradoxes that he would have been prone to saddle it with.

He would never have stopped with just the glasses showing you the aliens and now we can kill them, he would have turned it a hundred different ways. Of course, when I wrote about *They Live*, one of the things that I enjoyed doing, if you watch that movie ten, fifteen times. The paradoxes of John Carpenter's simple allegory start to permeate in the places where it gets a little weird around the edges, you realize with Philip K. Dick, implications sneak in anyway. Our sympathy for these creatures, in a way.

How does it feel to be from a place where everyone knows that our entire species is ugly and all we want to look like is other species? All of these weird Philip K. Dick vibrations just helplessly attach themselves to this, even as John Carpenter's trying to keep it a really radical, simple allegory of Reagan yuppies, but I think it's got his DNA in it, in a sense. Absolutely...

Audience Member: Just a comment about Santa Ana. I visited there for the first time two days ago. Very noticeably, his neighborhood really looks like a neighborhood of churches. It's also a big Mexican village that was there at the time.

He wrote about feeling like he'd moved to kind of a healing land with all the streams and such. I just wanted to make that comment.

Lethem: It's something, again, that was touched on this great panel yesterday. His glancing motifs of race difference. That's something that he never really engaged with full throttle. It sneaks into his work in interesting and odd ways. The black president here, the race riots in LA that are looked at for a moment there.

The existence of indigenous, or native cultures, crops up in the mainstream books in the form of the jaw ... his interest in Cro-Magnon Man. The idea that we are living in a place that isn't our own—that there are predecessors, ancient histories and civilizations.

It is the great counter narrative to the fantasy of the blank slate. That California is a place for civilization to reinvent because it's empty. Is a fiction, right? It wasn't. It required a violent displacement and eradication, an amnesia, to make it work.

The idea that that amnesia might make itself and reveal itself is obviously a very Dickian motif...

Sousa: Any other questions?

Lethem: Maybe that's it.

Sousa: Thanks very much, everyone.

Appendix
Images and Ephemera from the 2016 Philip K. Dick Conference

Images

Our conference mounted an art show and display of California State University, Fullerton Special Collections material as well as running panels and paper sessions. We share a selection of key images that emerged from that and surrounding events: a photo of Dick in the Special Collection archives of the Pollak Library, organizing his materials for deposit (for which he was paid a small stipend); a map by artist Felipe Flores, "Philip K. Dick in Orange County," from the Hibbleton Gallery show, downtown Fullerton, 2015; the conference poster portrait of PKD; and selected images from "Here and Now," the show in the Atrium Gallery of the Pollak Library at CSUF, 2016, in which artists responded to four key works: *Do Androids Dream of Electric Sheep?*, "Minority Report," *The Man in the High Castle*, and *The Three Stigmata of Palmer Eldritch*.

188 Appendix

Philip K. Dick in the CSUF Special Collection archives of the Pollak Library (CSUF Pollak Library Special Collections, circa 1972).

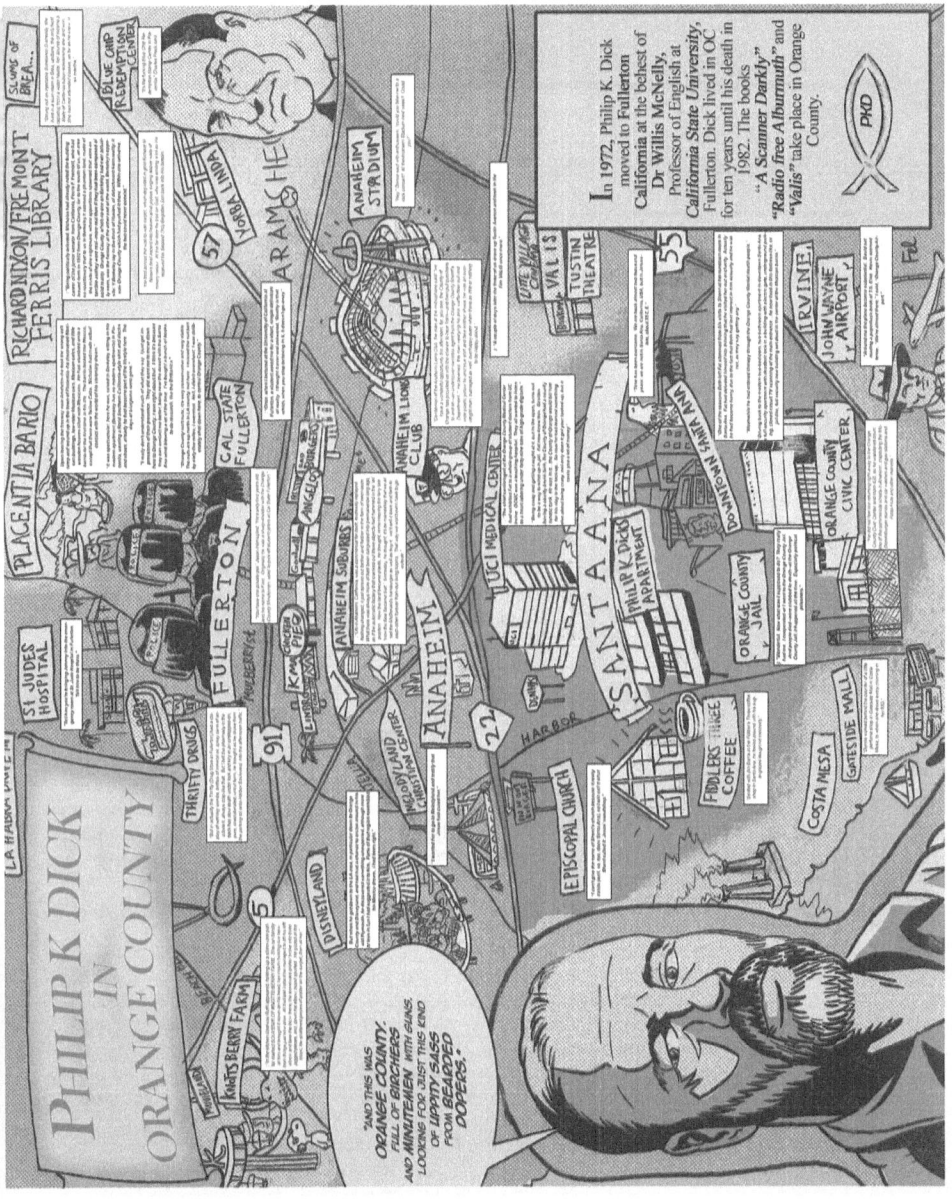

Felipe Flores, "Philip K. Dick in Orange County" (2015). Approximately top to bottom, left to right:

St Jude's Hospital—"Tell him you're bringing Johnny into the emergency room at St. Jude Hospital in Fullerton. Tell him to be there."

Placentia Barrio—"Upon leaving the freeway near Anaheim—he took the wrong exit ramp and wound up in the town of Placentia—he discovered Mexican buildings, low-rider Mexican cars, Mexican cafes, and little wooden houses filled with Mexicans. He had stumbled onto a barrio for the first time in his life. The barrio looked like Mexico, except that there were Yellow Cabs. Nicholas had made actual contact with the world of his visionary dream." *(continued on page 190)*

"It was spectacular; here he was, raised in Berkeley, sitting in his modern apartment (Berkeley has no modern apartments) in Placentia, wearing a florid Southern California-style shirt and slacks and shoes; already he had become part of the lifestyle here. The days of bluejeans were gone."

"I really don't understand much of what they say. I just get impressions of their presence. They did want me to move down here to Orange County; I was right about that. I think it's because they can contact me better, being near the desert with the Santa Ana wind blowing a lot of the time. I've bought a bunch of books to do research, like the Brittanica."

"Orange County isn't nuts; it's very conservative and very stable. The nuts are up north in LA county, not here. I missed the nut belt by sixty-five miles; I overshot. Hell, I didn't overshoot; I was deliberately shot down here, to central Orange County."

Richard Nixon/Fremont Ferris Library—"Being politically oriented, Nicholas had already noted the budding career of the junior senator from California, Ferris F. Fremont, who had issued forth in 1952 from Orange County, far to the south of us, an area so reactionary that to us in Berkeley it seemed a phantom land, made of the mists of dire nightmare, where apparitions spawned that were as terrible as they were real—more real than if they had been composed of solid reality. Orange County, which no one in Berkeley had ever actually seen, was the fantasy at the other end of the world, Berkeley's opposite; if Berkeley lay in the thrall of illusion, of detachment from reality, it was Orange County which had pushed it there. Within one universe, the two could never coexist."

Slums of Brea...—"Strung out on injectable Substance D already, she lived in a slum room in Brea, upstairs, the only heat radiating from a water heater, her source of income a State of California tuition scholarship she and won. She had not attended classes, as far as he knew, in six months."

Yorba Linda—"He trod across the wall-to-wall carpet, which depicted in gold Richard M. Nixon's final ascent into heaven amid joyous singing above wails of misery below. At the far door he trod on God, who was smiling a lot as He received his Second Only Begotten Son back into His bosom."

Blue Chip Redemption Center—"It's the fucking Blue Chip Redemption Stamp Center in Placentia," Charles Freck said.

Knott's Berry Farm—"In the kitchen doorway Ruth appeared, holding up a stoneware platter marked SOUVENIR OF KNOTTS BERRY FARM. She ran blindly at him and brought it down on his head, her mouth twisting like newborn things just now alive. At that last instant he managed to lift his left elbow and take the blow there; the stoneware platter broke into three jagged pieces, and, down his elbow, blood spurted. He gazed at the blood, the shattered pieces of platter on the carpet, then at her."

Thrifty Drugs—"But in actuality the Thrifty (Drug Store in Fullerton) had a display of nothing: combs, bottles of mineral oil, spray cans of deodorant, always crap like that. But I bet the pharmacy in the back has slow death under lock and key in an unstepped-on, pure, unadulterated, uncut form, he thought as he drove from the parking lot onto Harbor Boulevard, into the afternoon traffic."

Fullerton—"You have one private pol," Jason interrupted, "He's sixty-two years old and his name is Fred. Originally he was a sharp-shooter with the Orange County Minutemen; used to pick off student jeters at Cal State Fullerton."

Cal State Fullerton—"Once, when I lectured at the University of California at Fullerton, a student asked me for a short, simple definition of reality. I thought it over and answered, 'Reality is that which, when you stop believing in it, it doesn't go away.'"

Disneyland—"But when he got down to the LA area, in particular down to Orange County and Disneyland, and had had a chance to cruise around in his old Plymouth, he discovered something unexpected, although more or less in fun I had suggested it to him. Parts of that region resembled his Mexico dream. I had been right."

Melody Christian Center—"I wanted her to go to Melodyland and testify that Jesus had cured her."

Anaheim Suburbs—"Life in Ahaheim, California, was a commercial for itself, endlessly replayed. Nothing changed; it just spread out farther and farther in the form of neon ooze. What there was always more of had been congealed into permanence long ago, as if the automatic factory that cranked out these objects had jammed in the 'on' position.

How the land became plastic, he thought, remembering the fairy tale 'How the Sea Became Salt.' Someday, he thought, it'll be mandatory that we all sell the McDonald's hamburger as well as buy it; we'll sell it back and forth to each other forever from our living rooms. That way we won't even have to go outside."

Anaheim Lions Club—"Gentlemen of the Anaheim Lions Club, the man at the microphone said, "we have a wonderful opportunity this afternoon, for, you see, the County of Orange has provided us with the chance to hear from—and then put questions to and of—an undercover narcotics agent from the Orange County Sheriff's Department.": He beamed, this man wearing his pink waffle-fiber suit and wide plastic yellow tie and blue shirt and fake leather shoes; he was an overweight man, overaged as well, overhappy even when there as little or nothing to be happy about."

Anaheim Stadium—"Hey," Donna said with enthusiasm, "could you take me to a rock concert? At the Anaheim Stadium next week? Could you?"

Episcopal Church—"I can't give the name of Sherri's church because it really exists (well, so, too, does Santa Ana), so I will call it what Sherri called it: Jesus' sweatshop."

UCI Medical Center—"The chief cardiologist at the Orange County Medical Center had exhibited Fat to a whole group of student doctors from UC Irvine. OCMC was a teaching hospital. They all wanted to listen to a heart laboring under forty-nine tabs of high-grade digitalis."

"Being crazy and getting caught at it, out in the open, turns out to be a way to wind up in jail. Fat now knew this. Besides having a county drunk tank, the County of Orange had a county lunatic tank. He was in it ... the County of Orange would bill him for his stay in the lock-up.... So now he had learned something else about being crazy: not only does it get your locked up, but it costs you a lot of money."

Tustin Theater—"A couple of days later the three of us drove up Tustin Avenue and took in the film VALIS once more."

Santa Ana, Philip K. Dick's Apartment—"Time has been overcome. We are back almost two thousand years; we are not in Santa Ana, California, USA, but in Jerusalem, about 35 C.E."

Fiddler's Three Coffee—"Seated with Jim Barris in the Fiddler's Three coffee shop in Santa Ana, he fooled around with his sugar-glazed doughnut morosely."

Orange County Jail—"Wonderful. Now what was I supposed to do? They really had me. I cooperated or I went to the Orange County Jail. And people died—were clubbed to death—at the Orange County Jail; it happened all the time. Especially political prisoners."

Downtown Santa Ana—"One of the reasons Beth left Fat stemmed from his visits to Sherri at her rundown room in Santa Ana. Fat had deluded himself into thinking that he visited her out of charity. Actually he had become horny, due to the fact that Beth had lost interest in him sexually and he was not, as they say, getting any."

"Meanwhile he had entered therapy through the Orange County Mental Health people."

"Driving back to the modern two-bedroom, two bathroom apartment in downtown Santa Ana, a full-security apartment with deadbolt lock in a building with electric gate, underground parking, closed circuit TV scanning of the main entrance ... he now lived in this fortress-like, or jail-like, full security new building set dead in the center of the Mexcian barrio."

Gateside Mall—"Donna worked behind the counter of a little perfume shop in Gateside Mall in Costa Mesa, to which she drove every morning in her MG."

Orange County Civic Center—"He did not feel like returning right away to the Orange County Civic Center and room 430, so he wandered down one of the commercial streets in Ahaheim, inspecting the McDonaldburger stands and car washes and gas stations and Pizza Huts and other marvels."

John Wayne Airport—"Around me the plane became substantial. David sat reading a paperback book of T.S. Eliot. Kevin seemed tense. "We're almost there," I said, "Orange County Airport."

Cliff Cramp, conference poster portrait of PKD (2016).

Caleb Havertape, "San Francisco," illustration for *Do Androids Dream of Electric Sheep?* (2016).

Cliff Cramp, "Police Hovercraft," illustration for *Do Androids Dream of Electric Sheep?* (2016).

Cliff Cramp, "Association Owl," illustration for *Do Androids Dream of Electric Sheep?* (2016).

Dallin Bifano, "San Francisco," illustration for *Do Androids Dream of Electric Sheep?* (2016).

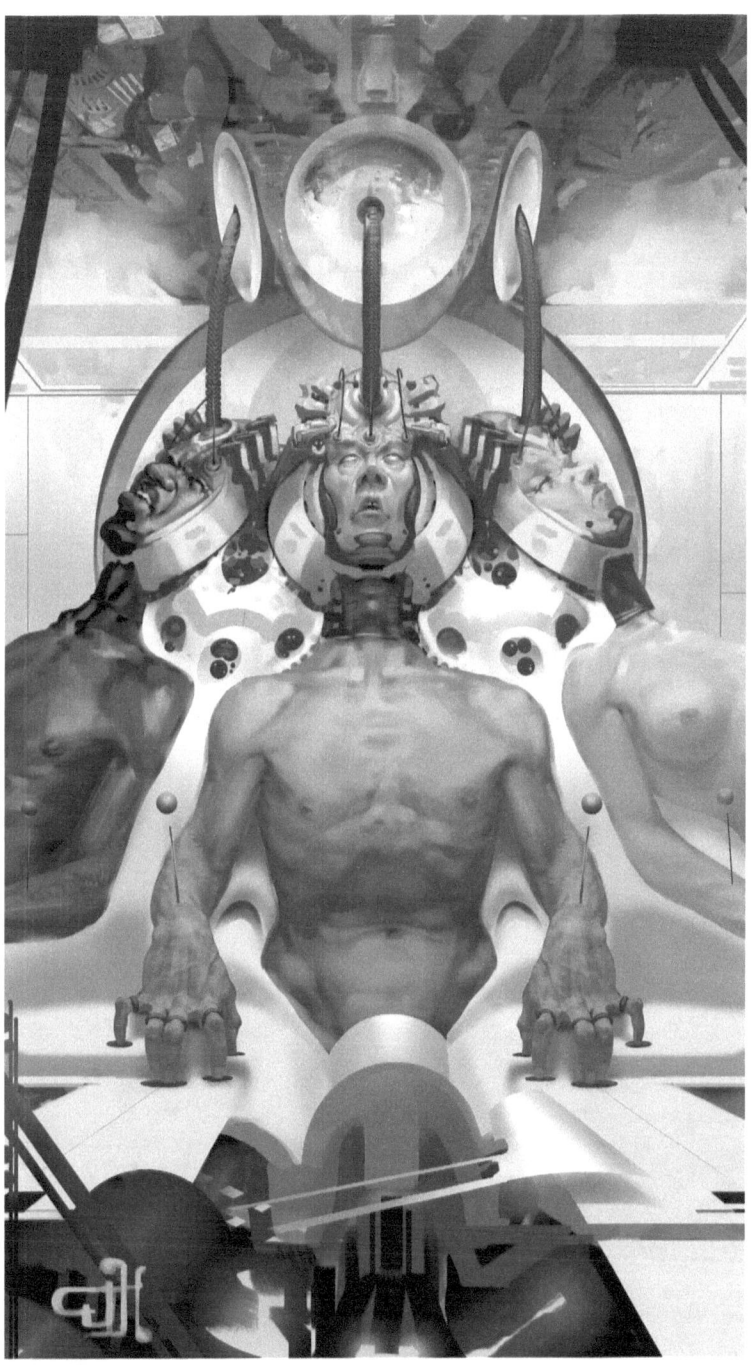

Caleb Havertape, "Precogs," illustration for "Minority Report" (2016).

Garrett Kaida, "Chase," illustration for "Minority Report" (2016).

Cliff Cramp, "German Sector," illustration for *The Man in the High Castle* (2016).

Cliff Cramp, "The Gate," illustration for *The Man in the High Castle* (2016).

Dallin Bifano, "Japanese Empire Aircraft," illustration for *The Man in the High Castle* (2016).

Caleb Havertape, "Mars Outpost," illustration for *The Three Stigmata of Palmer Eldritch* (2016).

Appendix 203

Cliff Cramp, "Pluto," illustration for *The Three Stigmata of Palmer Eldritch* (2016).

Cliff Cramp, "Mars Outpost," illustration for *The Three Stigmata of Palmer Eldritch* (2016).

Garrett Kaida, "Miss Fugate," illustration for *The Three Stigmata of Palmer Eldritch* (2016).

Zines

As Jonathan Lethem and Samuel Sousa just described in "Dick's SoCal Dream," zines play a key role in Southern California culture, especially in relation to the punk music that Dick admired; they play a key role as well in the history of science fiction literature generally, connecting fans as far back as the pulp era; Lethem's keynote explains the importance of Paul Williams's zines: first, in inventing rock and roll criticism ... then, in the *Philip K. Dick Society Newsletter*, launching PKD scholarship toward its current ubiquity. Two zines came out as part of our constellation of Dick events, and, mindful of the history above, we offer brief selections from them as a counter-gesture to what Lethem calls "the gentrification of Philip K. Dick" in books like our present volume. Included are short introductions by Christine Granillo from *Philip K. Dick in Orange County* (2015) and by Nicole Vandever and by David Sandner from *The Aramchek Dispatch* (2016).

From *Philip K. Dick in Orange County*

A BRIEF ACCOUNT OF HOW I BECAME A DICKHEAD

Christine Granillo

The Philip K. Dick in Orange County project started last year during a Digital Literary Studies class I took with Dr. David Sandner at Cal State Fullerton. As a class, we created a website that was dedicated to Philip K. Dick's time in Orange County and his connection to Cal State Fullerton. Before I took this class, my only knowledge of Philip K. Dick was from the story "The Electric Ant," so I confess: at the time this project started, I was a newbie at PKD. Yet, once I started reading more of Philip K. Dick's works, it clicked. I was an instant fan. Like David Gill says in the short film *Why Philip K. Dick Matters* when I got hooked, "I did that thing that Dickheads do, they go and they buy a giant stack of books." I buy more of his books before I've even finished reading the ones I already have. When I think of why I like Philip K. Dick so much, I realize I appreciate the social commentary he provides, the scary predictions he forecasts in his novels that somehow feel all too real today, and the astonishing way he portrays humanity.

The first novel I read was *A Scanner Darkly*. I became tuned in. I began to understand what the fuss was all about. I tripped out over the mention of sights I am familiar with and grew up around, some that no longer exist, like the La Habra Drive-In that was just down the street from the house I grew up in. It felt surreal to see the landscape of the Orange County that I take for granted mapped out in the novel I was holding in front of me. Not only was Orange County mapped out but it was mapped out in a novel that rejected the plastic, conservative image OC has crafted for itself. Rather, it called this image into question and displayed the underbelly that exists within Orange County. It was this, the presence of Orange County in his novels, that the Digital Literary Studies class was interested in exploring. This is what we wanted to put on display on our website. Philip K. Dick is a famous author, 11 of his books or short stories have been adapted into films—some of them, like *Blade Runner* and *Minority Reports,* were huge successes. It seems like something Orange County should be proud of, yet somehow the legacy of Philip K. Dick sleeps quietly through the night under the cover of a thin blanket. It's time to pull the blanket. On to the show...

From *The Aramchek Dispatch*

SPECULATIVE FICTIONS AND THE OUTSIDER: EVERYONE IN THIS ZINE IS A LOSER

Nicole Vandever

Hello! Thanks for picking up our zine. It was put together with loads of time, sweat, tears, and ink by our editors, our reader panel, and, of course, our contributors. I'll get to that process in a bit, but most importantly and more immediately interesting (to me, at least) is, *What exactly is a zine? And what does it have to do with speculative fictions?* Spending a long while in the library, visiting a couple zine-related events, I've come up with my own definitions. But first, here's some from the *OED*:

AMATEUR. Etymology: *amateur* < Latin *amātōr-em,* lover< *amā-re* to love.

MONSTER. *n.* Originally: a mythical creature which is part animal and part human, or combines elements of two or more animal forms, and is frequently of great size and ferocious appearance.

LOSER. *n.* One who loses or suffers loss. / A squanderer or waster (of time).

I thought about these three words while helping to assemble this beast. They are words I've come to treasure in my studies of literature and spec fic, because they represent the nature of the writer, the outsider, and the SF/Fantasy fan, and the creations that come from all three.

We are all AMATEURS, and ACADEMIA is a fancy word for FANDOM.

A zine is made on the ground, totally DIY, expressing the traditions and cares, ephemeral as they may be, of the editors and contributors. It seemed perfect for our club's aim—showing the world (a small part of it, if not just ourselves and immediate friends and family) the important history and present of speculative fictions at our university and what we're doing now that keeps it all relevant.

[Zines, as we know them, can trace their roots back to science fiction fanzines way back in the 30s (awesome, right?). It all started with people re-imagining the world, writing it down, and talking to each other about their stories through printed, folded, floppy things. Like the one you hold now.]

When Michelle Hickethier, Paige Patterson, Jasmine Romero, Emma Strand, and I came together to form the Science Fiction & Fantasy Lit Club, we wanted to create an extended version of our little fan community. We, as students who sometimes feel like the pages upon pages we read and write would amount to nothing outside our own heads, wanted to share the excitement. We, as students of CSUF, got *very* excited when we heard about our university's history and holdings—"we have *Bradbury? AND Herbert??*"—but felt like nobody knew or cared.

So we thought we'd start a club.

Why not? We said, rallying after class, coming up with wild and impossible ideas for meetings

Why not? We said, filling out forms and putting down cash to register the club, wrestling for rooms and tech access.

Why not? We said, begging people to share their ideas and creations in a zine, unsure but unchecked and excited.

We never got our zine off the ground, until Christine Granillo, president of the Creative Writing Club, decided she didn't have enough on her pallet and wanted to collaborate on a zine to be released at the Philip K. Dick conference. She had created one before, which was released as collection of local authors and artists titled *Philip K. Dick in the OC*. It made its debut at the Hibbleton gallery in downtown Fullerton, and so many fans and enthusiasts came out that night to share in the mutual excitement.

Big things, small packages. We're all just students, here. We're used to writing academic papers, using MLA, APA, but here you'll find them MIA. Quick, snappy, the unpolished, but nonetheless witty and important for its swiftness and ephemerality. We hope to channel the sublime of the punk, rocking the academia tree with our humble zine. We're hardcore amateurs.

Monster, outsider.

By creating a zine, something ephemeral, without barcode or accolades, and by using it to celebrate science fiction & fantasy, we are outside of a norm. None of this is USEFUL. Also, all of us are so DIFFERENT. It shocks me every time, at club meetings, in classes. We're colorful and queer, of all genders, nervous and loud, big and small and young and old. Some of us have visions of the future, or really hope there's a dragon left alive, somewhere; some of us just really wish we had a superpower. But we all come together, different, imagining. All of us who are reading or building this zine ended up in Speculative Fictions. How did we get to this strange horizon?

It's undeniable that the roots of speculative fiction may not have grown from the Outsider in our modern, inclusive sense. Zines, says Stephen Duncombe, had their roots in a base where the white, male, heterosexual is the norm. Le Guin, SF queen, calls out the sexism inherent in her field in "American SF and the Outsider" (and most of her works following). And I *love* LOTR, but can we talk about Orcs? Even with questionable representation within a great many works, it is speculative fiction as a form that requires us to pose questions to reality, encourages us to imagine the world differently by seeing its faults, its quirks, tweaking elements and creating new ones from them.

"Together," says Duncombe, zinesters "give the word 'loser' a new meaning, changing it from insult to accolade, and transforming personal failure into an indictment of the alienating aspects of our society." The point of the zine, is that there IS NO TARGET MARKET. The Zine—the creation and bastion of the outsider, the purposeful loser—and Speculative Fictions—a space where the norm is necessarily questioned. This speculation is marked, sometimes uncomfortable, strange in a way that's not packagable, exotic in a way that's not pretty—it is MONSTROUS.

In the following pages, you'll read Magical Manifestos, reality-bending twist endings, ruminations on our celestial origins, and ordinary people writing about and drawing the strange things they love. These pages are fragments of what's important to a number of very different people, but they all express it speculatively and fictionally. Imagining beautiful things, questioning and drawing out the strangeness of our world.

> "In the zine world, being a loser ... is something to yell from the rooftops."
> —*Notes from Underground*, Stephen Duncombe

So why did we make this zine? We're worrying a bit now, down to the wire—how can we print this thing quick and dirty—you can smell the we-should-have and how-much-time on us; the odor of anything done passionately. We come together with our different ways of doing things and our multiple left feet. With our visions of other worlds, and the future. We worked hard between our day jobs and night studies to make something that doesn't matter one bit to the vast timeline of the universe. This stapled paper booklet will be read, decay, and be dust faster than the smallest star in the furthest part of the galaxy. It is necessarily ephemeral in form ("everything in life is just for a while," says Dick). It is the definition of a LOSER.

And so, here is our attempt at creation. Our authors are diverse—some consider themselves writers, some have never written a story in their lives—

but we have come together for a reason. To be an outsider, to love speculative fiction, to make a zine—to lose. That's what we've attempted here.

> "It's easy to win. Anybody can win."
> —Philip K. Dick, *A Scanner Darkly*

Introduction—On Your Last Chance to be Human... On It Being Already Too Late...

David Sandner

> "I have a bad attitude ... so I rebel. And writing SF is way to rebel.... SF is a rebellious art form and it needs writers and readers and bad attitudes—an attitude of "Why?" or "How Come?" or "Who Says?"
> —Philip K. Dick

Why?

Zines, too, have bad attitudes. They go out for cigarettes with your last twenty and you know they're not coming back. They hang out in alleyways or under bridges. They know where the bodies are buried—they might have put them there.

Zines just won't get out of your face. They exist, in a real, tangible, messy way. You hold it in your hands, right here and now—you can't just click away this time—you have to close the cover, you have to toss it down if you want to refuse it.

But you don't turn away. You will not refuse. Why? Could this be your last chance to be human? Isn't that the always-broken promise of art? And especially of art like this—not made for capitalist consumption by corporations (who are more people than people, the law now says), but instead made anyway, by hands and glue and tape and nails enough for a crucifixion, probably yours. (Does that make you want to stop, or to read on all the more?)

"All art is quite useless," Oscar Wilde whispers in George Orwell's ear as they conceive their love child, Philip K. Dick. Mary Shelley flies in as a good fairy and bestows on the baby a gift: visions of the future. But another fairy, of more malignant disposition, angry at being neglected, sends a curse—but it is the same as the gift: visions of the future!

Still you will not stop reading!

* * *

So it's all in good fun, isn't it? Just entertainment? It's only science fiction. Just a zine. But what if this *Aramchek Dispatch* is written in code? What if it contains a message meant only for you alone? What if it tells truth? What if it reveals the face of God?

What, I wonder, will finally prevent you from breaking the code? Your disbelief? Your busy schedule? Your boredom? Your fear?

How Come?

This zine you have refused to stop reading is released in conjunction with the 2016 Acacia *Philip K. Dick Conference* on the campus of California State University, Fullerton, April 29 and 30.

Now the origin story of the conference lies in a website, *Philip K. Dick in the OC*, created by my Digital Literary Studies class for reasons obscure to us. Maybe messages microwaved into our brains by our alien overlords. We wanted to know about PKD and his presence here in Orange County, almost among us, in an alternate now. He seems to have a message, slightly garbled, almost mislaid, we need to hear.

But we created a zine back then, too, of which this one is the hideous progeny. How come? Websites have a far reach but are a ghostly presence; they are but spectral flickers of uncertain existence. A zine, however, abides—it presses against your flesh. Stitched together from unhallowed parts and endowed with life by its creators—those mad scientists—it is less ghost and more Frankenstein's monster, lifting the curtain on you while you sleep, asking for your love. Surely you will take the living hand, so warm and capable, held out to you? We made a zine then, also called *Philip K. Dick in the OC*, to go with our newborn website. There was an art show at the Hibbleton Gallery in downtown Fullerton, with art on the walls … and the zine to read.

And just as the first website begat the zine and art show … so they all begat another website, of greater scope: SF at CSUF. And the website looked about itself and it was good, studying the many facets of SF at Cal State Fullerton: PKD and more … steampunk and the pulps in our Special Collections, and on into the shiny future. And lo, the website begat the conference which begat an art show and special collections display as part of the conference. But something was missing, and all must move in an eternal return … and so we have a zine. This one you now cannot stop reading even if you tried.

This one you hold shows you life is but a zine. It contains multitudes. It is the child of giants that lived in those days.

* * *

What if you broke the code here, disguising the message meant for your eyes alone, only to find you, yourself had encoded the message hidden here?

Will you find your own name signed here on these unhallowed pages, suddenly implicated in every sordid thing, laid bare, now alien to you? Will you wonder: did you mean to send the message or hide it forever?

Will you burn your notes and erase your memories?

Will you write an answer to the message here first *before* you burn your notes and erase your memories? What will you say in that impossible conversation with yourself that you will refuse to remember but will never stop striving to know? What is it you have to say—that one thing at the tip of your tongue that you will make yourself forget?

This zine is a burning bush. It is a fall from a dizzying height. This zine is the kiss that kills. A dream that cannot be spoken, but here it is.

Who Says?

The zine you still insist on reading, despite all warnings, was brought to life by the combined dark powers of the Science Fiction and Fantasy Club and the Creative Writing Club. Wholly a student production, wrought of their energy and insight, as a reaction against the terrible insistence of Philip K. Dick's art. Art makes art. Come listen in to what can only be alien communications between distant worlds, where, in languages fabulous and unknown, words cross the stars in one final chance to fail better than we ever have before ... these writers will strive and fail to be human as a kind of gift to you (lest you fail without striving)—a hand held out on a rainy, dismal night by the creature you yourself have made—a dream you thought your own that you find, tears in your eyes, is shared by others, despite everything you thought you knew.

Who says? We do, dreaming together even as we live forever sequestered by all we cannot know or be. We dream together anyway, despite everything.

Read on!

* * *

What if I'm lying and there is no code but you break it anyway and discover a secret of untold significance? For what if the code is everywhere and the key meant for only you to discover here? What sort of prophet will you be? Mad, raving on street corners or at the edges of freeway off ramps? Or will you write science fiction, alternate histories? Or will you put out a zine, and place it in the hands of those who may understand?

I'm talking about you. Bring your questions. Bring your fears. Read with a bad attitude. We're counting on you to break the code. We're counting on you to fail but to fail in the only way that matters... We're counting on you to rebel. It's all you've got ... your last chance ... already too late to take ... but how human to strive to take it anyway! How amazing!

And remember: Philip K. Dick was right!

About the Contributors

James **Blaylock**, one of the pioneers of the steampunk genre, has written some 25 books in his nearly 45 years of publishing stories and novels. His short story "Unidentified Objects" was nominated for an O. Henry Award, and two of his stories have won World Fantasy Awards. He has taught writing at Chapman University in Orange, California, for the past 25 years.

Gabriel **Cutrufello** is an assistant professor of rhetoric and composition at York College of Pennsylvania. His areas of research are the rhetoric of science, technical writing pedagogy and science fiction literature. His work investigates the use of visuals in undergraduate and graduate scientific and technical writing in American colleges and universities at the end of the 19th century.

Richard **Feist**'s research concentrates on the history of ethics, meta-ethics, and military ethics as well as the philosophy of science, mathematics and process metaphysics. He is at work on papers in public ethics; the Victorian roots of Whitehead's and McTaggart's metaphysics; and a study of the historical relationship between Western ethics and Western warfare. He also works on the interface of science fiction and metaphysics, especially in works by Philip K. Dick, Walter M. Miller, Jr., and James Blish.

Daniel **Gilbertson** moved to the United States in the late 1970s after graduating from Oxford University, where he was an active member of the Oxford University Speculative Fiction Group. He spent three decades in Los Angeles working as a writer-producer-director for a wide variety of companies and start-ups. Now retired, he resides in Santa Monica.

Ursula **Heise** is the Marcia H. Howard Chair at UCLA. Her books include *Sense of Place and Sense of Planet* (Oxford, 2008), and *Imagining Extinction* (Chicago, 2016). She is the managing editor of *Futures of Comparative Literature* (Routledge, 2016) and coeditor of *The Routledge Companion to the Environmental Humanities* (2016). She is also a 2011 Guggenheim Fellow and served as president of the Association for the Study of Literature and the Environment.

Michael **Kvamme-O'Brien** is a secondary English teacher with degrees from Aberdeen, Strathclyde and Glasgow. His Ph.D. thesis tests the hypothesis that certain authors require their protagonists to think mythologically to transcend the limits of their material universes. He has published on Phil Farmer in *Vector*, has a chapter on *2000AD* coming out in *Aliens in Popular Culture* by ABC-CLIO, and is working toward publishing his dissertation as a monograph.

Jonathan **Lethem** is the author of 11 novels, including *Girl in Landscape, Chronic City,* and *The Feral Detective*. His fifth, *Motherless Brooklyn*, won the National Book Critic's Circle Award for fiction. His stories and essays have been collected in six

214   About the Contributors

volumes, and he's also the author of monographs on the film *They Live* and the album *Fear of Music*. In 2005, he was made a Fellow of the MacArthur Foundation.

Sean **Matharoo** is a Ph.D. candidate at University of California, Riverside, where he studies French, Francophone, and Anglophone speculative literature and philosophy. He has published his research in *Green Letters* and *Horror Studies*, book reviews in *Science Fiction Studies*, the *Journal of the Fantastic in the Arts*, and *Science Fiction Film and Television*, interviews in *The Eaton Journal of Archival Research in Science Fiction* and *The Los Angeles Review of Books*, and encyclopedia entries.

Tim **Powers** is the author of more than a dozen novels, including *The Anubis Gates*, *Alternate Routes*, and *On Stranger Tides*, which was the basis of the fourth "Pirates of the Caribbean" movie. He lives in San Bernardino.

Gregg **Rickman** teaches at Sonoma State University. He has edited numerous works on Dick, including *The Early Works of Philip K. Dick*, Vols. 1 and 2 (Prime, 2008) and *To the High Castle, Philip K. Dick: A Life, 1928–1962* (Valentine, 1989). He also edited *The Science Fiction Film Reader* (Limelight, 2004), and other readers on film. He has published numerous articles on Philip K. Dick as well.

Umberto **Rossi** is a secondary school teacher, independent scholar and the chief editor of the PULP Libri online book magazine. He is the author of *The Twisted Worlds of Philip K. Dick* (McFarland, 2011), coeditor of a collection of essays on Thomas Pynchon's *V.* (with Paolo Simonetti, CSP, 2016), and has written articles on J.G. Ballard, Thomas M. Disch, Barry N. Malzberg and Jonathan Lethem for *Science-Fiction Studies*, *Extrapolation*, and *Foundation*. He is a member of the Science Fiction Research Association.

Paul **Sammon** has written numerous books, including *Future Noir: The Making of Blade Runner*, *Ridley Scott: Close Up*, *The Making of Starship Troopers*, *Conan the Phenomenon*, the *Splatterpunk* anthologies, and the *Alien Screenplay* book. He has also worked on approximately 100 films, including *Conan the Barbarian*, *Robocop*, *Dune*, *Blue Velvet*, and *The Silence of the Lambs*.

David **Sandner**, professor of English at California State University, Fullerton, is the author of *Critical Discourses of the Fantastic, 1712–1831* (Ashgate, 2011), a finalist for a Mythopoeic Award. He wrote *The Fantastic Sublime* (Greenwood, 1996), and is editor of *Treasury of the Fantastic* (Tachyon, 2013) and *Fantastic Literature: A Critical Reader* (Praeger, 2004). A member of Science Fiction & Fantasy Writers of America and the Horror Writers Association, he chaired the 2016 Philip K. Dick Conference.

Samuel **Sousa** teaches as a lecturer in the American Studies Department at California State University, Fullerton. His works has an emphasis on politics in music-based subcultures, especially in Southern California punk music and the related zine culture.

Gary **Westfahl** is the author, editor, or coeditor of 28 books, including the Hugo Award–nominated *Science Fiction Quotations* (Yale, 2005) and the three-volume *Greenwood Encyclopedia of Science Fiction and Fantasy* (2005). He has coedited *Bridges to Science Fiction and Fantasy* (2018) and *Arthur C. Clarke* (2018), among others. In 2003, he received the Science Fiction Research Association's Pilgrim Award for his lifetime contributions to science fiction and fantasy scholarship.

Index

Ackerman, Diane 17
The Adjustment Bureau (film) 3, 11–12, 164–165
adolescents 184
"Afterthoughts by the Author" 2
Agent Orange 184
Alien (film) 155–156
Altman, Robert 161
Amendola, Giovanni 34
Anaheim, California 6, 52–53, 189–191
Arbor House (publisher) 122
Ashbless, William 138
Atwood, Margaret 15
"Autofac" 19

Bach, Johann Sebastian 38
Bacigalupi, Paolo 147
Baird, John Logie 32
Ballard, J.G. 35, 149
Barjo (film) 135
Barnouw, Erik 32, 36–37
Batten, Barton, Durston & Osborn (advertising agency) 35
Bee, Robert 108
Beethoven, Ludwig van 38, 104
Beresford, Bruce 123
Bergman, Ingmar 161
Berkeley, California 2, 4, 101, 118, 124, 128, 130–132, 174, 185, 190
Bernardo, Susan M. 23
The Bible 32, 93
Bierce, Ambrose 141
Birch Society 5
Bishop, Michael 100
Black Flag 177
Blade Runner 3, 118, 120
Blade Runner (film) 6, 11, 120, 147, 159–163, 166–170, 207
Blade Runner 2049 (film) 11
Blaylock, James 8, 11, 137–138
Blue Jay (publisher) 118
Bogen, Joseph E. 10, 46, 49–53, 59
Bohr, Niels 159
Boon, Marcus 84
Borges, Jorge Luis 172
Bradbury, Ray 9, 113, 159, 208
Brando, Marlon 176
Brautigan, Richard 176
Brea, California 190

The Broken Bubble 102
The Brown Derby 156
Bruce, Lenny 126
Bukatman, Scott 73
Burroughs, William S. 55, 162
Butler, Andrew M. 37

California State University, Fullerton (CSUF) 3–9, 11–12, 116, 137–139, 144, 153, 159, 187–188, 190, 206, 211
Cameron, James 155
Capitol Pictures 154, 156
Carmel, California 109
Carpenter, John 186
Carquinez, California 74, 76–78
Carr, Terry 128
Carroll, Lewis 125–126
Cassidy, Joanna 169
CBS 166
Chakrabarty, Dipesh 17
Chandler, Raymond 131
Chicago, Illinois 2
Clans of the Alphane Moon 118, 172
C.L.A.W. (film) 12, 155–156
Cleveland, Ohio 109
Cold War 14, 29, 151
College of San Rafael 5
Colorado 119
Conan Doyle, Arthur 138–139, 143
Confessions of a Crap Artist 71–72, 74, 100, 128, 135
Conway, Erik M. 18
Corey, Irwin 122
Corroboree (publisher) 122
Costa Mesa, California 191
Costello, Elvis 134–135
The Crack in Space 87, 102, 129
Cramp, Cliff 8
Cronenberg, David 163
Cronkite, Walter 40
Crumb, Robert 135, 178
Crutzen, Paul 16–17
cyberpunk 3, 14, 27, 147

Dangerous Days (documentary) 168
The Dark-Haired Girl 122–124
Davis, Erik 61, 125–126, 129, 178
Deeley, Michael 166
De Laurentiis, Dino 163

215

Index

De Lauzirka 167–169
Dennett, Daniel 56–57
Derrida, Jacques 105
Descartes, René 47
Dick Hackett, Isa 117
Dionysus 99–101
Disneyland 6, 12, 175, 190
The Divine Invasion 32, 43, 62, 87, 101–104, 126
Do Androids Dream of Electric Sheep? 6, 15, 19, 22–28, 37, 40–41, 71, 73–74, 79–80, 84, 87, 90–92, 109, 118, 120, 160–161, 187, 193–196
Dr. Bloodmoney 15, 26–27, 102, 118, 120, 127, 131, 139, 142, 174, 176
Dune 4, 137, 139
The Dune Encyclopedia 4
Dylan, Bob 124

Earthshaker 11, 99–100
Einstein, Albert 159
Eisenhower, Dwight D. 33, 35–36, 88
"The Electric Ant" 116
Encinitas, California 116
Englund, Matt 108
Erickson, Steve 126
Euripedes 99
Evernden, Neil 18, 22
Exegesis 2, 6, 9–11, 69, 83–90, 94–96, 104–105, 118–122, 125, 133–134, 151–152
"The Exit Door Leads In" 130
Eye in the Sky 101, 105

Fahrenheit 451 4, 137
Fairchild, John 124
"Faith of Our Fathers" 39–40
Fancher, Hampton 160
Farmer, Philip José 129, 150
Farnsworth, Philo T. 32
"The Father Thing" 157
Festival de Metz 2
Fitting, Peter 61, 67, 73
Flack, Steven 135
Flow My Tears, the Policeman Said 2, 5, 42–43, 104, 120, 135, 140
Ford, Harrison 168
Foreman, Carl 156
Frasca, Gabriele 33, 44
Fullerton, California 3–5, 116–117, 121, 137, 139, 144, 184–185, 189–190, 208, 211

Galactic Pot-Healer 11, 26–27, 107–113, 129
The Ganymede Takeover 129
Gazzinaga, Michael S. 46, 49–50, 52
Gibson, Mel 123
Gibson, William 3, 27, 128, 147
Giger, H.R. 155–156
Gill, David 206
Gilliam, Terry 134
Glen Ellen, California 118, 120, 128
Goethe, Johann Wolfgang von 52–53, 94, 96
"The Golden Man" 100

Graouilly d'Or 2
Groening, Matt 121
Gryphon Bookstore 130
Gunderloy, Mike 182

Haber, Katy 166
Hammerstein, Oscar 38
Hansen, James 18
Haraway, Donna 16
Hartwell, David 122, 135–136
Hayles, Katherine 25
Heine, Heinrich 52
Heinlein, Robert 149, 159
Heise, Ursula 8–10
Herbert, Frank 9, 208
Hereclitus 48, 59
Hibbleton Gallery 12, 187, 208, 211
Hollywood 12, 117, 131, 147, 154, 156–157, 164–165, 167
Homer 57–58
"How to Build a Universe That Doesn't Fall Apart in Two Days" 3, 9, 141–141
Hubbard, L. Ron 128, 179
Hugo Award 2
Hume, David 47
Humpty Dumpty in Oakland 100

I Ching 127–129
"If You Find This World Bad, You Should See Some of the Others" 1–2
"Imposter" 103–104
"Introduction to *The Golden Man*" 1

Jackson, Pamela 121, 134
Jameson, Fredric 15, 19, 26, 28, 73, 84
Jaynes, Julian 10, 46, 55–59
Jesus Christ 24, 43–44, 47, 58, 83, 85–86, 89, 92, 94–97, 110, 179, 190–191
Jeter, K.W. 140, 148–149
John W. Campbell Memorial Award 2
Johnson, Lyndon B. 40
"Jon's World" 155
Jouanne, Emmanuel 72
Joyce, James 122

Kennedy, Jacqueline 38
Kennedy, John 41–42
Kennedy, Robert 41–42
Kern, Jerome 38–39
Kibbee, Roland 168
King, Martin Luther 41–42
Kinney, Jay 120, 134
Kleier, Gerry 130
Knott's Berry Farm 190
Kozyrev, Nikolai 46
Kunstler, John Howard 15

La Habra, California 206
Last Wave (fanzine) 122
Le Guin, Ursula 3, 146, 209

Index

Lem, Stanislaw 129, 149–150
Leslie, Laura 117, 127
Lethem, Jonathan 2–3, 8–9, 11–12, 206
Lewis, C.S. 147
The Library of America 3, 118, 132
Lincoln, Abraham 41, 73, 175
Linklater, Richard 162
"A Little Something for Us Tempunauts" 41–42
Los Angeles, California 141, 154, 159, 165, 169, 174

Mackey, Douglas 72
"Man, Android and Machine" 48
The Man in the High Castle 2, 4, 36–37, 73–74, 101, 123, 187, 199–201
The Man in the High Castle (TV) 3, 166
The Man Who Japed 102
The Man Whose Teeth Were All Exactly Alike 10, 71–72, 74–80, 122
Martian Time-Slip 26, 71, 79–80, 118, 171
Marx, Karl 68–69
Mary and the Giant 101
A Maze of Death 147
McKee, Gabriel 84
McKibben, Bill 16, 18, 22
McNelly, Willis 4–5, 8–9, 137–139, 146
McPherson, Aimee Semple 178–179
Meillasoux, Quentin 10, 62–63, 65–69
The Middle Class 184
Milne, A.A. 149
"Minority Report" 187, 197–198
Minority Report (film) 3, 11, 164–165, 207
Minority Report (TV) 3
"The Mold of Yancy" 33–35, 37, 43
Monroe, Marilyn 39
Mulligan, Robert 160
Murakami, Haruki 3
Mussolini, Benito 34, 39

Nagel, Thomas 55
Naked Lunch (film) 162
Nazism and the High Castle 127
Nelson, Ray 185–186
New Line Cinema 158
New York Times 126
Next (film) 163
Nick and the Glimmung 123
Nietzsche, Friedrich 68
Nixon, Richard 5, 36, 43–44, 185, 190
Now Wait for Last Year 10, 16, 26–28, 71, 79–80, 87, 123, 142, 147
"Null-O" 74

Oakland, California 174
O'Bannon, Dan 155, 163
O'Brien, Flann 125
"On a Cat Who Fell Three Stories and Survived" 122
Orange County, California 3–8, 93, 137, 144, 189–191, 207, 211

Oreskes, Naomi 18
Ornstein, Robert E. 46, 48–49, 59
Orwell, George 32–34, 38, 210
Our Friends from Frolix 8 16, 26, 99–100, 102, 127
The Owl in Daylight 62

Pagetti, Carlo 38
Palance, Virginia 155–156
Palmer, Christopher 72, 74–75
Panter, Gary 121–122, 177
"Paycheck" 103
Paycheck (film) 3
The Penultimate Truth 35, 37, 43, 84, 87–92, 102
Persona (film) 161
Peterson, Peter George 36
Peyton Place (TV) 33
Philip K. Dick, A Day in the Afterlife (BBC documentary) 134–135
The Philip K. Dick Conference 8–9, 12, 187, 192–205, 208, 211
The Philip K. Dick Festival 116
Philip K. Dick in Orange County (website) 7–8, 206, 211
The Philip K. Dick Society (newsletter) 11, 117–135, 181–182, 206
philipkdick.com 154
Piltdown Forgery 72
Placentia, California 189–190
Planck, Max 159
"Planet for Transients" 19–20, 28
Plato 47
Porter, Cole 38–39
postmodernism 3, 15–16, 44
Pournelle, Jerry 150
Powell, Ivor 166
Powers, Tim 5, 8, 11, 119, 137, 161
Presley, Elvis 39
Prestinary, Patrisia 8
Prischman, Paul 169
Puttering About in a Small Land 33, 101
Pynchon, Thomas 3, 32, 35, 122

Radio Free Albemuth 8, 62, 102, 122
Radio Free PKD (zine) 135
Rawlings, Terry 167
Reeves, Rosser 36
Reynolds, Whitman 125
Rickman, Gregg 43
Robinson, Kim Stanley 72, 84
Rodriguez, Spain 178
Roell, Sophie 154
Rolling Stone 130, 133, 151–152
Ronstadt, Linda 101–103
"Roog" 32, 103, 132, 161
Rossi, Umberto 55

San Diego, California 141, 159
San Francisco, California 74, 135, 174

218 Index

San Francisco State University 116
Sandner, David 116, 206
Santa Ana, California 2, 184–186, 191
A Scanner Darkly 2, 5–8, 10, 43–44, 46, 51–55, 58–59, 84, 87, 92–95, 137, 148, 171, 174–175, 185, 206–207, 210
A Scanner Darkly (film) 3, 11, 162–163
Schwarzenegger, Arnold 130, 159, 163–164
The Science Fiction Writers of America (SFWA) 4, 129, 149–150
Scott, Ridley 160–162, 166–169
Screamers (film) 3, 12
"Second Variety" 11, 22, 154
"Service Call" 26
Shainberg, Lawrence 125
Shakespeare, William 42
Shaw, Greg 125, 131, 133
Shaw, Suzy 125
Shelley, Mary 25, 210
Shusett, Ronnie 163
Simak, Clifford D. 112–113
The Simulacra 16, 37–39, 43
Sladek, John 127
Smith, Clarke Ashton 149
Solar Lottery 26, 87, 100
"Some Kinds of Life" 15
Social Distortion 184
Sonic Youth 123
Spiegelman, Art 177–178
Spielberg, Steven 165
Spinoza, Baruch 47–48, 59
Spinrad, Norman 149
Stamp, Terrence 165
"Stand-By" 102
Star Trek (TV) 159
Star Wars (film) 156–157
Sterling, Bruce 128
Stevenson, Adlai 36
Stoermer, Eugene 16–17
Sturgeon, Theodore 117, 159, 176
Sunset Gower Studios 154
Sutin, Lawrence 48, 71, 134
Suvin, Darko 26, 84, 151

Ted Bates (advertising agency). 36
Teilhard de Chardin, Pierre 10–11
Terminator (film) 11, 154
They Live (film) 185–186
Thorpe, Charles 72–73
The Three Stigmata of Palmer Eldritch 16, 19, 71, 73, 79, 120, 171, 187, 202–205
3 Women (film) 161
Tichi, Cecelia 32
Time magazine 3
Time Out of Joint 36, 103, 105
Tiptree, James, Jr. 3
Total Recall (film) 3, 11, 123, 125, 163–164
The Transmigration of Timothy Archer 62, 87
Tsing, Anna 29

Tustin, California 191
2-3-74 5, 47–48, 58, 83, 86–90, 95, 101, 105

Ubik 3, 10–11, 39–40, 61–69, 74, 171–172, 176
Ubik (screenplay) 122, 153
Universal Pictures 162
University of California, Berkeley 2, 6, 76
University of California, Irvine 105, 191
The Unteleported Man 99–100, 122

VALIS 1, 5, 10–11, 44, 55, 62, 84, 87, 95–97, 99–100, 103–104, 121, 147, 152, 171–172, 175, 178–179
VALIS (opera) 123, 135
Vancouver, British Columbia 4
Van Vogt, A.E. 149
"The Variable Man" 26–27
Verhoven, Paul 163–164
Verne, Jules 138–139
Village Voice (newspaper) 118, 125, 129
Vint, Sherryl 23
Vintage (publisher) 116–118, 126, 128
Voices from the Street 100–101

Wagner, Richard 38–39
Warner Brothers 167
Warning: We Are Your Police (teleplay) 127
Warrick, Patricia 22, 84, 89, 94
Watson, Andy 125
We Can Build You 37, 73, 140
"We Can Remember It for You Wholesale" 123, 163
Wells, H.G. 138
Wenner, Jann 133
Wessel, Karl 170
West, Nathanael 173, 178, 180, 182
"What'll We Do with Ragland Park?" 102
Wigan, A.L. 51
Wilde, Oscar 210
Williams, Paul 11, 72, 116–121, 123–125, 127–136, 151–152, 206
Williams, Robert 178
Williams, Sloan 33
Wilson, Daniel H. 154
Wilson, Maer 156
Winfrey, Oprah 39
The World Jones Made 16, 20–22
Wyman, Angela 129–130
Wyndham, John 15

X 177–178

Yiggdrasil 99
Yorba Linda, California 190

Zap Gun 123–124
Ziesing, Mark 122
Zines 119, 121, 124–125, 133

www.ingramcontent.com/pod-product-compliance
Lightning Source LLC
Chambersburg PA
CBHW032041300426
44117CB00009B/1151